PERFECT IMPERFECTIONS

CONNIE RAE STRAIN

ISLE OF DOGS

PUBLISHING COMPANY
San Diego • London • Seattle

www.isleofdogspublishing.com

HARDCOVER "COLLECTOR'S" EDITION
First Printing
ISBN 0-9741321-0-1

SOFTCOVER EDITION
ISBN 0-9741321-1-X

Library of Congress Control Number: 2003105987

PRINTED BY GORHAM PRINTING, ROCHESTER, WASHINGTON USA

COVER AND BOOK DESIGN BY KATHRYN CAMPBELL

AUTHOR PHOTOGRAPH: TED CASE PHOTOGRAPHY, SNOHOMISH, WA

DEDICATION

This book is dedicated to Shane, the paint, for his inspiration. Over many years of writing, I often laid down my head in weary frustration, thinking I just can't do this anymore. At those moments, your sweet memory uplifted me. I would have my cry, shake away the late night cobwebs, and get down to work again, always repeating the same affirmation: I will write Shane's book. I will make it the best it can be.

ACKNOWLEDGMENTS

In loving memory of my stepfather, DAREN L. AREND, Daddy Mike. Thank you for sharing the dream. It is my hope that one of this world's most colorful characters will be remembered and savored through the pages of this book.

Adoration to my father, RAYNOR E. HORTON, Daddy Ray, for giving his daughters a foundation so solid to stand on. Thank you for being our hero. It is my hope that one of the world's greatest fathers will be remembered and savored through the pages of this book.

Special appreciation to my mother, AGNES O. AREND, who refused to allow this manuscript to slip into a drawer. Thank you for your exuberant pride in me, Mom. Thank you for the faith you have invested in me.

Last, praise for my husband, JOSEPH R. STRAIN. What a joy it is to live and work with someone so dedicated to the pursuit of excellence. We may never achieve it, but we're sure giving it all we've got. I love you.

AUTHOR'S NOTE

Perfect Imperfections is a Pacific Northwest story based on true events in my life. It is written as a work of creative nonfiction. Due to limitations of memory, as well as literary factors, it is not intended as an exact recreation of events. The timeframe of the story has been compressed from a two-year period down to one year: my age during these adventures was thirteen to fifteen, rather than fourteen to fifteen as written in the book. Events, circumstances, and the names of family and friends are as stated. However, names related to the Murphy farm and the trail ride have been changed.

TABLE OF CONTENTS

A gift for my family

CHAPTER ONE

August 1966

Incredible! My two fathers, Daddy Ray and Daddy Mike, had at last succumbed to my years of deep-kneed begging, and had agreed to share the expense for their daughter to own a horse. It was to be the most magical time of my life.

The Horton and the Arend families lived near each other, separated only by a two-mile stretch of road that wound through connecting neighborhoods. Both homes were nestled in the beautiful Pacific Northwest, east of Seattle, in the tidy, residential community of Bellevue. At fourteen, I was a girl raised in the suburbs who had met scarcely more than a handful of horses. I had ridden even fewer. In fact, except for two recent, overly-exhilarating encounters, most of my riding experience had been on an hourly rental or astride trusty old Nellie as she plodded around a pasture at a family friend's ranch. However, despite scant physical contact with horses, I felt fully prepared to own one.

If time spent dreaming, asleep or awake, could be counted—and in my mind it could—my entire childhood had been spent with horses, wondering at their majesty and racing them across the Western plains. Further, beyond merely dreaming about them, I had spent years with them in more practical ways through reading and study. Over time each breed from Thoroughbred to Arabian had been thoughtfully investigated. Which kind would be best for me? I had memorized the various parts of a horse's anatomy, and the names of the intricate parts of the saddle and bridle as well. Then there was the Horsemanship class at summer camp. The class didn't involve much riding, though I did get to watch the instructor groom, bridle, and saddle a horse. Finally, and likely bolstering my self-assurance, even Daddy Ray, who knew little about horses himself, felt justified in trusting his daughter's horse sense. I had impressed him through the years—as well as annoyed and exhausted him—with my knowledge on the subject.

For all these reasons, I felt prepared for this day, even confident. Caring for a horse? A cinch! I had blissfully no concern nor dawn of thought that I might reveal to myself or anyone else how incompetent I truly was.

The magic began on a Sunday morning when a man from Rodeo Ranch called to say they had purchased a horse from a ranch in Oregon—a strikingly marked paint that was good-natured and gentle. Although the call came in quite early, the Horton family was already up and racing to be the first water-skiers on a mirror smooth Lake Sammamish. Of course, some members of the family raced faster than others. Dad and I had just finished hitching the boat and trailer to the station wagon. We were ready to go. "Let's round 'em up," Dad said, as we headed for the house.

Stepping inside, we saw that things were progressing at a more fitful pace. A yawning Momma Darleen was standing at the kitchen counter making sandwiches. She had lunch underway, which was good, but she was still in her bathrobe. The baby, button-nosed seven-month-old Julie was ready to go. She was strapped into a carrier chair beside her packed diaper bag near the front door. But Cher, my attractive, sixteen-year-old sister hadn't budged from the bathroom, and three-year-old Wendy was still in pajamas hanging comatose over her breakfast.

"It's hopeless," I commented. However, Dad, who was comfortable with his women, wasn't troubled by the peaceful, restful scene. He knew exactly what to do. Striding to the hi-fi, he put on a record of loud, rousing marching music.

Now Mom was marching in place at the kitchen counter. Cher marched past with an armload of towels and suntan lotion heading for the car. Wendy was upright making an effort to finish her breakfast, while I tried to untangle her long blond hair. And Julie was kicking her chubby legs along with the music, watching the action contentedly. We barely heard the telephone ringing. Luckily, Mom was standing right over it.

"Ray!" she called excitedly. "Turn down the hi-fi!"

We all wondered why someone would be calling so early on a Sunday morning. Cher stopped, poised by the open front door. At this hour, it could only be the Wellmans canceling. The Wellmans were our family's closest friends. The family of four consisted of the lovely, vivacious Robin, the jolly, big-hearted Harley, and their two children, the athletic, good-looking Gary, who was Cher's age, and the smart, mischievous Gail, who was my age. To hushed expectation, Dad took the phone.

"Oh," Dad said. "Yes . . . yes, a big paint, very gentle." I leaped up instantly, quelling a rapturous scream as Dad motioned for me to stay quiet. "Yes, I think we might be interested," he said, giving me a wink. "Well, I guess we'll have to come right over then."

Cher's face fell with disappointment as he hung up the phone. She set the armload of towels down. Dad, Cher, and Gary needed a smooth lake surface for their extra-fancy skiing. Once other boaters were on the lake the water got too choppy.

"Darleen," Dad began, "why don't you go ahead and meet the Wellmans at the boat launch. Harley and Gary can put the boat in the water, and Connie and I can meet you at the park later." Cher's face lit up, and the towels were quickly regathered.

"Now, where are the car keys?" Dad asked himself, searching his pockets. Automatically reacting to what was an ongoing frustration for all of us, I began a frantic search of the kitchen junk drawer and Mom started sifting through the pile of mail and papers on the kitchen counter. "Darleen, could you check your purse, please," Dad said, taking up her position. He sorted quickly through the odd items that collected on that one small space of countertop most convenient to the traffic of the front door, such as important papers-in-waiting, several pairs of sunglasses, a tool awaiting return to the garage, the very necessary, not-to-be-lost, blue, elephant-shaped, Woodland Park Zoo key, the Popsicle man money, someone's Bible, various games to be played in the car, and more. "I wish we could keep these things off the counter," Dad muttered, more to himself than to any of us.

Mom dug through her handbag, saying, "I haven't driven the Fiat lately."

"Connie," Dad called absently to Cher as she returned from depositing her load at the car. "Would you please check my white jacket pockets?"

"Yes, I will," she called back. "But I'm not Connie."

"Here they are!" I cried holding up the keys like a prized trophy. The keys had slipped under the toaster, which happened all the time.

Dad nodded in approval. "Now, where is that checkbook? . . ."

* * *

Rodeo Ranch would be a drive east to Issaquah and then south to Maple Valley. "If we decide to buy this horse," Dad said, backing down the steep driveway of our middle-class, rambler-style home. "I want you to promise that you'll still go down to visit Grandma with the family next weekend."

"I wouldn't miss going to Grandma's," I assured him, thinking back on the wonderful times spent at the farm in Oregon. Summer impressions of playing with the old straw hats the strawberry pickers once wore, somehow got mixed up with Thanksgiving dinner and homemade raspberry juice, which led on to Christmas musings. And I remembered Dad at Christmas time, climbing high into a huge oak tree and leaning out dangerously far to gather mistletoe. Worried, we had called up to him, "Dad, we have plenty!" "I want to get some for the fellas at Boeing," came the reply. "Raynor!" Grandma had ordered sternly, "You get right down here!" Grandma would send us home with a generous bagful of hazelnuts freshly picked from her trees.

All thoughts were abruptly brought back to the present.

"And," my father was saying, "I told your grandma to go ahead and tell them at Gaston that you girls would be happy to sing for church next Sabbath." He had probably been chatting away for the last several minutes, but I hadn't heard a word he was saying, until now.

"Aw, Dad!" I whined, although I knew there was no getting out of it. Sick or dying, there was no getting out of it. It seemed that Grandma had a remedy for any illness my sister or I might contract. It was amazing how many sore throats Cher and I had come down with at our grandma's house. All the same, like it or not, after a miserable night of trying to sleep with a liberal slathering of Mentholatum applied to our throats and a steaming wool sock pinned around our necks, we would be miraculously cured and able to sing at some local church in the morning.

"Dad," I said, waiting to get his attention. He was pulling onto the highway. "Dad! Are you listening? I asked you not to tell me so far in advance when we have to sing. Now I'll have plenty of time to get worked up. I'll probably break out in a rash," I said bitterly, adding, "I hate to sing for church . . . especially Gaston church."

Dad wasn't sympathetic, only curious, as he asked, "Why Gaston? It's the smallest church you sing for and the people there appreciate your singing so much. I can't understand why you girls want to be so selfish with your talent."

Dad was right. Of all the churches for which Cher and I sang, Gaston was the smallest. It was an ordinary, innocent-appearing, small white clapboard church. So what was my problem? Even now, merely thinking about the place as we drove, I could feel my skin crawl and my face start to burn. Yep. I could definitely detect the beginnings of a rash.

From experience I knew that, as the singers at Gaston church, Cher and I would be ushered to the very front pew. That's where we always had to sit waiting until it was time for us to sing. It was supposed to be some kind of honor—at least that's what Dad told us. I dreaded it. For one thing, sitting up front forced us to listen to the sermon, instead of playing our usual games of tic-tac-toe or hangman to get us through it. And for another thing, sitting there in the front pew without those distractions I'd be panicked, absolutely panicked, feeling the entire congregation staring at the back of our necks.

When our time came to sing, we'd be introduced as, "The Horton girls . . . they have come all the way down from Seattle just to sing for us here today." I don't know why, but that familiar line would make me want to drop right through the floor. By that point, my legs would be trembling uncontrollably, yet somehow we'd climb the three steps to the pulpit and smile, the two city slickers from Seattle, all spruced up in whatever loathsome frilly or matching apparel Dad had selected for the occasion. No doubt, some unimpressed country brat would be sticking his tongue out at us from somewhere near the back.

Our mutual fear was that we'd start giggling. Cher and I were notorious gigglers. To avoid this most horrifying scenario, my sister and I never looked at each other or talked before, during, or after we sang. As he always did, Dad would watch us sing from the back, peeking around the half-closed door of the foyer. Although never admitting it, he was nervous, too. Then, when the little church became quiet, except for a few stifled coughs and the creaking of the old wooden benches, our Momma Darleen would play the introduction on the piano. I could always tell her hands were shaking. Every face would be fixed upon us. I don't know why, but I'd have been less terrified if we'd been singing to a crowd at the Seattle Coliseum.

At last, we'd begin to sing with clear, strong voices, in perfect harmony. Then, and only then, would I begin to feel some relief. We hadn't started giggling; we were remembering all the words; we were almost through this grim task and on to a more pleasant weekend. On every occasion, stepping down from the platform after singing, Dad would be beaming great smiles at us while making silent clapping motions. Dad was our biggest fan. Still, we wouldn't be able to go to the back with him. Instead, we singers had the honor of returning to that same unhappy front pew, forced to sit through the rest of the service.

"Have you had a chance to see this pasture where Big Mike plans to board your horse?" Dad's voice interrupted my thoughts.

What? Horse? Pulled back into the present, I asked, "Did you say something, Dad?"

"Yes. I asked if you've had a chance to see this pasture where Big Mike plans to board your horse?"

"No," I admitted cautiously. "But I'm sure it will be fine. He knows the people who own the place through his work somehow." When no further comment from Dad seemed forthcoming, I added, "It's over in Redmond."

With raised eyebrow, Dad glanced my way. "Isn't that kind of far?"

"He said he got us a really good deal," I defended.

"That's exactly what worries me."

"He's compulsive. He can't help himself."

Slowing the car as we left the highway, Dad assured me, "Don't worry. I'm not going to say another word about it."

Changing the subject, I said, "It sounded, from what the man said on the phone, as if this could be the perfect horse. I'm so excited!"

"What kind of horse is a 'paint,' anyway?" Dad asked.

"I don't know," I answered thoughtfully. "It might refer to his markings."

"Hold on, there," Dad said, somewhat disconcerted, as he was now heading off to purchase a horse with less than an expert. "I thought you knew everything about horses."

"Well, you stumped me on this one. Guessing though, I'd say paint is a color, not a breed. I don't know if you can breed a horse for color."[1] Then, mumbling to myself, "As long as he's not anything like that other horse, whatever color or breed, I'm certain to like him just fine."

"What did you say?" Dad asked, his concentration now more on fiddling with the radio, trying to tune in his jazz station, than it was on listening to me, which had worked out well.

"Nothing," I said. It was best that he didn't know about the other horse.

Now, as we drove, with jazz horns blaring, piano rifts vibrating up and down our spines, and further conversation out of the question, I couldn't help but think back to the recent, absolutely awful day, when, without my asking, Daddy Mike had helpfully picked out a horse for me. I'm sure he had meant well, when he had dropped me off at a stable on his way to work at the car lot. He had said I was to "check out the horse, take her for a spin, and I'll be back by noon to scratch out a check."

Skat Kat had been everything I didn't want in a horse. A short woman with graying hair led the chestnut mare from her box stall. The horse was saddled and ready to ride. However, the leather trappings didn't conceal her muscular body, thick neck, powerful shoulders, and plumpish rear. "I really think this horse is too much for you, child," the woman said, peering at me over her glasses with a disapproving eye, which, though she was no

---

[1] American Paint Horse Association, founded 1962, www.apha.com

taller than I, made her seem to be looking down on me as she spoke. Skat Kat wore the same snooty expression as her owner. "I told your father, but he insisted that you were an excellent rider." She gave me a doubtful look, adding, "We'll see soon enough."

We were standing in the center of an open grooming area, inside an expansive, aluminum-sided building. "I took the liberty of bringing sugar cubes for you to give to Skat Kat," the woman was saying. Something about that name gave me an unpleasant warning. "It's a little get-to-know-you gesture for you to make," she added, placing the sugar cubes in my right hand. I didn't mention that I was left-handed. I offered the sugar cubes awkwardly with my right hand, noting, when the horse lowered her head to sniff at the cubes, that her entire mane had been shaved, cropped close to her neck. I can't explain why, but I was fairly certain that my dream horse had a mane. The mare blew warm air on the palm of my hand while nibbling at the sugar cubes daintily. As I tried to hold my unsteady hand still and flat, I saw the animal suddenly flatten her ears, bare big yellow teeth, and make a grab for my exposed fingers. I jerked my hand back barely in time, flinging the sugar cubes to the ground. Skat Kat tossed her head, snorting indignantly, whereupon I quickly stooped to retrieve the cubes, and then caught the horse on her chin with the back of my head as I came up.

"An unbelievable performance," the woman said, shaking her head. I would have sprinted out of there right then if there had been somewhere to go. The woman, having similar thoughts but also unable to escape, sounded resigned to her fate. She said, "I can see we'd better start with the basics," and grudgingly recited, "This is a saddle . . ."

I wasn't hearing much of her lesson, though. Instead, I was inwardly seething, thinking, I'm going to have to kill Daddy Mike for this. This time, I'm really going to kill him. Both him and his deals be damned! How could he drive off and leave me here with this . . . this . . .rude . . . All the while these thoughts were whirling around in my head, they were accompanied by the woman's voice droning on in the background.

"Gosh, I hope I haven't missed anything too important," I thought, when I finally tuned back in, just in time to hear, "And you must never mount Skat Kat inside the barn, any barn . . . ever. She has a tendency . . . as so many high-spirited horses do," she quickly added, "to rear up unexpectedly." My blank expression prompted her to continue. "She could hit her head. She could give herself an expensive injury."

Still not understanding the point my instructor was trying to make, I glanced upward. "The ceiling looks plenty high to me."

The woman dipped her chin to take a long assessment of me over her glasses. She shook her head in wonderment that one of her own kind could be so dense. "I meant," she said, "not to ride her through a doorway," she pointed to the barn door.

Turning in that direction, I understood what the woman had been trying so hard not to say. Skat Kat would only rear up when passing through the doorway if she were purposely intent on hurting her rider. "Understood," I said.

Next, I followed my reluctant instructor as she led the mare outside, stopping at the gate of a small corral. "You'll have to take charge to show her who's boss right away," she told me, opening the gate and stepping aside so I could mount. "No matter what happens, you get right back on."

I'll kill him! raced through my mind again. Trapped as I was, contemplating my tightening grip around Daddy Mike's throat had become my only relief. I was barely able to raise my leg high enough to get my foot into the stirrup. Skat Kat was a tall horse, and apparently an impatient one. While I was mounting, the mare wanted to pull away, but the woman had a tight hold on the reins. At that point, I couldn't tell whether the mare was merely enthusiastic about being taken for a ride, or eager to get away from me. As soon as I was in the saddle, wondering if there were some adjustments that were going to be made to the equipment, the woman, quite unexpectedly, handed over the reins with a wicked smile. Skat Kat took advantage of the handoff to thrust sideways through the gate, brutally scraping my leg on a fence post when I couldn't get my foot out of the stirrup fast enough. Before there was even time to register the pain and regain a proper foothold in the stirrup, I found myself lying breathless on the ground, gazing up at a blue sky and swirling white clouds.

"What happened?" I asked the face peering down at me.

"It's called a crow hop."

With Skat Kat being led my way, "I can't kill him," I decided, thinking again of my dad. "Hell's too good for him!"

"It's very important that you remount immediately," the woman was saying. "Otherwise, you could lose control of your horse permanently." The mare gave me a menacing, sneering sizing up as I walked up to the saddle, forever branding her face on my memory. Despite her attempt at intimidation, I made a much better second mount, and took up the reins with hope and determination. "Just walk your horse around the arena," my instructor said, almost pleasantly, trying to impart confidence. "I'll tell you when to change gaits."

"Okay," was all I managed to get out before the face was again peering down at me.

"I'm certain your father said you were an experienced rider," the woman said, helping me to my feet.

"He's a salesman," I defended, brushing myself off. "He tends to exaggerate things. He probably meant that I'm an experienced rider when compared with any other fourteen-year-old girl who has never ridden a horse before."

"Yes. I'm sure that's what he must have meant," she agreed. "Shall we try again?" Amazingly, I felt my head nodding an affirmative. So this is what it means to be knocked silly, I thought. We walked over to where Skat Kat was absorbed in trying to remove her bridle by rubbing her head aggressively on the top of a fence post. "Stop that!" the woman ordered fiercely. "I'm about to lose my patience with you!" And grabbing the reins, she jerked the mare's head away from the fence.

Again, I remounted. Round three. Skat Kat made a lunge forward even before I was properly seated with the reins securely in hand. No time for heroics, I dropped the reins and grabbed for the saddle horn in front and the cantle in back. Skat Kat made erratic, violent, stiff-legged hops around the corral. I imagined these to be the crow hops the woman had spoken of earlier. I knew I wasn't going to be able to hold on long. Seeming to read my mind, the mare twisted her head around to give me another hateful snarl, and then renewed her enraged efforts to unseat me by rearing high into the air. Convinced that the heavy horse would fall over backwards, on me, I leaned far forward to help keep our balance, loosening my grip on the back of the saddle. I realized my mistake immediately as I went sailing high over the fence.

Dad punched the Off button on the radio at the same moment our car tires crunched on gravel. Daddy Ray and I had arrived at our destination.

Rodeo Ranch was exactly the kind of place young, horse-crazy girls such as myself visualize in their dreams. The pastures were scenically dotted with grazing horses and there was a corral area where there were even more horses. An enclosed, full-sized riding arena contained horses with riders, and there were adjoining barns with rows of horse-filled stalls. If you got tired of horses, as if such a thing could ever happen, you could wander through stacks of saddles and other wonders inside the well-outfitted tack shack. Rodeo Ranch had it all—even a cute, young, cowboy-type, who knew everything about horses and lived in a trailer out back.

Although it was still early when we arrived, the place was bustling with activity. There were other cars on the lot—other buyers. At first, Dad and I stood around, waiting to be noticed, waiting our turn outside the tack shack. But soon, as we began feeling more adventurous, we decided to start our own search of the many stalls in the multi-acre complex for a "strikingly-marked" paint.

"Here's a beauty," I said jokingly, calling Dad over. From my viewing angle at the rear of the stall, all that could be seen was a big black rump protruding from its close dark quarters. As I came up beside the huge horse for a better look at the whole animal, the horse shifted positions, mashing me against an unforgiving wall. "Ugh," was my muffled cry for help.

"Well! You knucklehead!" Dad said, rushing to my aid. "What did you expect?" Gallantly, at some risk to himself, he pushed as hard as he could on the massive hindquarter, which only served to make the horse press harder against me.

"Need help, partner?" a man asked.

"I think we do," Dad answered.

"Kind of a predicament," the man said, addressing me. He was an older man, hatless, with thinning gray hair. "You stay right still, little lady." He received only a grimace in reply. Turning, he took hold of a nearby pitchfork.

"I'll have you out in a jiffy. Stand back," he said, waving Dad aside. With the pitchfork and practiced expertise, the man administered a healthy jab to the flank of the unbudging horse, at the same time pulling me free of the possibility of flailing hooves.

Taking a deep breath, I gratefully thanked the man. "Thank you. I think I may have just learned an important lesson."

"Is this place always so busy?" Dad asked.

"Sometimes." We followed the man outside. "Had two truckloads of horses arrive this mornin'."

"That's why we're here," Dad said. "We came to see the paint they brought in."

"Someone's taken him out for a ride," the man answered. "Nice horse," he added.

"There he is!" I cried, spotting a group of horses and riders coming up the lane. My horse was easily recognizable, a large paint, prancing proudly in the lead. As they rode past, I took the opportunity to look the horse over, noting his striking markings. The horse, which was predominately a pleasing reddish-brown color, had a mostly white rump, splashes of white on his sides, neck, and shoulders, and four white stockings that extended above his knees. He also had a long mane that was a mixture of his red and white coloring, and a full, long, white tail. His handsome head had a white blaze that spread across his forehead and all the way down his face to include a pink muzzle.

"Hold on!" Dad said, hanging on to me as I started with purpose toward the horse and dismounting rider. "We'll have our chance." I was anxious, worried that the dismounting rider was going to buy my horse.

We waited for a few minutes, and then followed when the paint was led into the arena, careful to keep a polite distance. Once inside, the man who had helped us earlier motioned for us to come over. "This here's Wild Bill, little lady," the man said, attempting a formal introduction. "And they call me Hank."

I nodded to the young man who had been riding my horse, relieved that he worked at the ranch and wasn't going to buy the horse. "Wild Bill Hickock?" I asked stupidly, flustered by his good looks, as well as admiring his Western garb: black cowboy hat, black cowboy boots, fringed black leather chaps, and beaded buckskin jacket.

"No," came the smiling reply, "Wild Bill Smith. Would you like to take a ride?"

Suddenly, I felt mortified at the prospect of riding before the scrutiny of these two experts, as it occurred to me then that maybe I didn't know how to ride a horse, since most of the horses I had ridden had been in a line of horses, following other horses.

"No, thank you," I started to say.

"Don't be ridiculous," Dad said, hustling me forward.

On the way to the saddle, passing by the head of the horse, I peered into his brown eyes giving him a most pleading "please be nice" appeal. The paint stood quietly for me to mount, which impressed me. He wasn't pulling away, as Skat Kat had done. Then, he was patient as we rode, when I proceeded to give him the confusing cross signals of a novice rider who knows not one whit of riding protocol. The men watched, chatting, while we circled the arena several times.

When finished riding, I led the paint over to where the men were talking. "So what do you think, Con?" Dad asked—as if he didn't know.

Next Dad and I got some needed instruction about what to consider before purchasing a horse, and about how to tell if a horse is healthy. Wild Bill pulled up the horse's lip to expose his teeth for our inspection. "His teeth and gums are healthy," the young man pointed out. "I'd say his age is close to six years."

Dad and I looked at each other. Yes, we agreed, the horse had teeth. "There's no bit on this bridle," I said questioningly.

"That's right," the young man explained. "This is a hackamore. Instead of a bit, there's a chain under the chin." He pulled back gently on the reins to show how the chain strap tightened.

"Isn't that painful?" I asked.

"It would be if you began jerking on the reins. Instead, use quick, easy pulls." He demonstrated, saying, "I suggest you stay with the hackamore, since that's how this horse was trained."

Next we were invited to inspect the horse's hooves. Wild Bill lifted each hoof as he gave a lengthy lecture about healthy hooves and a happy horse. Dad's hazel eyes studied each hoof intently, his blond head nodding in agreement with everything Wild Bill said. Dad's tennis shoes and white shorts stood out in citified contrast to the fringed chaps and cowboy boots. When the young man was finished, Dad and I looked at each other. Yes, we agreed, the horse had hooves. The horse was standing, and he was definitely the right price. Dad pulled the checkbook from the back pocket of his shorts. "I'll have to call you about where to deliver the horse," he said. We watched the paint being led into an empty stall, and then followed the older man to the tack shack.

"This here's where you really get to put that checkbook to use," Hank said with a knowing smile, opening the door for us. "You for sure need a bridle and halter."

Entering the tack shack, my nose came happily alive at the sweet smell of leather, and my hands joyously touched everything within their grasp. It was a large room, but it felt cramped with the many hats hanging overhead, and every sort of bridle, bit, halter, coils of rope, and more, bulging out from straining pegs on every wall. Packed shelves consisted of boxes over-flowing with clothing, boots, brushes, oils, and medicines. The haphazard arrangement of saddles, mounted on wooden stands, made the tack room floor an obstacle course. Making my way to the bridles on the far wall, I stumbled over a stack of buckets, sending a pile of catalogs sprawling. Dad hardly noticed—he hadn't made it past the price tag dangling from the first saddle he'd encountered. His face was ashen.

"What's wrong, Dad?" I asked, bending to regroup the catalogs. Then, receiving no answer, I went over for a look. "Gosh!" I exclaimed. "The saddles cost more than the horse! Lucky we won't be needing one."

Dad's face showed dismay. "Of course you'll need a saddle."

"Indians ride bareback, Dad," I said solemnly. "You must know that." In reality, it wasn't anything to do with my courageous, best-of-the-best, alter ego–Apache self; it was about the expense. But I knew he would fall for it.

Dad studied my blue eyes and nearly white, shoulder-length hair skepti-cally. "Right," he said, shaking his head. "For a minute there I forgot you were part-Apache."

"That's right," I said, somewhat defiantly. "I am."

"Well, you'll have to excuse me if I don't see it."

"That's okay, Dad," I then softened. "It's the part you can't see."

"The part that asks for an archery set or a rifle every Christmas? All the same, I'm sure you'll need a saddle."

"I can't imagine why I would," I said, leading him toward the bridles. "Besides, if I ever do, we can find a used one."

"That makes sense," Dad agreed, sounding cheered and reassured.

I led Dad around the saddles over to where Hank was untangling a jumble of bridles, talking to them all the while. He seemed to need the one attached to all the others. "Here you are, you little devil," he said at last, giving the errant bridle a chastening shake. "This is your bridle," he said then, presenting me with a confusing bundle of leather straps. The leather of the bridle was the same reddish-brown color as the horse. The man returned the rejected bridles to their peg in one tangled mass. "And there you be," he told them kindly.

The halters were arranged on pegs by color. Hank held up a green one. "Here's a fine specimen," he said.

"I'm sure white would be the best color for the horse," I said decisively.

"Maybe so," he reluctantly agreed. "Sorry, old boy," he said to the green halter, gently putting it back. "Now I'd better help you pick out brushes."

With Dad outside opening the car trunk for Wild Bill to load in a sack of grain, Hank and I stooped together over a big box of assorted brushes, all sizes and all prices. "Hank," I said, taking the opportunity now that we were alone, "I want to thank you again for coming to my rescue earlier."

"It happens," he said, not looking up. "Some horses, they're just plain spiteful."

"I already found that out," I said grimly.

Pausing in his search through the brushes, the man looked over at me, saying, "Your horse, though . . . I guarantee he's a sweetheart. I knew it right away, the first time I laid eyes on him. I've been in this business over fifty years, and I can always tell. I can always tell by their eyes. Your horse has honest eyes."

From the brushes, I chose a metal currycomb with a red leather strap, a wood-handled bristle brush, a hoof pick, and a metal comb for untangling the horse's mane and tail. We found a yellow, plastic bucket, which, Hank assured, was the perfect size for giving the horse his grain.

While Dad wrote out the check for our purchases, I admired the silver objects in the glass case. There were shiny silver spurs and buckles, fancy silver bits, and other parade-quality finery.

"We sure appreciated all your help, Hank" Dad said, offering his hand to shake as we stood by the car. Everyone had been so friendly to us there, at Rodeo Ranch, that they had taken away much of the stress we had felt making our decision about purchasing the horse.

"Glad to be of service," Hank said. "Call if you ever need any help. I mean it, little lady." He looked at Dad, "We'll be hearing from you then about where to deliver that horse."

"'Bye, Hank. Thanks again!" I waved as we headed for our rendezvous at the lake.

CHAPTER TWO

The first place we boarded the horse was the cheapest place Daddy Mike could find. My girlfriend Karen and I begged an early ride out to the pasture from my mother, who had to drive quite a distance out of her way to take us to Redmond and beyond, and then drive back to Bellevue where she worked as a receptionist in a doctor's office. Now my friend and I stood together at the pasture gate, waving good-bye to my mom as she drove off in a cloud of dust. I had halter in hand.

Once the car was gone, there was silence, a country silence unfamiliar to me. Karen and I climbed up on the lowest rail of the rickety gate to survey our surroundings. It was the first time I had seen the place. My eyes, completely dismissing the house, scanned beyond for a barn. There was no barn, only a very rough and small lean-to where grain could be stored. Standing there, in the summer sunlight, I studied the lean-to critically. I gulped. No barn—that meant there would be no refuge from Seattle's frequent rain, or, for that matter, from any inclement weather. As it was already late summer, and the fall rainy season would soon be upon us, this was definitely a concern.

Moving on, past the lean-to and the tiny corral to which it was attached, I noted that much of the property didn't even have a sturdy fence. Instead, a carelessly strung up mixture of barbed and electric wire was used to keep the animals enclosed. Gosh, I hope the horse likes it in this pasture, crossed my mind, since it would sure be easy for him to escape. I turned back for a thoughtful inspection of the house and yard area. There was a rundown old house, a small rambler. Then again, maybe it wasn't rundown, or old. It was hard to tell since much of the house was covered with ivy and concealed by overgrown gardens. With no car in the driveway, and not even a dog to greet us, I found the deserted appearance of the place a bit unsettling, maybe even a little eerie.

"It sure doesn't look as if anyone is home," I said.

"I guess you have to work all the time to afford a place like this," Karen commented. She wasn't seeing the spooky house, or the disappointing lean-to, or the sagging fences, only the lush field of tall grass stretched out before us. Daddy Mike had said that we wouldn't need to buy hay.

Now, opening the pasture gate, we stepped inside. The only horses to be seen from where we stood were grouped in the distance grazing near a grove of trees. In addition to the paint, we counted five Shetland ponies. There may have been horses elsewhere on the place, as the large field stretched into the distance, around the back of the house, and all the way to the other side of the driveway as well.

"Do you just whistle?" Karen asked.

"I can't whistle. Can you?"

"Sometimes," came the guarded reply.

Karen was my best friend. We lived close to one another and attended the same junior high school. My friend had short dark hair, and some would say she was a bit chunky, although she looked perfectly fine to me. She was of Alaskan native decent, a Tlinget, who had been adopted as a baby by a wonderful family. Sadly, however, my friend knew nothing about being a Native American and, in fact, was prone to yawn in boredom at the mere mention of the subject.

We began advancing toward the horses, taking one halting step at a time in an effort to keep from spooking them. "You can start whistling," I prodded. Obligingly, Karen pursed her lips, slowly sucking in air, and finally emitting a quiet, moaning sound. Midway to the horses, we stopped our advance so that she could concentrate while trying again. She certainly made an effort, puckering her lips, licking her lips, puckering again, blowing and sucking every which way, with the same quiet, moaning result.

Disgusted, I said, "That's it? He'll never hear that. Can't you whistle any louder than that?"

"I can only whistle when I suck in," Karen explained defensively. "Besides, what would you do if I wasn't here?"

We had attracted the attention of all the horses the moment we had come in at the gate. The paint had raised his head from grazing and had been watching our approach the whole time, somewhat warily, his ears pointing toward us in a listening attitude. The ponies, also watching us the whole time, were more curious than cautious, one even taking a few steps in our direction. And now, as we started forward again, that pony, a gray, ambled right up to greet us. It was clearly disappointed when we shooed it away, and it only retreated a step or two.

By now, we'd abandoned the whistling and our reproaches. "Here, old boy," I said in my sweetest, softest tones, again, while inching forward, and wondering how I'd neglected to ask them at Rodeo Ranch if the horse had a name. "Easy, old boy." The other ponies straggled over to join their gray friend; perhaps they thought I was calling to them. We were surrounded. The paint, still at some distance, no longer seeing us as a threat, returned to his grazing.

"These ponies are sure friendly," Karen said. Then she became apprehensive when one of the ponies began nibbling at her sleeve, and said, "Are they dangerous?"

At any other time, on any other day, I would have enthusiastically welcomed the attention of ponies, but right then, I was concentrating on trying to catch my horse. "Let's clap our hands," I suggested. "That will scare them off." We clapped loudly, and sure enough, the startled ponies reared back and then raced around the pasture like a miniature herd of wild mustangs. The paint had raised his head to watch the activities, so I decided to take advantage of his distraction. "Here old boy," I said again, slowly proceeding one step at a time. I was allowed within a tantalizing few feet of the animal before he turned his back and walked away. When I followed, he quickened his pace, always staying a frustrating step or two ahead. Finally, turning away in despair, I saw that Karen was, yet again, completely surrounded by ponies.

"Help!" she cried, shuffling toward me.

"Can't you keep them busy while I catch my horse?" I said, thinking that sounded like a logical plan.

One of the ponies gave her a shove with its head. "Help!" Karen cried again. That's when, patience gone, I picked up a dead branch, and waving it, ran at the ponies, determined to be done with them once and for all. The ponies, however, were delighted with what they thought was a game. They weren't afraid or running scared, but instead took off galloping and cavorting around the pasture, kicking and bucking, and playfully nipping at each other's heels. They were putting on quite a show.

"See that one in the lead?" I pointed. He was a beautiful brown pony, with a long, flowing mane and tail. "Let's call him Comanche," I suggested. Frustrated by many unsuccessful attempts to catch my own horse, I said, "I wonder if he's tame? Maybe we can ride him." We watched the pony herd race down the pasture, disappear into a forested area, and less than a minute later, emerge from the other side of the forest, where the herd slowed to make a sharp turn to avoid a section of fence before thundering back up our way.

Now ponies pressing inward from every side surrounded us again. Only Comanche kept a reserved distance outside the circle. I tried approaching him, but he reacted in the same manner as my horse had, trotting off and only returning after he felt I had lost all interest in him.

"Karen," I said, feeling a brainstorm coming on, "have you noticed that the ponies always go the same way? I mean, have you noticed how they always have to slow to make that turn when they come out of the trees? Why don't I go down there, hide in the woods, and you chase the ponies down. Then, I'll jump on Comanche just as he makes that turn."

The ponies had worn a path around the pasture and through the trees that was easy to follow. I hid in the woods at the spot in the trail where the racing pony herd would have to make their turn. Waiting there, Karen's yells and the sound of pounding hooves could be heard. Peeking out from my hiding place, I could see that Comanche was, as usual, in the lead as the herd raced down the far side of the pasture and entered the wooded trails. I waited. Very soon, Comanche appeared at the end of the trail where I was hiding and now had to slow to make that sharp turn. That was the moment I grabbed hold of his long mane and swung onto his back for a wild, bucking ride up the pasture. This sport would never have been possible except for the lush carpet of grass that softened our falls. Karen and I took turns chasing the ponies down the pasture and riding Comanche until we and the ponies were completely exhausted.

After that we rested, lunching in the shade of the trees in the middle of the pasture. "I think my butt is totally bruised," I said, munching on a sandwich while watching the ponies grazing in the distance; they were having their lunch, too. "Look at that," I said quietly, in some wonderment, to Karen, noticing that the paint had come quite close to us while we rested. His behavior was particularly strange, since it was such a large pasture, stretching all around and out of sight, that he certainly didn't need to be anywhere near us—unless he chose to be. Deciding to take advantage of the situation, groaning, I rose stiffly to my feet. "I think I'll make another effort to catch my horse," I said.

"Good luck," Karen answered, with little interest.

The minute I began to advance toward the paint, he turned away.

"Why don't you hide the halter behind your back," Karen suggested with a yawn.

"Could he be that stupid?" I called over my shoulder, though I switched the halter to my right hand, and held it hidden behind me. Then, at a complete surprise to me, I slowly walked right up to the horse, where he merely stood there waiting. At first, I wasn't sure what to do. Standing next to him, he seemed so tall, especially after having spent time with the ponies. I rubbed my hand along his neck, while at the same time he sniffed me curiously. My intent was to slip the halter over his head when he wasn't looking, but when I brought the halter around it dawned on me that I didn't know how to put it on.

"That can't be right," Karen said, popping a grape into her mouth, eyeing the horse critically. "He won't be able to see with the rope over his eye that way." Then, "That's a little better. But what's that ring thing on the top of his head for?" Although he could have easily walked off at any time he chose, the horse remained patient while the halter was changed around until it looked right.

Turning back to my friend, who sat comfortably leaning against a tree with her legs sprawled out in front of her, I said, "I'm going to lead him around the pasture. You stay where you are for now so he won't get nervous." Clipping the lead rope to the ring, now correctly placed under the horse's chin, I started off at an easy walk. I was surprised when the horse came right along, and then became anxious as he was practically walking over me. I sped up to get out of the way of his huge hooves, but he stayed right with me, his head directly over my shoulder. Remembering Skat Kat, I was worried that he would take a bite out of my shoulder. But moving to the side didn't help either; the horse stayed right with me.

"What are you doing?" Karen called. "You look ridiculous jumping around like that."

"He's going to trample me," I explained. "Why is he following me so closely?"

"You're asking me?" Karen said in mock amazement. "When you're always saying how you know everything about horses?"

Accompanied by Karen's merry laughter, the paint and I walked around the pasture as if we were a comic act in a circus. For although the halter was equipped with a sufficiently long lead, the paint insisted on following too closely. He was crowding, as if he were attached to me, with his head positioned directly over my shoulder. This was very disconcerting. If there was one thing to be noticed about this horse, it was his remarkably huge hooves. But race forward, lunge to side, arms extended, no matter what was tried, the big paint walked with his head directly over me, his huge, clomping hooves not a half-inch from my moccasin-clad feet.

"Karen," I called, "Why don't you stop laughing and come on over here. Let me give you a leg up, and I'll lead you around the field."

"Are you sure it'll be okay?" she asked attempting to sober up. She came over, wiping the tears from her eyes, but still emitting little choking laughs. Except for Comanche, as far as I was aware, old Nellie had been the only other horse that Karen had ever ridden. Dropping down on one knee, I cupped my hands, and whooshed Karen into the air, precisely at the moment the horse sidestepped away. So we moved a foot or two over to try again. Suddenly, the paint lowered his head and flattened his ears, while at the same time, pawing and pounding the ground with his massive left front hoof. From *Black Beauty* to *National Velvet*, I had never seen anything like it. Karen and I fled screaming across the pasture, a specter horse snorting and snapping at our heels.

"Gosh! I thought we were goners," I panted, peering out from behind a protective tree.

"I thought he was right on our tail!" Karen agreed. "But he's just standing there now," she added in disbelief, "just where we left him."

It took some convincing, but I assured my friend that I had never heard of a horse attacking its master. Surely, we had imagined the whole ugly incident. With summoned bravery, we cautiously approached the horse again. Indeed, he was standing exactly in the same spot where we had so quickly left him. He appeared calm, innocently switching at flies with his tail. He even gave me a friendly nudge with his head as I took hold of the lead rope again. However, as soon as I tried to help Karen up a second time, the horse lowered his head, ears flattened, his massive hoof pawing and pounding the earth 'til it shook. That was it. Karen and I raced in outright terror to the nearest fence and dove under.

Now from the safety of our position behind the fence, we studied the horse that was, again, standing so quietly. Not only was he now standing quietly, he seemed to be studying us as well.

"Is he laughing at us?" Karen asked.

"Apparently this game is to his liking," I answered.

"What should we do?" Karen asked expectantly.

Standing up and dusting myself off, I said, "I don't know."

"But you always say . . . ," Karen began.

"Please, Karen," I said. "Would you, this once, forget what I always say." I gave my friend a hand up. "See that big stump over there?" I pointed. "Let's put you up on that stump. I'll lead the horse by, and you jump on." Karen's face showed skepticism. "Just like Comanche," I added. And, further explaining my strategy, "He can't paw the ground while he's walking."

"Okay," Karen said dusting herself off. Sighing, she said, "My mom's going to kill me when she sees me." Karen's mom always had her well-dressed in starched and ironed clothing, and most times, like today, her play attire included a nice white blouse with a lace collar. In contrast, I was dressed in cut-off blue jeans and an old flannel shirt I had borrowed, without asking, from one of my brothers.

"Aw, you don't look so bad," I said cheerfully, picking grass from her dark hair.

My plan with the stump worked. I led Karen and the horse around the field with the ever-friendly ponies following in procession. Suddenly, behind me, the paint tripped, staggered, and nearly tumbled. It was a dramatic, all-out stumble to his knees, hard to miss, even though I had been turned away.

"What happened?" Karen exclaimed, white-faced, having been pitched forward almost over the horse's head.

Scanning the ground under the horse and all around, I said, "I guess he tripped on something."

"What was it?" Karen asked.

"I don't see anything," I said, somewhat concerned. "I guess he must have tripped over his own big feet."

With me still leading and Karen riding, we took several more turns around the upper pasture, and then headed down into the wooded area with its labyrinth of trails. There we were winding our way through the woods along a particularly narrow section of trail, when Karen gave a quiet cry. At the same time, the horse balked, refusing to take another step. What could be wrong? My view was blocked. With the trail so narrow, all that could be seen was my horse's big head. Finally, I had to squeeze past him to have a look. That's when I saw a frightening situation. Karen was pushed far back onto the horse's rump, hanging in an upside-down position, with her head between his back legs. She had a two-handed grip on his tail. A branch had pushed her back and had her wedged down tight. The horse had barely stopped in time. Visions of a kicking, bucking horse, and all of its certain consequences, rose before me.

"Karen," I whispered. "Don't move."

"I'm pinned!" Karen exclaimed, her face appearing strange talking in its upside-down position. "I can't move!"

Standing as I was, at the side of the horse, I attempted to pull my friend back up onto the horse's back. But I soon realized a push was needed, and that I would have to get completely around behind the horse to get any kind of leverage. With the lead too short to stretch any further, it made me very nervous because it meant no one would be in control in front of the horse. Thinking it was a bad idea, I dropped the lead and moved behind.

All the while, as I pushed and Karen struggled to get free, we had to wonder what the horse was thinking about all this commotion at his rear. Why didn't he simply walk away, letting Karen fall? Finally I said, "I hate to say it, Karen, but you'll have to let go of the tail. We can't push you back up, so I'll have to help you slide down." Holding my friend's shoulders, I braced for her weight. Karen let go of the tail. Nothing happened.

"Move . . ugh . . . move the branch." Karen, who had regained her two-handed grip on the tail, was finding it difficult to speak. I put on an aggressive show with the heavy limb, with much leaf rustling and groaning, though from my position at the back of the horse it could barely be reached, as it was up and over Karen. I had to push up on it with only one raised hand, as the other was needed to support her in case she began to fall. Still, with all the effort, the branch hadn't moved more than an inch. "This isn't going to work," Karen finally said. In the end, we could see only one sad solution to our problem. There would be no budging the branch unless I moved around to the other side of the horse and got directly under it. Then I would have to push up as hard as possible on the branch, and, completely unaided by me, my friend would have to let go of the tail and fall backwards, headfirst, off the horse.

When at last we had accomplished the deed, I rushed around to her. "Are you all right?"

"I think so."

"Your beautiful blouse is torn," I said woefully, helping her to her feet. "Let's not do any more riding today," I suggested.

As both of us led the horse back up the pasture, "Your horse sure is nice," Karen said. "He could have walked away, any time, and let me fall. I was terrified he would start kicking."

"So was I," I admitted. "And did you notice how he waited for us even after you fell?"

We then lavished the paint with petting and praise to make sure he realized how much we appreciated his good-natured and gentle behavior during our difficult maneuverings. It was late in the day and we were tired and dirty, but we were beginning to like the horse and feel more comfortable around him. I knew horses could be vicious biters and sneaky kickers. However, I felt reasonably certain this horse didn't bite or kick. If he did, he would have availed himself of one of the many opportunities presented during the afternoon. Still, I knew it would naturally take time to build the trust so important between a girl and her horse.

Deciding to give the horse his grain and brush him before freeing him in the field, we led him across the pasture, around the back of the lean-to, and into what could only be loosely described as a corral. The lean-to made up one side of the small enclosure, with barbed and electric wire making up the other three sides. After leading the horse inside, I tethered him to a hitching post. Once the big paint was inside, the corral shrank even more in size, making it difficult to maneuver. The door to the shelter could barely be opened wide enough to get the brushes and grain for the horse. Working within the tight space, I scooped two generous helpings of molasses-sweetened oats out of the bag, and poured the oats into his new round plastic dishpan, munching a few as I worked. Then Karen and I rested, sprawled in the grass outside the enclosure, while the horse ate his meal.

"What will you name your horse?" Karen asked lazily, chewing on a piece of grass.

Replying absently, "Nothing has come to mind yet," as I eyed a nearby garden hose, wooden bucket, and bottle of liquid dish soap, all conveniently placed as if someone had recently washed their car. We were in fact lying on the grass next to the gravel drive. "Karen, let's give the horse a bath," I suggested.

Karen gave me a suspicious glance, "Why would we want to do that?"

"I think it would be fun, that's why. I'll let you work the hose and I'll scrub."

Karen was dubious. "I don't know," she said. "He doesn't look dirty."

"Oh, come on, Karen," I said enthusiastically. "It'll be fun."

"You mean fun, like getting up at 5:30 in the morning is fun for you?"

"I promise not to set the clocks ahead anymore, Karen. I promise." And, begging, "Please, let's give the horse a bath."

"Oh, all right," Karen shook her head, giving in, "but I already know I'll regret it."

We decided to wash the horse in the same way you would wash a car. Karen would operate the hose; I would suds and scrub. I set the bucket partially under the barbed wire fence at the head of the horse, filling it with soapy water. Then I stood trying to calm the paint, whose breathing had quickened and whose nostrils had flared, as he was beginning to understand what we had in mind for him.

Again, hesitating, "Are you sure this is a good idea?" Karen said, eyeing the horse's distress.

"Are you going to help or not?" I answered, probably sounding somewhat annoyed. "You can spray from where you are. You don't even have to come inside the enclosure." Still shaking her head with misgivings, Karen began spraying the horse with water. Things were going well, until I bent down to retrieve the soapy brush from the bucket. At which point, the paint, politely taking several steps back to afford me more room, gave himself a nasty jolt of electricity on his rump. Lunging forward, the startled animal propelled me face first through the barbed wire fence.

"Owwwch!" I cried. "Owwwch!" My chin was torn and bleeding.

My friend, panicked by my unabashed yowling, lost control of the hose. It now flip-flopped, freely spraying us all. "Grab the hose!" I yelled. Meanwhile, the paint, rearing back to avoid the spray in his face, had pulled the hitching post straight up out of the ground. Now he was dripping wet and anxious, pressing against the corral gate, with the fence post half-dangling from his lead. The message was clear; this horse had had enough for one day.

Karen and I were waiting quietly at the entrance to the gravel drive when my mother arrived to pick us up.

* * *

The Arend family lived in a two-story house in the sprawling Lake Hills residential area. We ate our meals together at the kitchen table, which was actually a built-in, peninsula-shaped bar. Daddy Mike encouraged all hands to attend every meal, and he did much of the cooking himself. According to him, there were three squares each day, as he called them, with breakfast being the most important. If the phone rang during a meal, Dad answered and had whomever it was call back later—unless it was business. With a salesman and so many teenagers in the house, the phone was in constant use.

Around the crowded kitchen bar that evening, sitting on high stools, were my mother, Aggie, my brother, Little Mike, my sisters, Cher and Lindy, and me. Only our oldest brother, Walt, was missing from the table, as he was in the Marines at the time. Dad joined us, sitting down after everyone had been served. "Mike!" Dad barked. "Would you stop!" Our brother had been discussing my injury as it compared to some food on the table. It was a ploy to sicken his sisters, thereby getting more food for himself. We sisters merely giggled. However, his nauseating comments had worked on Mom, whose request to be excused had been denied.

"You know, Con," Dad started, "If you get hurt again, we might have to rethink this whole horse thing." Luckily, though, my wound wasn't the main topic of conversation that evening. Addressing my sisters, he continued, "And you two, with your loud music!" Our neighbors across the street, a patient family, were complaining again. "One more complaint from Mr. Hargrave and I'm throwing that hi-fi out the window."

"But," Cher interjected, as the spokesperson for the two, "but we . . ."

"'But we,' nothing," Dad cut her off. "Mr. Hargrave mentioned that there was, pretty much, a party going on here all day." That ratfink, we kids were all thinking. Dad, reading our minds, warned, "I'd better not hear about another snake in their mailbox, either. And, Mike, I don't know how many times I've told you I don't want your friends over here when we're not home." Dad was concerned about Little Mike's good-looking, football playing friends from high school hanging around our house on long summer days when he had two attractive, voluptuous, boy-crazy, unchaperoned, teen-aged daughters at home, dancing around the house. At that point, the dinner conversation turned to pleas for spending money. Little Mike wanted gas money, Cher wanted money to go to the movies with her friends, and Lindy wanted money to go shopping at Crossroads Mall with her friends, and so on and so on.

After dinner, and after having waited for my turn to use the phone—the youngest always last—I called my friend. "I'm grounded," Karen said.

"Mom says you're a bad influence. She says just because you have a horse doesn't mean that I have to get myself killed, too."

"Great. How long this time?"

"She said two weeks."

"Which translates to one," I added knowingly.

Lying in bed that evening, gently fondling the stitches on my chin, I tried to think of a name for my horse. I thought back over some of my favorite Westerns, and the names of famous Indian chiefs and tribes. Sugarfoot came to mind—too cute. I thought of Cochise, War Chief of the Apache, who was my personal hero. I loved the name, "Cochise," but I was concerned that it might be disrespectful to name a horse after such a distinguished historical figure. Then I thought of Shane. The name came from a popular Western at the time. Somehow, Shane seemed right.

Mom poked her head around my bedroom door. "Are you asleep?" she asked softly.

"No, Mom," I answered, sliding over to give her room to sit down on the edge of the bed.

My mother was a beautiful woman of Swedish decent, who had blue-green eyes and wore her honey blond hair in a French roll. "How do you feel?" she asked, lovingly caressing my forehead with a cool hand.

"I feel great, Mom," I said enthusiastically. "I'm trying to think of a name for my horse . . ."

Mom interrupted. "You must know that your dad was worried sick about what happened to you today."

"Nothing happened," I said defensively. "I'm fine."

"You know that your dad's uncle was killed by a horse," Mom continued.

"Daddy Mike's uncle was killed by a horse, too?" I exclaimed in astonishment.

"No. I'm talking about your Daddy Ray. That's why your Grandma Hanes doesn't allow horses on her farm."

"I know that, Mom."

"Well, then, you understand how shaky he is on this whole deal."

"I'll be more careful, Mom. I promise."

"I know you will, sweetheart. I know you will." She kissed me on the forehead as she got up to leave.

"Don't close the door all the way, Mom," I reminded her.

From my bed, with the bedroom door left slightly ajar, I could watch my mother sitting at the kitchen bar. I couldn't see into the kitchen, but I could see her silhouette, framed in a narrow band of light, sitting on a stool just inside the kitchen archway. It was there, after everyone else had gone to bed, and while she was still tending the washer and dryer cycles downstairs, that she smoked, sipped a toddy, played solitaire, and worked crossword puzzles late into the night. Staying up late was her way of stealing a moment of peace from our house of bedlam. I loved to watch her sitting there, comfortable in her robe and slippers, and enjoying herself so completely, marveling at the hushed household, when she thought she was at last alone.

CHAPTER THREE

I was eight, and my sister, Cher, was ten when our parents divorced. Our mother had fallen in love with a salesman who was the manager at the car dealership where she worked.

Until that day, my sister and I had lived a sheltered, religious life of ordered serenity. In fact, it seemed as if our whole life revolved around the church and church-related activities. And there were lots of activities, from Friday night worship, to Sabbath morning church service, to Saturday afternoon potlucks and picnics. Usually we went to someone's house, often our own, for a multi-family dinner. We also enjoyed frequent Saturday night church socials, where a nature film might be shown and vegetarian hamburgers, called Shamburgers, might be served. Although we took our worship seriously, we weren't a sober, always-kneeling group; we liked to laugh, play, and have fun, too. During the week, my sister and I attended a private church school. The word "divorce" was unknown to us. The church had guidelines for conduct. No jewelry, not even a wedding band, was worn. Dancing was taboo, any movie suspect, and absolutely no profanity was used. Smoking and drinking were unheard of. But none of this seemed strange to us. Our parents were raising my sister and me strictly and lovingly, in the same manner in which they had been raised by their parents. Until I was eight, I lived in a world largely comprised of devout Seventh-day Adventists.

Our family of four had moved to the Seattle area from California when I was two, and our father had accepted an engineering job with Boeing. All our roots and relatives were in the Washington and Oregon area, so for us, our move to the Northwest had represented more of a return home from California, where Dad had been working for Standard Oil after completing his Master's at Oregon State University. We had settled quickly into our new life. Our parents, both young and attractive, were a popular couple with lots of friends. These were not only friends from church, but friends from our neighborhood, and friends from Boeing as well. Our father was appreciated as one of those upstanding guys, always eager to offer assistance, the kind of person on which one could depend. The news of our parents' breakup was shocking, as we all, especially my sister and myself, thought the couple was blissfully happy. The news, however, particularly sent shock waves through our cloistered community, since divorce, rare at that time, was almost unheard of among our Adventist friends. Our father was devastated. Everyone knew how much he loved Mom, and everyone knew how important his family was to him.

The unthinkable happened one cold January night, when Mom said she was taking us girls shopping, but instead drove us to the parking lot of a strange apartment building. There she gently informed us that this was where we were going to live with a new family. Leave our father? Leave Dad? Who would take care of Dad? Cher and I cried for a very long time. In many ways, as children of divorce, we never stopped crying. Sobbing, we listened to our mother explain about falling in love, and about how she had to live her own life. She told us she was marrying a widower, Mike Arend, who had two sons and a daughter. Then, after drying our tears, she took us on a tour of a bleak, empty apartment, explaining that we would be living there with her and our new brothers and sister during the week, and spending our weekends with Dad.

When Cher and I met the Arend family, on a Sunday afternoon in January, they were in the process of moving into the apartment, unpacking boxes and putting their things away. Mom introduced us to Big Mike, who was exactly that—big! He was a tall, stout, barrel-chested man who had a slightly receding hairline and pale blue eyes. Cher and I peered out from behind our mother at the three children who peered back at us from behind their dad. The boys were Walt, fourteen, and Mike, eleven. Their sister,

Linda, was about our age, actually right in between, seven months older than I and nine months younger than Cher. All three had the same pale blue eyes as their father.

"Well, here we all are," the man said, breaking the ice by pointing out the obvious.

"Yes, here we all are," our mom agreed. Then added with a gulp, "All seven of us."

"You, Walt," the man barked, "and you, Mike . . . What are you waiting for? Start bringing in their things."

"Let's have them show the girls their room first," Mom suggested.

The apartment, which was small, had only two bedrooms, so we five children had to sleep in one bedroom on two sets of bunk beds and one twin bed. The older boy, Walt, chose the twin bed, Mike and Cher chose the bottom bunks, and Linda and I got the top bunks. I would sleep over Cher, and Linda over her brother. Linda, who was a pretty child with a fair, lightly freckled complexion and shoulder-length sandy hair, showed me the best way to climb up into my bunk. Her brother, Mike, kept grabbing at her ankles as if to pull her off the rails as she climbed up. Whereupon, she, accidentally on purpose and with a wink in our direction, stomped on his fingers, which he had left carelessly lingering on one of the rails as she climbed back down.

As soon as her brothers had left to bring in our things, Linda informed us she was a Roman Catholic. I thought she meant "roaming" Catholic, something like "wandering" Jew. Then she demonstrated for us how to say the rosary. Cher and I admired the beautiful beads she held in her hands and the small cross she wore on a chain around her neck. Linda had a few possessions that had belonged to her deceased mother, which she showed us with great reverence.

We got to know more about the two boys as they carried in our things. Walt was a quiet, good-looking boy, who had dark, wavy hair and a captivating, shy smile that made Cher and me feel welcome without his ever having uttered one word. He had only brought in one or two boxes from our car when he was sent off on his bike to a nearby grocery store to purchase a sponge for his father. Then, as soon as he returned from that errand, and after looking in on us for only a moment, he was sent off again, to a different store, for nails and screws. Even while Walt was off on a mission, his father would call for him. "Where is that kid?" he would bark loudly. "What the hell happened to that kid?" That left the younger brother to unload our car.

Little Mike, as he was called, was quite the opposite of his reserved brother; he was an extrovert who only appreciated his own space when there were lots of other people in it. Every time he delivered a box to our room, he hovered over our conversations with his sister, eager to join in. Little Mike was very cute, with short sandy hair, twinkling pale blue eyes, and a mysterious, Cheshire-cat kind of grin. It was a playful, self-satisfied, somewhat mocking kind of smile, which, somehow, would seem to appear just before he did, and then seem to fade away slowly after he'd gone. For me, the fading away part of the grin's effect was particularly strong, and I quickly made it my habit to stare at the spot where he had most recently been to make sure that he had truly gone. He liked Cher and me right away. We soon suspected that it was the prospect of having two more sisters to tease and torment that so delighted him. We had already seen him taunt Linda by threatening to take her jewelry box away, trap her in the bathroom with the light off, and leap from concealment to frighten her. I caught him eyeing my baby blanket and clutched it tightly. That was the first time I saw the grin.

It didn't take long, as the afternoon progressed, for Cher and me to figure out that Little Mike was fond of his sister, yet he demonstrated his affection by continually picking on her. It didn't help matters for the girl that she looked up to her big brother, and believed, without question, every word that came out of his mouth—prized qualities that made her the perfect target for brotherly pranks. She accepted his attentions with good humor and grace, yet, at the same time, she was fully prepared to defend herself when necessary. Our new sister, Linda, was overly sensitive, hopelessly gullible, and quick to laugh wholeheartedly at herself, especially when she discovered that she had been duped by one of her brothers. All in all, Cher and I found her to be a very easy person to like.

That first night at the Arend household, we children had difficulty getting to sleep. For one thing, once we were tucked in and the lights turned out, our room remained well lighted by a floodlight in the parking lot below our window. Also, the crowded, jungle-gym-like arrangement of beds added to a slumber party atmosphere. Little Mike, wide-awake and full of questions for Cher and me, wanted to know all about us. Then, despite his brother's protests, he insisted on entertaining us all by reciting every offensive, off-color joke he knew. And he knew plenty. He kept Cher, Linda, and me giggling and rolling around in our beds. Even Walt sometimes chuckled between his earnest efforts to restrain his brother. "Not that one," Walt would beg. Then, "Please, don't, not that one, too!" Little Mike was also intrigued by the fact that he could lie in bed and kick up at the underside of his sister's bed, startling her, whenever he thought she was dozing off.

That night, as the volume of the chatter in our room increased, every few minutes or so Big Mike would pound on the wall that divided the two bedrooms, and, in a booming voice, yell oaths and tell us kids to shut up. Cher and I, who had never heard such language, were amazed that their dad's yelling seemed to have so little effect on our new brother and sister, who would wait only a short time before resuming their giggling and loud talking. The pounding and yelling, followed by the boisterous giggling response, went on for some time. At last, bursting in, wearing only his briefs, Big Mike described for us, in the most colorful terms, what would happen to us if we didn't SHUT UP! It had something to do with our being keel-hauled and then strung up by the yardarm. This last tirade, as well as the first (and all the others), had convinced Cher and me of his seriousness. But again, amazingly, their dad's graphic threats of our impending torture on the high seas only served to send our new siblings rolling around in their beds with glee. "Please," the man pleaded. Then, in a most quiet voice, "Please. You have to get up for school in the morning. We all have to get up." This final appeal proving effective, we all settled down to sleep.

When the smells and sounds of breakfast cooking woke us, the problems of one bathroom for a family of seven instantly presented themselves. Big Mike was forced to divide himself between cooking and orchestrating the order and duration of each one's bathroom visit. "Mike! That's it!" I heard him call from the kitchen. Digging through my cardboard boxes, dragged out from under the bed, I found my school clothes and hurriedly dressed. We had yet to work out where we would find a dresser large enough for the clothes of five children, or where we would find a place to put that dresser once we found one. Then, with Cher and Linda both waiting in the hallway outside the bathroom door, and things so desperate there, I continued on to the dining room.

Rounding the corner, I stopped short, aghast at seeing my mom smoking a cigarette.She was sitting at the dining table visiting with the man who was busy in the kitchen.

"We're going to need a bigger frying pan," the man was saying. "Be sure to get that on the list for us, won't you, Ag." Since the breakfast table was already set, I joined Mom, sitting down next to her to watch the man cook. At the same time, I continued to sneak sideways peeks at my mother, as I was so absolutely fascinated by seeing her puffing and blowing smoke. Big Mike was equally fascinating to watch. He filled the apartment's compact kitchen with his size. Stepping aside to open the oven door, he shoveled bacon onto a cookie sheet, already heaped high. Then he cracked eggs into a skillet expertly, using only one hand, while the other hand raised the lid on a different frying pan to check on hash browns, all the while monitoring the toast, with one ear tuned to the whining in the hallway. "Walt!" he boomed, "Your turn's up! What's wrong with that kid, anyway?" he seemed to ask himself, my mother and I merely shrugging. And only minutes later, "Your time's up, you girls!" he called, stooping to take the toast and bacon from the oven. "Everyone to the table!"

The dining table was hopelessly inadequate; it would be a tight squeeze. "Walter," Big Mike pointed, "you there. Agnes, by me. Linda, go tell Mike to get in here. Connie, you sit here."

"Connie can't sit there," Cher broke in. "She's left-handed."

"Is that true, Connie?" he asked, bending to the level of my face. I nodded. Everyone switched places, and plates were passed. Big Mike heaped each plate with eggs, hash browns, toast, and bacon. "You there!" he said to Linda, "Don't be picking at your food. Mike, you slow down. Walt, don't reach your arm across the table again or you'll pull back a bloody stump! Connie, eat some of that bacon."

"But I'm full," I pleaded.

"We don't eat pork," Cher volunteered. "It's against our religion."

"Jesus Christ, Agnes!" the man boomed, turning to our mother. "What kind of a religion is that, where a child can't even eat a decent breakfast?" And without waiting for her reply, "You there," he wagged a finger in my direction, "finish your eggs and milk then. Agnes, get everyone a vitamin." Whereupon, following instructions, our mother passed out vitamins to everyone at the table except me. Then she went to the kitchen counter to crush my vitamin into a spoonful of honey. "What are you doing there, Agnes?" Big Mike asked, leaving the table to hover over her.

"She's crushing Connie's vitamin," Cher volunteered. "Connie can't swallow pills."

"Is that true, Connie?" the man asked, turning to me. I nodded. "Agnes! You stop that right now!" he ordered. "What kind of a kid are you raising here? Who can't swallow a pill, for Christ's sake?" Then, "Connie!" he boomed. "You come around here!" And then, in a most gentle tone, which was almost a whisper, he added, "There's nothing to be afraid of."

My eyes must have been wide with confusion and fear as I came to stand between the knees of the big man who had pushed his chair back from the table. His frequent outbursts were quite unsettling. However, much of my apprehension subsided when I peered up into a kind and sympathetic face. "No one's going to hurt you," the man assured me again. "Now," he said, bending toward me, "you simply stick out your tongue, like so . . . ," He demonstrated. "Can you do that for me?" I stuck out my tongue. "We put the tiny red pill way back, like so . . . a sip of water . . ." He held the glass to my lips. "And then we swallow." I took a good-sized gulp, held my breath until my face turned red, and then almost drowned when I tried to swallow, dramatically choking, and finally coughing the pill onto the floor. All the while, my mother stood protectively near, somewhat behind the man, wringing her hands helplessly. Cher, who had rushed to my side, was boldly giving hate stares to the strange man who was humiliating her little sister. Cher was my defender. "Superman," some of the boys in my class at school, who chased me and tried to kiss me, had called her. She was not afraid of this man, or anyone else for that matter. The other kids watched from the table. "Okay, let's just everyone calm down," Big Mike said, leaning back in his chair. "Agnes, go in the other room if you need to be hysterical." He waved her away. "Cheryl, get back to the table! You kids there! What are you gaping at? Finish your breakfast."

We tried again. "Maybe you need the pill placed on the tip of your tongue," the man said thoughtfully. "Yes. Maybe the tip of the tongue is the thing." At that, everyone raced to resume their original places, Mom standing to the side and somewhat behind the man, Cher prudently but protectively near, and the other children leaning out expectantly from the table. The room fell silent. "Now, we stick out our tongue, just so," the man said softly, placing the pill carefully on the tip of my tongue. "Okay, now drink this glass of water. Don't think about the pill. Don't even let it enter your mind."

Everyone watched as I drank the entire glass of water, all hopeful, including me, that this whole episode could then be over. But when I stuck out my tongue for inspection the second time, the pill was still there. The man's face fell in disappointment, and my sister flashed an I-told-you-so look to the other kids.

Thoughtful for a moment, Big Mike said, "I think we might have been on the right track the first time," as he got up to refill the glass at the kitchen sink. "Yes, we'll try that again. And, returning to his chair, "Agnes!" he barked. "Please stand back! I'm not going to kill her!" Then, spreading his arms to encompass the scene, "Is anyone being murdered here?" he asked, turning to the other children for confirmation. Again, I stuck out my tongue. "We put the pill as far back as we can . . . like so. Now this time, you take one big gulp," Big Mike instructed. So I took one big gulp, gargled, gagged, and swallowed. The pill was still there. It was such a tiny pill. How could it be? Both the man and I were disappointed. "Maybe we should try this again another time?" he suggested gently, now sounding somewhat defeated and reaching to take the glass from my hand.

Determined not to give up, and to everyone's surprise, I pulled the glass back. All watched as I took another gulp. This time I threw my head back and waited until I felt the pill sink to the bottom of my throat. Then I swallowed all at once. My ears popped and my eyes bulged, but remarkably the pill was gone! I was so pleased with my accomplishment that I gave the man an appreciative hug and danced around the room. "I did it! I did it! I swallowed a pill!"

At our father's fervent request, it had been decided that Cher and I would continue to attend the private church school. The Arend children attended a nearby public school. Big Mike drove us to school on his way to work, dapperly dressed in cranberry colored slacks, pink shirt, gray sport jacket, black tie, and shiny, black, French-toe shoes. Cher and I sat next to him on the front seat of the car with our lunchpails on our laps. When we pulled into the parking lot of the school, which was busy as parents dropped off their children, I waved to my special friend, and Cher leaped from the car, running to catch up with one of her friends disappearing into her classroom. Nervously, I gathered my things. Alone with the man, this was my chance. "Do you think . . . I could have a goldfish?" I asked, giving the man a sideways begging look, with what I hoped to be a disarming smile. I was holding my breath.

"Hmm . . ." Big Mike considered carefully, hesitating, his pale blue eyes studying me while he tapped on the steering wheel thoughtfully with his ring finger. His hands were large with thick fingers, one of which bore a sizable gold ring. It was an Elk's ring, with the Elk's emblem set with a diamond. It looked like a king's ring to me.

"I'll take good care of him, I promise."

"Hmm . . ."

"I'll feed him every day."

"Well. I guess I don't see how one little goldfish could hurt."

"Oh boy! Oh boy!" I cried. "Thank you! Thank you!" I ran to tell my friends.

At first recess, our classmates surrounded Cher and me. "What's it like to have a stepfather?" they asked, having seen the man who had dropped us off. "Is he mean?"

"Not yet," I answered. "But he yells for us to keep quiet a lot."

It was natural for our classmates to be inquisitive, since at that time divorce was so uncommon, even outside our religious community. Suddenly, as children from a broken home, my sister and I were curiosities to the other children at our school, not outcast by any means, but different, perhaps even pitied. "Are you sure he's not mean?" they asked again, thinking that because we had a stepfather, surely, we would be abused and beaten. All in all, though, our classmates were kind, and more curious than they were accusing. Some of their parents felt differently, however. For some reason, my special friend's parents told her she could no longer play with me, apparently thinking that divorce was catching. I tried to understand, but it was hard because I had lost my best friend.

Cher comforted me. "I will always be your best friend," she promised. Then, and forevermore, my sister and I kept our grieving about the divorce strictly between ourselves.

Meanwhile, back at the apartment, my treasured baby blanket was gone. Covered with brightly colored giraffes, I considered it to be irreplaceable. Little Mike was the obvious culprit, but my heart wrenching crying, foot-stomping, pleading performance brought about only a widening, appreciative grin. "What did you do with my blanket?" I demanded accusingly, following him around.

Little Mike's face was hard to read, because his eyes and his mouth never seemed to be in agreement, making it impossible for me to know what the truth might be. "I have no interest in your blanket, Con," his mouth solemnly swore, but at the same time, his eyes were twinkling mischievously, and I was certain, even though I knew he didn't have one, that I could see his tail twitching. Yes. Little Mike reminded me of the Cheshire cat in *Alice in Wonderland*. The cat was probably up to no good, but who could tell? It was useless. The more I pestered him, the more he enjoyed himself. I knew I would never see my baby blanket again.

Then, not long after, my young life was shattered once more. I was standing on a stool at the kitchen counter visiting with Big Mike while he was peeling potatoes at the sink. The water was running, and from time to time he would reach over to flip on the garbage disposal for a second or two as he worked. I had recently fed my goldfish, and Harold the fish was still enjoying his meal. He was happily swimming around in his small bowl, which was placed on the windowsill above the sink. While we talked, to my horror, I saw Harold take a leap, and fall from his bowl into the sink exactly at the moment that Big Mike flipped on the garbage disposal. The vibrating stainless steel sink sucked the slippery fish right in.

Wailing and sobbing, I cried as my mother held me on her lap trying to calm my desperate tears. At the same time I uncontrollably vented my grief for my friend, so did Big Mike give way to his emotions. At first standing over us, feeling utterly helpless, then pacing, and then standing over us again, he gave heated proclamations. "No more pets!" he thundered. "This child is to have no more pets!" Then, coming alongside us again, handing Mom another tissue as my wailing continuing unabated, "Agnes!" he roared above my crying. "Agnes! You are my witness!" Mom dutifully nodded to indicate she was listening. "None, I tell you! None! Absolutely no more pets for this child!" Then, stooping closely to examine my swollen face and stricken eyes, and in an attempt to soothe me, "There, there, now," he said softly, kindly.

"Harold!" I cried. "I want Harold!"

"Agnes!" he barked, upright again. "For Christ's sake! Get her a tranquilizer, can't you! She's making herself sick. This kid is to have no more pets . . . and that's final!"

My sobbing stopped as I tried to figure out the reason for Little Mike's contortions in the hallway, where he appeared to be in considerable distress. I wiped my swollen eyes to better see. He was reaching out . . . Little Mike was reaching out . . . was he turning on a switch, I wondered? Now he was writhing on the floor . . . flopping about . . . ripping at his throat. The gruesome picture, all at once, painfully dawned on me. Little Mike was miming the death throws of Harold in the garbage disposal.

"Mike!" Big Mike roared when my crying intensified. "Agnes!" he pleaded. "Can't you do something with these kids?"

*   *   *

Very soon, I got my pet parakeet, followed closely by a cat, two turtles, an aquarium, and many other beloved pets.

CHAPTER FOUR

The question of who would take care of our father was soon answered. On our first Friday night home we found that our wild Aunt Barb had moved in, having officially left the farm at Gaston, Oregon, to move to the city, eager to help her big brother in his time of crisis. She had moved into our room, and was sleeping in my bed.

Our dad, who was a self-sufficient person, didn't actually need his sister's help. Still, as it turned out, having Aunt Barb move in was a good thing, as she was not only a much needed and effective distraction, but more important, over time, she gave our father the extra urgency he needed to find a new wife, and a mother for his children. Aunt Barb meant well, but with her loud rock-and-roll music, cherished stack of 45s, and love of Elvis Presley, she was hardly the influence Dad had in mind for his two young daughters, who were now suddenly gyrating around his house. Worse yet, she insisted on calling our dad, "Raynor," no matter how many times he asked her not to. Aunt Barb had to go.

One Sunday morning with summer approaching, Dad took Cher and me aside. "Say, you girls," he said. "Come sit down here a minute." He motioned for us to sit across from him at the dining room table. "I have something we need to discuss." Pausing, he waited for us to get settled in our chairs. "I've been . . . thinking," Dad finally continued haltingly, "that . . . well . . . maybe . . . I mean that . . . well . . . maybe . . . we should start looking for a new wife for me and a new mom for you girls." It had been painful for him to get those words out.

And it had been painful for us, waiting for him to get those words out. "Yes!" we both agreed enthusiastically.

"Well . . . ," Dad said, taken aback by how quickly Cher and I had embraced his idea. "I guess this means that you girls don't need any time to think this thing over." He wasn't aware we had been thinking the same thing for some time.

"So, how will we find her?" Cher asked.

"I've been thinking about that, too," Dad said. "And I've been thinking that maybe we'd all be better off if I try a more rational approach to romance this time."

"Rational?" I queried.

"Yes, rational," Dad said. "It means not being mindlessly carried off by every ridiculous whim." And then, when we appeared confused, added, "You'll understand one day," he said softly, taking a moment to gaze sadly out the window into the distance. Then, cheerful again, "But for now, let's just say that it starts with having a plan, and then sticking to it . . . I hope."

"So how will we find her?" Cher asked again, and, glancing my way to include me, added, somewhat defeated, "We don't know anybody." Dad hadn't a clue that, for months, Cher and I had been critically eyeing, and then disqualifying, every unmarried woman we knew or saw, elbowing each other in church whenever a likely candidate passed by, studying women at checkout counters, following prospects down store aisles, scoping the neighborhood on our bikes, or just generally on the lookout.

Still sitting together at the dining room table, and eager to do anything to get started, it was decided that Dad would write down our wish list while we tried to think of the many essential qualities we would be seeking in this mystery mother and wife. Dad told us the list would be our compass, and it would be something we could refer back to when things of the heart inevitably got convoluted. We agreed we needed to find someone who liked kids. That made the top of the list. We put a star beside that one. Dad wanted someone with deep religious convictions. He underlined that one. We all hoped she would be a good cook. Sitting across from Dad at the table, whenever he looked down to write, my sister and I cast each other excited glances. With Dad on board, and with an actual plan in the making, we could again feel quite optimistic about what had become a stalled search. Besides, we were both thinking, Dad had everything to recommend him. He had blond good looks, an athletic build, a steady, well-paying job, abundant friends, and a wide variety of interests. My sister and I could have been considered his only liabilities as we had heard the words "brats" and "spoiled" associated with our names on more than one occasion.

To get things underway with vigor, and sticking to our plan of finding someone with deep religious convictions, the very next Sabbath friends at church were informed of our intent. Presto! Overnight, we three became the most sought-after bachelor family around, with so many invitations to lunches, dinners, and parties that each weekend was a whirl. We were introduced to everyone's single sister, sister-in-law, aunt, distant relative, or friend of the family. We met them all, and dated a fair number, no doubt leaving many a broken heart in our wake. Usually, we arrived home late from our dates with Cher and me asleep in the back seat of the car. As time went on, Dad, who was wide open to any suggestion, even let me talk him into a date with my teacher at school. We were invited to her house for dinner. Although we all liked her, and she was a good cook, the consensus on my teacher was only so-so. Still, we agreed she had been the closest prospect we had come upon thus far.

Then, at church one Saturday, Dad accepted a blind date with a distant relative of a friend. By this time, there was no particular reason for us to be hopeful, but of course, we always were. We would all meet at Herb Brown's house before leaving to go swimming with a large group at an indoor pool that same evening. I remember we first saw Darleen across a crowded living room, where she was sitting in an overstuffed chair visiting with friends. Herb pointed her out. A cute number, we thought. The petite, poised young woman who rose to greet us as we came toward her, shook Dad's hand and gave Cher and me a warm smile as we were introduced. I thought Dad brassy when he asked her to ride to the pool with us in our car; however, she graciously accepted his invitation.

As we drove, we learned that Darleen was the registrar and secretary at the private boarding academy affiliated with our church. The school was at least an hour's drive away, but she had driven up, finally giving in to Herb's frequent appeals. We also learned she was a widow who had lost her young Marine husband, and then her unborn child. As the young woman chatted, asking us questions, and candidly telling us about her life, she had the most captivating way of talking. It kept us all mesmerized. Speaking softly, with perfect diction, she turned sideways on the front seat to face Dad more easily, and glanced back at us often as she spoke, including Cher and me in every conversation. Turning back to Cher and me, Darleen then told us she had heard about our singing. She sang herself, and played the piano. While she was telling us this, watching Dad in the rearview mirror, we could see his face was beaming. Best of all, Darleen, who had short brown hair, lovely blue eyes, and a Hollywood smile of perfectly straight, white-white teeth, seemed to understand and appreciate our Dad's wry sense of humor. She frequently smiled at his comments, jabs, and teasing, or responded with the most delighted, lilting laughs. We three were thoroughly smitten.

Driving home late that same evening, Dad, Cher, and I were all wide-awake, exhilarated, and chattering. It was so unlike all the other times when we had driven home from a date, Dad demoralized, Cher and I disappointed and passed out in the back. "So what do you think?" Dad asked. He was unable to keep from beaming as he drove. "Tell me the truth. Do you think she liked us?"

"I hope she didn't see you pull my hair," I said, scowling at Cher, "or try to drown me."

"Yes. Let's hope she didn't see that," Dad agreed, also scowling at Cher. Then, he laughed. It was good to hear him laugh in such a special, happy way. "So, what do you think?" Dad asked again. Then we all laughed.

"Are we rational?" I worried.

"Not completely," Dad admitted. Then we laughed again.

Heartbeats fluttered and hopes soared, as we three committed ourselves to the immediate and expedient courtship of Darleen. As we drove, we strategized. It was agreed that Cher and I would be on our very best behavior. We promised Dad there would be no fighting or roughhousing in the back seat of the car, and that we would keep our voices down, suppress our frequent outbursts of giggling, and try not to interrupt when other people were talking. For Dad's part, we would trust in his natural good looks and charisma. But, my sister and I admonished him, lots of compliments and absolutely no engineer humor. "Engineer humor," as we called it, was humor that no one except another engineer could ever possibly understand, much less appreciate or hope to find funny.

The next morning, Cher and I stood expectantly near while Dad called to thank Darleen for the enjoyable time we had all had the night before. He was quite nervous with his daughters hovering over him, especially after having consulted with us for our opinions on just when this strategic after-the-first-date call should be made. "Right now!" had been our thinking. My sister and I held our breaths when he asked her if we could pick her up early next Saturday morning, bring her up to Seattle for church, and then spend the day and evening together. We could see by our Dad's delight that she had said yes. Wildly relieved, we planned the following Saturday over Sunday breakfast. Dad wondered about having a small dinner party Saturday night. He proposed that we invite Herb's family and a few other friends whom Darleen knew. We would make tacos. Dad was a master at cooking taco shells in the deep fat fryer, something he had perfected during our years in California. Cher and I, along with some of the women, would help with the cooking. There was no point in letting ourselves get serious about someone who didn't like tacos. It was agreed.

We three then spent the rest of our Sunday, as usual, together—exactly as we had done before the divorce. First, we straightened up the house, and then we helped Dad work in the yard. Years before, Dad had landscaped the yard of our new home himself—with his little girls help of course. All our childhood friends played in our yard because we had the greenest, most lush lawn in our neighborhood.

From the earliest time I could remember, Cher and I had followed our father everywhere he went as he did his chores, working in the yard, washing the car, or building something in his basement shop. Dad could putter in his shop for hours, and it seemed as if he could fabricate or fix anything. As little girls, we had tried to be helpful, but many times we were not. If my sister and I got in the way, which we often did, he would give us an important job to do. Sometimes, he would give us each a hammer, and set us about cracking hazelnuts on the cement floor of his workshop. We always had a huge bag of hazelnuts to crack that we'd brought back from our grandmother's farm. And if we had particularly misbehaved, he would turn on the saw and cut up several scraps of wood. The noise of the saw would chase us into another part of the house. Occasionally, he even made wooden toys for us. He fashioned hydroplane boats for us during Seafair when the hydroplanes were in town for the Gold Cup race. We tied the boats to the back of our bicycles with string, so that we, like other North-west children, could race our brightly painted hydros all around the neigh-borhood.

When our Sunday chores were done, we helped Dad do his grocery shopping for the coming week, and helped him shop for other supplies as well. Cher and I chaperoned Dad when he was in the hardware store, which was our most important job; otherwise, he would have remained in there all day, wistfully pondering his next year's purchases. We would watch his eyes actually glaze over in Sears—a particular trouble spot. My sister and I were patient, however, following him through the aisles while he marveled at everything, occasionally letting slip the word "tape" or "rake," or what-ever the name of the item for which we were shopping. If not vigilant, it was still possible to lose him even after we had urged him to the check-out stand.

Our Sundays weren't all about work, though. Together, we went snow skiing, waterskiing, hiking, and camping. We spent lots of time walking in the woods where Dad taught us to respect every living thing. Pointing out snakes and frogs, Dad explained to us why they were our friends. Also, on our walks, he taught us the names of many of the Northwest trees, plants, and flowers, and which berries were safe to eat. He also taught us about fossils and rocks, demonstrating how to search for fossils along stream banks, and how to hunt for the beautiful clear rocks called agates, along streambeds and at Pacific Ocean beaches. Our father wasn't one of those suddenly- single, weekend dads who now managed to find time for his chil-dren. These were all the things we had done together as a family before the divorce, and now merely continued to do on our own. Even without us, Dad kept busy. He was a mountain climber who had climbed many of the peaks in Washington and Oregon.

Although we lived in the suburbs, Dad often took us to nearby Seattle.

He loved the city. There we frequented museums, art galleries, and especially the zoo, where we used our elephant-shaped key to turn on the story boxes placed in front of each exhibit. Besides the zoo, there were many other exceptional parks to visit, such as Seward Park with its views of Mount Rainier, the fish hatchery, and eagles nesting in the treetops, and the Arboretum, where my sister and I skipped along trails lined with azaleas and rhododendrons. Along with enjoying Seattle's many parks, we attended special events, such as the Ringling Brother's Circus, the Ice Follies, and the Torchlight Parade, a summer event that was part of Seattle's annual Seafair celebration.

In the city, we sometimes had lunch at Ivar's on the Seattle waterfront. Ivar's had the best fish and chips anywhere. This was a special treat for kids, or anyone, as Ivar's encouraged everyone to feed the seagulls that lined the roof of his restaurant waiting for handouts. Sometimes, weather permitting, we bought our fish and chips and continued on to picnic at the entertaining Hiram M. Chittenden Locks. All day, every day, recreational craft from dinghies to luxury yachts, and working giants, such as Alaska fishing trawlers and tugs, were heading out through the locks to the saltwater of Puget Sound. At the same time, just as many boats were returning to the freshwater interlocking system of channels and passages that separated Lake Union, Portage Bay, and Lake Washington. Standing at the railing, snacking on fish, and tossing French fries to the seagulls, my sister and I were encouraged to keep watch for our namesake tugboats, the Cheryl Ann and the Connie Rae. We considered these tugs to be phantoms that Dad swore he had seen before. As it turned out, many years later, I actually saw the cute little Cheryl Ann tugboat tied up at a dock on Lake Union.

Much of the time when we were driving we were singing. We sang hymns, folk songs, and popular songs of the time. And when we weren't singing, we had a special game we played in the car, called "Beetle." At that time, there were lots of Volkswagen bugs on the road, so many that merely driving to church we could easily spot a hundred of them. Whoever saw a Beetle first would call out, Beetle!! Beetle One! Beetle Two! And so on. We always had to say the number of the Beetle we were on, so the others in the car could keep track and make sure we weren't cheating, as it was a competitive game and the score was usually close. The most important rule of the game was someone else in the car had to confirm they, too, saw your Beetle; otherwise, your Beetle didn't count. This rule often forced us to backtrack, or circle the block to search out someone's shady Beetle. There were lots of these suspicious sightings, because Dad was so hard to beat at this game. Cher and I only beat him, rarely, by resorting to watching down side streets, taking advantage of his having to pay attention to the road in front of us.

When we weren't singing or playing Beetle, we would beg Dad to sing to us. He knew the words to many old cowboy ballads, such as, "Little Joe the wrangler, will wrangle never more/His days on the chaparral are through . . ." They were sad sagas, but Cher and I never tired of hearing them sung again and again. Although we were generally loud children, my sister and I were quiet and respectful when Dad was singing, as he sang these songs in soft, hushed tones.

Dad often took us to visit his mom, so we spent many weekends at our grandmother's farm in Oregon, playing in the long abandoned turkey shed, where we were never supposed to play, and chasing the cows around the pasture, something we were absolutely forbidden to do.

When Darleen joined us on our weekend outings, we all wondered how we had ever gotten along without her. Conversations were livelier, playing Beetle more exciting, and her lovely singing voice made the four of us practically a choir. Cher and I were very glad when Dad married our wonderful Momma Darleen.

CHAPTER FIVE

It didn't take long for us to realize that we needed to board my horse closer to home. Driving me to and from Redmond soon became a hardship for everyone. Naturally, I wanted to visit Shane as often as possible, which quickly turned into another, albeit new, form of parent badgering. Searching for a place with a barn, at my request, we were surprised to find the perfect location a mere three blocks from my school, Highland Junior High, where I had started ninth grade.

The Murphy farm[2] was a country oasis amid suburban sprawl. It was conspicuously located on a huge corner tract, with its red barn and two-story white house prominent atop a hill. We found it hard to believe that we had probably driven past the farm many times over the years without noticing it. Yet there it was. A place so otherworldly that from the moment our car turned onto the long gravel drive my vision narrowed, excluding the residential areas just across the roadway. And as we continued up the gently sloping drive, approaching the weathered barn and the scenic, clapboard farmhouse, even the garish sign of the nearby convenience store faded quietly from my consciousness.

On a Sunday afternoon in September, the Horton family pulled into the gravel parking area at the top of the Murphy's drive. Right away, we felt the slower pace of life, when Dad was forced to creep behind two dogs ambling in front of our car. The dogs, both cordial, with waving tails, leisurely led us toward the barn on the left, which was the only way we could go anyway.

---

[2] Original site of Hungerford Ranch

"Look! A teeter-totter!" Wendy cried, excitedly bouncing on my knee. She had spotted a children's play area on the side lawn of the farmhouse. "And swings!"

"Did you see the view as we came up the drive?" Momma Darleen asked. She was holding a struggling baby Julie on her lap who was trying to reach out to touch one of the dogs outside her open window.

Giving voice to all our thoughts, "I didn't even know this place was here," Cher said.

"Let's have you guys wait in the car until Connie and I unload her horse," Dad suggested.

"It's only for a minute," I whispered in Wendy's ear, sitting her on the seat beside me.

It was difficult to open the car door because the dogs were there to greet me. Both dogs wore collars with tags. One of the dogs, a black lab, sniffed my hand while I read his tag. "Water Dog—nice to meet you," I said, patting his head. The other dog was a small, stout I-don't-know-what. He was short, having the stubby legs characteristic of a basset, dachshund, or corgi, but he wasn't one of those breeds. "What kind of dog are you?" I asked him. Floppy, fold-over ears stuck out comically, in contrast to the intense hazel eyes staring up at me. "You have a terrier's coat," I told him, pondering his white and tan coat, which appeared scruffy, coarse, and sparse, yet felt silky when I stooped to pet him.

Hearing a screen door slam, my attention, which had been consumed with the dogs, was called away. A tall, slender girl, with dark, straight, shoulder-length hair, clomped down the stairs from the house's front porch and strode across the lawn toward us. She struck me as being very Western, with worn jeans tucked into high-topped cowboy boots. The small dog immediately went to her.

Scooping up the dog, "I'm Pat," she said. "Dad and I will be right out to get you settled. But first, I have to take Guthrie inside."

"He's not bothering us," I said, disappointed.

"He'll get underfoot," she cast over her shoulder, heading back to the house.

"Hey, Con. Back here," Dad called from behind the trailer. "Can you give me a hand?"

Unloading a horse from a trailer is easy; Shane was eager to set his four hooves on solid ground again. I led the paint around the lot in front of the barn to settle him down. He was unusually high-spirited and nervous. Everything was new to him. Nickering at the sight and smell of strange horses, his eyes darted about anxiously, and his prancing made him a handful. It also made his long mane and tail shimmer in the sunlight. At a nearby hitching post, a redheaded girl was grooming a stocky buckskin mare with a shaved mane. She stopped to watch. "Your horse is pretty," the girl commented as I led my prancing horse past.

The minute Shane was tied to a hitching post, the rest of the family piled out of the car. "This is a cool place," Cher commented. "Maybe I need a horse, too."

"Don't even joke about it," Dad said grimly.

Cher laughed, pleased with herself. She always knew just what to say to keep our dad on edge.

Dad had a meeting scheduled to talk about the financial arrangements with Mr. Murphy, so he and I were waiting by the trailer. "Darleen," Dad said. "Why don't you take the little girls to see those horses over there." He was talking about a group of horses gathered by the gate near the barn. "They look as if they could use some company." He added, "Take Cher with you, why don't you."

Mr. Murphy, who was tall and thin like his daughter, wore a yellow knit shirt, pressed tan slacks, and tan loafers. He didn't look anything like a farmer. "Beautiful day for golf, " he commented somewhat wistfully to Dad as they shook hands, but with a sideways glance aimed at his daughter.

"Or waterskiing," Dad agreed, also somewhat wistfully, with a sideways glance aimed at me.

"Let's let them talk," Pat said. "I'll show you the barn."

Following the girl, who I guessed to be at least sixteen, I asked, "What was that about?"

"You mean back there?" the girl said. "The 'I'd rather be golfing, I'd rather be waterskiing,' exchange?"

"Yes."

"Parental commiseration, that's all." Then she added, knowingly, "They need all they can get."

Entering the barn, Pat told me the front doors of the barn were always kept open. "Watch your step," she cautioned. "It can seem a bit dark in here when you first come in out of the light." In the center of the barn, running straight toward the back, was an aisle eight or so feet wide. There were three empty stalls on either side of the center aisle, which were oriented horizontally toward each sidewall, the last stall being the farthest from the center aisle. Pat explained the horses used the stalls only during feeding time, in that there were not enough stalls for every horse, and that there were plenty of wooded areas out in the fields where the horses could shelter.

At the far end of the aisle, toward the rear of the barn, were three steps that led to an open doorway. The doorway seemed small to me, yet I noted the tall girl passed through without stooping. "This is the tack room," Pat said indicating the long, narrow room to our right. "I'll show you where you can stow your equipment, but first, let me show you the hayloft." The tack room was so narrow that as soon as we passed through the doorway we had to take a sharp turn to the right or we had to immediately start climbing a ladder that was attached to the back wall—which is what we did. "Careful of your head," Pat said.

The loft was filled with the sweet aroma of alfalfa hay from the many neatly stacked bales that dotted the expansive floor. Pat pointed out that each girl had a section of the loft assigned to her for her horse's hay. I was already aware that there were so many horses on the Murphy place that the pastures were overgrazed and that every horse had to be fed grain and hay each day. We walked to the open window on the front wall of the barn where we could see out and over the pastures to view the Olympic Mountains far to the west. It was a very large opening through which hay was hoisted. "Watch your head here, too," Pat cautioned. "Sometimes this hook is left hanging down. And don't get too close to the edge. It's a long fall." Sure enough, now standing there with nothing in front of us but sky, I realized this was definitely not a window, but rather a wide-open doorway.

Leaving the loft, climbing back down the ladder, I noted a portion of the back wall of the tack room was actually a slatted board fence. On the other side of the fence was a box stall where a pampered horse was munching hay. The tack room had a low ceiling, but the stall across the rail fence had a high ceiling. It also had a private door at the back corner of the barn.

"Whose horse is that?" I asked.

"My horse," Pat said. "Swifty, come meet Connie." But Swifty was more interested in his meal than he was in me. "This is where your tack and grain will be stored," the girl continued. "You'll probably want to get a tack box, but for now you can stow your gear over in the corner." Pat then explained that each girl had her own tack box with a lock, where all her equipment was kept. The boxes lined the wall opposite Swifty's stall. Pat showed me inside her tack box where there were shelves for brushes and incidentals, and hooks for hanging bridles, ropes, and halters. She explained half the box was reserved for a galvanized garbage can that required a tight-fitting lid to thwart mice. This was how the grain for each horse must be stored.

Leaving the barn, we rejoined Dad and Mr. Murphy who were still talking. "Mr. Murphy says they'll feed your horse whenever you can't make it to the pasture," Dad said. "All we have to do is call to let them know."

"Your daughter told me that you ordered a ton of hay for us," I said. A ton of hay, I thought. A ton of hay! Gosh, I wonder how much that cost. I was quite concerned about how much this horse was costing my parents.

"That's right," Mr. Murphy replied. "You can use Patty's hay until yours is delivered later this week. Then you can pay her back. I was explaining to your dad that we'll put your horse in this pasture here," he said pointing to the front pasture that was on the barn side of the driveway. "This pasture is closed off behind the barn; we use it when a new horse comes in. We'll keep your horse separate from the other horses for the first few weeks. That way he can settle in and conduct his introductions safely from across the fence."

After Mr. Murphy and his daughter left, Dad said, "Well." We were both at a loss as to what to do next. "I guess we just put your horse in there then?"

A ton of hay, I was still thinking. "I guess."

"Let me get my camera," Dad said then. "I want to get some shots of you riding your horse in his new pasture."

At that moment, laughter drifted our way from across the back pasture where three girls were approaching on horseback. Thinking we were attracting an audience, with the girls getting closer, Pat sitting on the top step of the porch watching us, and the redheaded girl also having turned our way,

I began to feel apprehensive. "Do we have to do this today, Dad?" I pleaded. "I'll feel a little . . . uncomfortable, riding in front of these girls." Dad didn't know that because of difficulty getting to the other pasture, I had thus far only ridden my horse a few times.

"Don't be ridiculous," Dad said, starting for the car. "You'll do fine." Then, as if I didn't have enough of an audience, Dad had to call the family over from the yard where they were playing. "Come on," he called to them, an invitation for all to hear. "Connie is going to ride her horse for us!"

I followed Dad to the station wagon to get my bridle out of the back, all the while grumbling to myself, "Don't be ridiculous . . . don't be ridiculous." That was Dad's solution to my every problem. Now I found that the paint was also uneasy, snorting and shaking his head, and whipping his tail as I came up. Perhaps he was edgy about the group of girls now gathered across the fence, or perhaps he was merely trying to impress the buckskin mare that was being brushed at the adjacent hitching post. Either way, he was telling me his concerns. The three girls, astride their horses, all watched while I nervously bridled my fidgety horse.

Meanwhile, Dad had opened the gate to Shane's new quarters, and he was already in the pasture, his Exacta mounted on the tripod, fiddling with his light meter. With the family at the fence, everyone gawking, I led Shane into his new pasture. However, Dad waved us back. "I want to get a shot of you riding through the gate," he said, glancing up from his light meter. He must have mistaken his daughter's look of dismay for dimwitted confusion. "Go back out. Can't you?" he waved us back again. "I want to get a shot of you riding through the gate." Dad had all the camera's adjustments focused on the gate, and that was that.

Without a saddle, it was always a problem to get on my horse. I led Shane back and smiled at my audience. Mom was holding Julie up so she could watch her big sister. Cher was holding Wendy's hand, the little girl so short she had to peer through the barbed-wire fence. And now Pat and the redheaded girl also lined up along the fence. I glanced around. Where to find a place to mount? A bucket? A stump? A rock? There was nothing but a fence rail, so that had to do. I led the paint along close to the fence, then climbed up on the second rung, and before he had a chance to move away, leaped onto his back. I was grateful for success on the first try. The spectators could be impressed; however, I knew I couldn't take full credit for my nifty mount. Things had gone so well only because Shane hadn't been paying attention, so distracted was he by the horses across the way.

I rode Shane across the gravel parking lot approaching the gate, but when I tried to ride him through the gate, he balked. He flattened his ears, stretched his neck downward, and began pawing the ground with his left front hoof. The earth shook. I pulled his head up, urging him forward, but he reacted the same way, shaking his head no, stretching his neck far out to loosen my grip on the reins, and then pawing, pounding the ground till it shook. Dad, the family, and the observing girls were understandably taken aback by this display of insubordination. I heard gasps. "He doesn't like to be ridden through gates," I lamely explained to the astonished assemblage. "Can't I lead him through?" I asked Dad, who was flabbergasted, standing behind his camera, hands on hips. Embarrassed for us both, I was eager to dismount.

"Don't get down," Dad called. "Don't give in to him. Make him go through the gate."

Make him go through the gate? There was only one way to do that. I quickly tightened the reins, pulling Shane's reluctant, heavy head up, and then around to the left until we were looking at each other determined eye to determined eye. I had learned that this maneuver served to set him slightly off balance so he couldn't paw. Then his head was pulled around even further to the left, which forced the animal into making fast, tight circles. Round and round we went, three, four, and five times. Then, when he was dizzy, feeling him begin to sway, he was faced into the pasture, and at the same time given a nudge forward with my heels. A bewildered horse soon found himself on the other side of the gate.

At first, Dad was speechless. "That worked," he finally said, "But I didn't get the shot."

"That's okay, Dad. Let's forget it."

"Okay," Dad agreed, though disappointed. "I'll just get some pictures of you riding around the pasture."

"Okay."

Shane and I loped around his new pasture in less than poetic stride. We seemed to have no sync, no rhythm. I was feeling tense, knowing that Dad was taking pictures, and that everyone was watching. The three girls, now dismounted, the redheaded girl, and Pat were all lined up with the family, spread along the fence. Our ragged performance was surely a case of nerves. As time went by, and we rode around the field, I began to forget about our audience, relax, and enjoy the fact of being with my horse. Besides, I was riding a magical horse—my horse. By the time we cantered up the pasture for the last time, returning to the gate, I felt Shane and I had finally achieved a kind of fluidity. Therefore, relieved, as well as quite pleased, I patted his neck, praising him, before jumping down.

"That looked like fun," Dad said. "I think I got some good shots. How about I take a turn?"

"Sure," I said. "I'll take pictures of you."

Confronted with the issue of how to get on the horse, Dad said, "You'll have to give me a hand here." I braced myself, cupping my hands for his foot. Whereupon, Dad grabbed a handful of Shane's mane, as there was no saddle horn, and leaped, agilely, up onto Shane's back—almost. For at the precise moment of his leap, the horse stepped slightly away, which sent Dad tumbling. Somewhat chagrined, he stood and dusted himself off, surely thinking his poor mount had been his own fault. Embarrassed, he glanced back, shaking his head at the family, and at the girls who had started to leave but then decided to stay. Moving over, we tried again. At which point, at no surprise to me, the paint started pawing with his left front hoof. Dad leaped back. It was a natural reaction. For a moment, the paint continued his routine. With head lowered, he pawed the ground quite dramatically. "You'd better do something about this," Dad said, standing back, studying the horse.

"We have a few things to work on," I admitted.

Rethinking his ride, "Well, we can't let him get away with this kind of be-havior," Dad said. "Like it or not."

"He thinks this is funny," I commented.

"Well, he's the only one," Dad said grimly, glancing again at our audi-ence, all of whom had concerned expressions on their faces. Several frustrating mounting attempts later, the paint relinquished his game, and to clapping cheers from our onlookers, Dad was at last seated on the horse.

Now riding around the pasture, Dad appeared at ease, walking, trotting, and loping the horse, while I snapped shot after shot. Things were going so well the three girls, most likely bored by perfection, had returned to their interrupted day. Only the family, Pat, and the redheaded girl remained. By the time Dad was finished riding, he was exhilarated and smiling, having happily forgotten our previous trouble. "Good ride?" I called, as they approached at a jog. "Fun?" Then, before Dad had a chance to answer, Shane tripped. It was such a sudden, lurching, forward-falling stagger that it sent the animal nearly to his knees. Dad was thrown hard against the horse's neck, losing control of one of the reins. "What happened?" he asked, jumping down, shaken.

"Shane tripped."

"Over what?"

"Nothing that I can see," I answered, as Dad and I were both then searching the ground under and around the horse. It had been such a violent stumble that we were both convinced we'd find an open well, maybe a trench, or at the very least, a good-sized boulder. With the ground so obviously level and clear of obstructions, we turned, simultaneously and wordlessly, to contemplate the horse's big hooves. Dad ran his fingers thoughtfully through his hair.

Without another word spoken, I led Shane past Dad's questioning eyes, through the gate, to the nearest hitching post for his brushing. The redheaded girl, who had been watching our performance with some amusement, was leaning against the post, eyeing me, almost as if she had been waiting there for me. "Beautiful day," I said.

"Your horse is weird!" the girl said, shaking her head. At which point, she turned and abruptly left, leading her buckskin mare away.

CHAPTER SIX

Now that my horse was boarded at the Murphy farm, I could easily walk the three blocks to the pasture most days after school. Actually, it turned out to be much more than three blocks by the time I walked around the huge, front-corner pasture, and then up the gravel drive. I never minded the walk though, for the time was spent anticipating the first moment when the horse could be seen, quarantined as he was, on the opposite side of the driveway. At first, Shane didn't seem to recognize me, although walking up the long gravel drive carrying my schoolbooks, I waved to him and called his name. He was a spotted horse in a big field all alone, ignoring me. For now, the paint could afford to be standoffish, grazing in a seldom-used, lush and overgrown pasture. He could get along without oats, hay, or me. He was wild and free.

Every day, at the top of the drive, I stopped to pet Water Dog, waiting there to greet me. At least he was glad to see me. And I waved to the little dog, Guthrie, watching my arrival from the front room window of the farmhouse. On school afternoons, I had the place to myself. So entering the empty barn, I went to the tack room to change clothes and fetch Shane's halter. Then I'd made it a habit to stand at the gate calling to my horse, even though I knew he wouldn't come. Someday, he'll come when he's called, I told myself. Someday. Often, standing at the gate, I would take time to wonder at my surroundings, marveling about what a fortunate girl I was to be here. I remembered the other pasture where there had been no barn and no dog to greet me. If ever there was a horse heaven, I was thinking, this is it.

Then it was time to walk down into the pasture to catch my horse. The halter was held behind my back out of sight. Even so, for the first few minutes, I always had to follow the horse while he wandered slowly around the pasture keeping himself tantalizingly just out of reach until, eventually, he accepted the inevitable. Only then was he given a treat—a carrot, a piece of apple, or a sugar cube. And always, as the paint was led through the field, he was praised for being a good horse.

Knowing it was important to keep a routine when working with an animal, depending on the weather, I did everything in the same order and in the same way each time I went to the pasture. Whenever it wasn't raining, the horse was given his grain and groomed outside at one of the hitching posts. I held the plastic bucket in my arms while the paint ate his oats, turning the bucket as he ate so he could get hold of every last morsel. This was a more intimate way of feeding him than setting the bucket on the ground. This way our faces were very close together, and as he ate, I could smell his sweet breath and listen to the pleasant sound of his grinding the grain.

Once Shane finished, the lengthy grooming process began. There was a nice assortment of brushes from which to choose. First, a stiff-bristled brush was used for the main parts of the horse. I'd start at the top behind his ears, working with long strokes down his neck, across his back and sides, then over his rump, toward the tail. It seemed no matter how much the horse was brushed there was still plenty of dust, dander, and loose hair left to remove. He was so big and so very dirty my arms got tired and achy. Once finished with the stiff brush, a soft-bristled one was used. The soft brush made his coat shine. Then I'd clean gently around his eyes and along the lines of his face. The horse's legs and underbelly were usually spattered with dried mud. Those areas were done last, with the soft brush. There was a lot of brushing to do.

While working, I talked to my horse, telling him about my day at school and asking him questions about his day, and also about the life he had led before we met. Did he miss his horse friends back at the ranch in Oregon? What had his life been like there? Sadly, those questions would never be answered. I didn't fool myself into believing we would ever be able to communicate with words, the way humans do. Still, without words, somewhere along the line this horse had learned to say no quite clearly, with his clever, albeit annoying, hoof-pawing act. Also, while I worked, it would have been hard for me to miss the fact that my horse was talking to me in his own kind of language. For example, Shane had ticklish spots. The most ticklish spot was his flanks, an area distressingly close to the groin region. Shane would let me know when I was working in a tender area in three obvious ways. First, as soon as the brush reached his flanks, his skin would flinch. By flinching, he was telling me to be especially light-handed. Second, his head would pop up and his ears would point back, as if to say, "I'm watching your every move!" Third, he would cock his rear leg. A cocked rear leg on a horse is something to be concerned about, as it is often a warning the horse is positioning himself to be able to kick you if you do something not to his liking. My horse was clearly saying, "Don't try anything funny, or . . ."

Once the brushing was completed, a wide-toothed metal comb was used to untangle the coarse hair of Shane's mane and tail. Starting with his mane, which was streaked in a flattering combination of reddish-brown and white, I gently combed his forelock, the part that hung down on his forehead. Then I combed behind his ears. The mane of a horse is trained to lie smoothly against the side of the neck. However, Shane's had stubborn cowlicks that stuck up. One of these was at the top of his neck behind his ears. Shane's unruly mane sticking up and flopping onto both sides of his neck gave him a rakish, wild horse appearance, which was pleasing to me. Next, considerable time was spent combing his tail, which was always tangled and muddy. Most of the hair of his tail was white, which was not a very serviceable color, making it a challenge to keep presentable. There was some unavoidable tugging involved combing the tail. I had to stop when the paint became too restless, again talking to me by stomping his rear leg, as if to say, "That's enough now!" And then, if I didn't catch that, he would twist his head around to peer back at me, which seemed to say, "I really mean it!"

Next the horse's hooves needed to be cleaned. It was an important job, but one that was challenging for me. A hoof pick was used, which is a specially designed tool for digging out hard-packed mud and any stones the horse might have picked up in his metal shoes. The front hooves were cleaned first because I had an easier time with them. Facing the rear of the horse and close beside the front leg, I leaned against him, pushing him slightly off balance, which helped take the weight off the leg. The whole hoof-cleaning process had everything to do with getting proper leverage, and getting proper leverage had everything to do with the angle of my body in relation to the horse, the hoof, and the ground. When all these angles were properly aligned, Shane almost lifted his hoof for me. As I worked, my body kept pressing against the horse to keep him slightly off balance, or he would have dropped his hoof, very likely on my foot. Initially, I was so awkward I often lost my grip on a heavy hoof and had to jump back out of the way when it dropped with a thud. The rear hooves were trickier still, in that the rear legs of a horse are significantly heavier. Further, the rear legs lift at a cantankerously stiff and altogether disagreeable angle, making it difficult to get a solid grip. Shane was patient while I struggled to improve my technique.

Finally, I was almost finished. A thorough job had been done transferring most of the horse's mud, dust, dander, and loose hair onto myself. There were only a few more things left to do—taking care of a horse was a big job. Now medicinal salve was rubbed on any sore spots noticed during grooming. Shane was often bothered by biting flies, and sometimes cut or scratched himself on the barbed-wire fence. I also dabbed petroleum jelly in the corner of each eye to help keep the biting flies away. When all the grooming was completed, I stepped back to admire the paint, walking around him, praising him, telling him how handsome he looked. Then, hugging his neck, I thanked him for being a good horse.

Shane had to wait at the hitching post while the bucket, brushes, and other grooming aids were cleaned. All of this equipment was kept in a cardboard box in a corner of the tack room next to the garbage can that contained grain. I was always fumbling around in the dark tack room, never having found the switch for the overhead light. Once everything was cleaned, dried, and put away, it was time to give Shane hay. On school days I was the only girl at the pasture, so there was a choice of stalls. I led Shane into the first stall on the left. That way, I could watch him eat from the safety of the aisle outside the stall. Always, when I climbed down the ladder from the loft with one arm pressing the load of hay against me, some of it stuck to my clothes. I didn't like it when the itchy particles went down my shirtfront. Then, when I climbed the fence rail and tossed the hay into the bin, more of it rained down on me; it got in my hair and the dust stung my eyes.

It took the paint a long time to finish eating. He was slow, not because he wasn't an enthusiastic eater, but rather, I discovered, because chewing hay is wearying work. It is so tough and stringy that each mouthful requires a considerable amount of dedicated masticating before swallowing. Standing on the rail, watching, I learned it takes a certain amount of time for an animal to eat a certain amount of hay—no matter what. Hay cannot be gulped, wolfed, or gobbled. I respectfully watched my horse enjoying his meal—for the first few minutes. Then, the eventual boredom caused by the almost hypnotic effect of watching him tediously grinding away, would start to make me drowsy. My head would bob, and Shane's broad back would look more like a bed every minute. This overwhelming sleepiness, coupled with the fact that Shane was so conveniently positioned in the stall close to the fence rails, eventually, despite all better judgment, enticed me to climb up on his back while he ate. The paint didn't seem to mind when I stretched out contentedly on top of him, snuggled down, warmed my cold hands against his neck, and napped.

It was Mom's job to pick me up at the pasture on her way home from work at the doctor's office. She would be smiling and glad to see me, but sometimes her expression would change to outright horror when I got in the car. "Yuk!" she would say, recoiling. "You're filthy! Get out of the car and brush yourself off! Give those muddy shoes a good stomping. Just look at those shoes! What's that in your hair? How did you get that tear in your jacket? Just wait 'til your dad sees that!" (Mom didn't know that brandishing Daddy Mike as a weapon was ridiculous.) "Okay, you can get back in the car now . . . but don't touch anything!" And, then she would say, "Oh, by the way . . . I love you."

My mother was fond of telling friends, all the while rolling her eyes and shaking her head, that she didn't know whose kid I could possibly be, and that she didn't know where such a child had come from. This was especially true when I brought snakes, frogs, bugs, or any unlovely creature home begging my parents for it to stay. Mom saying I was certainly not her kid was a kind of loving joke, because I looked exactly like my mother.

* * *

When Shane's stint of solitude ended, he was free to roam the vast pastureland that made up the Murphy estate. He was also free to make a nuisance of himself with the other horses. Pat was always eager to relate the paint's daily transgressions. Although seeing very little of her before, now, on many afternoons, she came stomping across the lawn with a not-too-pleasant expression on her face. "Your horse is herding the other horses around," she would tell me. "He thinks he's a stallion. He tries to cut out the mares, and he chases the other geldings away."

It all sounded so bad. I was very worried. "What can I do?" I asked Pat finally.

"I don't know," Pat's tone softened. "I guess we'll have to keep an eye on him. If he injures one of the other horses though, you'll be responsible. You'll have to pay."

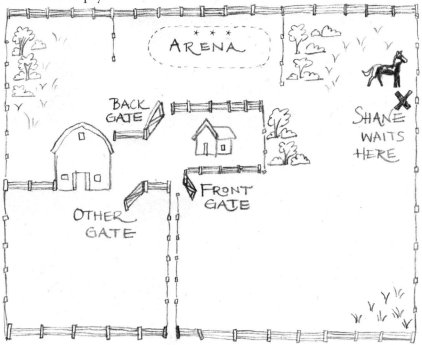

In his first pasture, the paint had only been able to see me approaching as I walked up the drive. However, now that he had been moved into the main pastures, he could see me from the minute I turned the corner after walking the first two blocks east from school. He could watch as I walked about a block north to the fence and all along the road around the front corner of the property, as well as all the while I was coming up the gravel drive.

The paint soon developed the habit of waiting at the bottom of the pasture where he could best see me approaching while I was still a block away. The first time Shane was there, waiting for me, I was surprised and excited to see him. I set my schoolbooks down on the side of the road, and jumped over the ditch into the tall grass to give him a proper greeting. To my astonishment, instead of shying away from my exuberant leap directly for him—which is what I would have expected him to do—the paint pressed closer to the barbed-wire fence, returning my wild welcome in kind. It was only then I realized that my horse had actually been waiting for me. This was beyond magic!

After our ecstatic reunion, I jumped back over the ditch to continue my way along the roadside. Shane followed. He kept my exact pace and hugged the fence, as it would allow. There were boggy areas along the fence, especially by the front corner of the property where the sloped front pasture drained into a depression. Since horses dislike mud, it's natural for a horse to avoid a marshy area. However, instead of going around the muck, the paint merely slogged on through, muddying his nice white stockings, staying with me as close to the fence line as possible. He was completely undaunted as I yelled and waved to spook him away from the mire. On that first day, the sight was so distressing—"Oh, those stockings!"—that even though I knew better, I decided to climb through the barbed-wire fence, and then walk diagonally up the pasture to the barn, thereby avoiding all boggy areas.

The decision made, I hesitated, studying the situation, for it wasn't easy to climb through a barbed wire fence, and tearing my school dress was unthinkable. Retracing my steps to drier ground, I searched for a spot where the wires were spread wider than most, my horse following along.

However, I still had to jump over the ditch, not too easy holding my schoolbooks, and then scramble up the other side. Shane liked the idea and eagerly pressed against the fence. It never occurred to him to back away so I could climb through. When I moved a little farther down, away from him, to give myself room, he merely moved down with me. Finally, exasperated with my failed efforts, "You know you are kind of weird," I told him, scooting the books under the fence. Literally, under my horse's nose, I climbed slowly and carefully through the barbed-wire. His head had to be gently pushed aside before I could stand up. Afterwards, he was praised and told he was a good horse—I didn't mention the muddy socks.

Now my horse and I began our first walk up the front pasture together. Right away, Shane was crowding me. He walked with his head directly over my shoulder, blowing warm air into my ear. I truly loved that part—the warm air in the ear part. But I didn't like the other part, where each step he took, his giant hooves landed solidly directly behind my heels. Walking along, I thought about Shane's bad habit of following too closely. So far, I hadn't been able to think of any remedy to correct the problem. I had observed the other girls leading their horses. They never appeared to experience any trouble. It seemed to me their horses just naturally stayed a prudent several steps behind. Their horses were being led, as if they were somewhat reluctant to go. The paint was not being led; he just happened to be going my way. Also, of course, as we walked up the pasture together, the paint wasn't being led because, having met him down in the field, he wasn't wearing a halter—not that having it would have made much difference. Anyway, what did I need with a halter when I couldn't get my horse to stop following me even if I wanted to?

That very day I decided to accept what I could not change. I would let it be okay that Shane followed too closely. I resolved that whenever I walked with my horse, I would square my shoulders and concentrate only on his warm breath in my ear, and forever erase from my mind the thudding distraction of his heavy hooves.

CHAPTER SEVEN

*A*fter years of parochial schooling, Cher and I finally convinced our father to allow us to attend public school with the Arend children. It had been a long battle, as our father had been concerned about the quality of our education. Sympathetic to Dad's argument, and although enjoying our other school, we still wanted to attend school with our brother and sister, and all of our neighborhood friends. Keeping the pressure on, "Oh, please, please, please!" we had begged together. Two against one was a mighty advantage.

"Okay," Dad had at last relented. "But I'm going to keep a sharp eye on your grades."

"Oh, we'll study hard," we promised.

Our new school, Highland Junior High, seemed vast and confusing to me. There were so many students it was easy to feel overwhelmed in the milling shuffle between classes. It helped that during my first year at public school, when I was in seventh grade, Linda Gail was in eighth, and Little Mike and Cher were in ninth grade. Except for Walt, already in the service, it was the first time we were all attending the same school. It was fun! Cher and I had choir together, and her friendly wave from out of the crowd was reassuring. Cher had a clear soprano voice, and she was also a member of the school's elite girls' singing group. Lindy and I didn't share any classes; however, she invited me to join her group of friends at lunchtime. With my two sisters keeping watch, I soon settled in.

Both Cher and Linda were popular, with lots of girlfriends and boyfriends calling at all hours of the day and evening. They were popular because they were so in style, with their enviable small waists and ample breasts, flaunted by the tight-fitting sweaters that were the style of the time. The two of them spent a great deal of time in the bathroom getting ready for school each morning. Linda Gail was the hair and makeup expert. She read all the movie magazines and fashion rags, keeping them up-to-date. Confiding and giggling about boys, they applied their makeup together, leaning close to the same mirror. They also helped each other rat their blond hair into ballooned and bloated bouffant hairdos. Oh, the hairspray! I was always choking and coughing whenever I was around them, peering in at the bathroom door, ever asking, "When will it be my turn?" I hung back, out of reach, during this whole operation, or before I knew what was happening I could find myself having to go to school ratted up and sprayed, too.

"Come on in here," they would try to lure me. "Let's see how this bow would look on you."

"Maybe later," I would cagily answer. They thought I was some kind of hairstyling manikin on which they could experiment. They were both able to stand fussing over me, and whatever the unfortunate outcome, in their opinion there was no harm done.

It was also intoxicating that, at my new school, we sisters enjoyed somewhat of a celebrity status because our brother, Little Mike, was a ninth-grade football star. Not only was he one of our school's top athletes, he was also good-looking and full of enigmatic smiles and pranks. Most of the time, he could be found hanging out in the hallways between classes. In my eyes he was foremost among his crowd of big, good-looking, football-playing friends. If I happened past, he would acknowledge me, his little sister, with a mischievous grin and a slight nod of his head. Even so, I left him alone in his school-world, never walking up to talk with him when he was with his friends, which was my way of showing respect. Besides, I knew he was there for me if I ever needed him. All sisters knew we only had to ask or hint of a problem, and the awesome outrage of an older brother would be unleashed on whomever. We used the powerful force of our big brother sparingly, as he could go off wildly crusading and was impossible to recall if he thought one of his sisters had been injured or wronged in any way. For these reasons, Little Mike was best kept as a recourse of last resort.

* * *

That seventh-grade year, with my older sisters and brother at my new school had been very exciting. However, by the time I was in ninth grade and just turned fifteen, I was on my own. Cher and Little Mike, then Lindy, had gone on to high school. I missed them, for without them things were different—Highland Junior High seemed smaller, as well as a whole lot quieter.

By now I had pleasantly discovered that many of my classes in public school were so easy I could daydream throughout most of my lessons, not do any homework, and still pull C's or even B's out of the courses. I did a lot more horseback riding daydreaming in class than I ever did in real life at the pasture. When not daydreaming, I was reading, scrunched low in a seat in the back row, engrossed in a book entirely unrelated to the current topic of study. I tended toward tangents in learning. If something interested me, it was explored. If, for example, on the first day of history, we were to see a film about World War II, I'd be off reading every book I could find on the subject, while the others continued on to the next war or subject without me. Of course, these two bad habits, daydreaming and reading in class, were damaging to my grades.

My best friend, Karen, and I became close in seventh-grade gym class because we had both disliked it. It wasn't so much gym we disliked as it was our teacher, Miss Cruel, as we came to call her. Miss Cruel had a squat, stocky build, and thick, bowed legs that made her appear bulldog tough. Adding to her no-nonsense demeanor, the woman carried a thin baton used to intimidate, to point, and to pounce, shaking the stick an inch from the nose of a cowering offender. She was much more like a drill sergeant than she was a young girl's gym teacher. Karen and I were frequently the recipients of her stern attacks. We'd sit together in the back during her lectures, exchanging barbs and witticisms that only we thought were funny. I had the stick thrust into my face more than most, as I was unable to suppress my appreciation for Karen's constant quips, which were often punctuated by hilarious impersonations. It was probably a good thing Karen and I only had that one class together.

Karen had one major issue in life: strict, overprotective, yet so-loving parents. They were an older couple who had adopted her after their own children were grown with families of their own. Her older siblings had turned out wonderfully, all gracious sorts, well-spoken, well-dressed, and nearly perfect in every way. Consequently, Karen's parents assumed they had a winner, a time-tested parental plan, and no matter what, they stuck to it. They had uncompromising standards that dictated how their daughter should act, what style of clothes she should wear, and even whom her friends should be—or not. The "or not" included me. They called me that spoiled rich kid. My friend deeply loved and respected her parents, and refused the thought of disappointing them in any way—so she was forced to lead a double life. At home, she was a dutiful, sweet, church-going young lady who took pipe organ lessons and played for her church. At school, we would meet in the girl's restroom in the morning before class, talking mostly about boys, since my friend wasn't interested in talking about horses, while she rearranged her wardrobe, unbuttoned the first two buttons of her blouse, hiked up her skirt, and applied her makeup. At the end of the school day, we were back in the girl's restroom, again talking mostly about boys, while she transformed back into her goody-goody, other self. She'd button up her blouse to claustrophobic extreme, lower her skirt length below her knees, and scrub her face with soap and washcloth. She kept her contraband makeup hidden in her locker at school.

Quite frankly, in junior high, I liked talking about boys with my girl-friends, but that was as close as I needed to get. Although boys in general had always been my friends, and were certainly nothing to be afraid of, once in junior high that comfortable, chummy feeling changed. This was especially true if I found out that a certain boy had a crush on me. It was usually hard to miss, as that boy would stare at me, follow me, or lurk outside my classroom whispering and joking with his friends. The whole gig-gling, gossiping group of them—yes, boys giggle and gossip—thought they were somehow concealed behind that one narrow post in the hallway. Sometimes, when I passed an unfortunate boy who had confided his feelings to his friends, his well-meaning band of cupids shoved him out in front of me. The boy was then as red-faced and as eager as I to bolt in the opposite direction. That's when the nerves truly set in. The raging, bashful embarrassment, wondering what could be wrong with that normal-appearing young man who had suddenly decided to torment me. There was also a certain resentment at the fact that I was now walking around school feeling altogether red-faced and awkward.

Part of my problem with boys, maybe even a big part of my problem, was the fact I was truly awkward—awkwardly left-handed. I was afraid that if a boy came too close, I would be sure to knock him down. I was always bumping into people, daydreaming and traveling on the wrong side of a busy corridor, or mindlessly hurrying up the wrong side of the stairs. And if someone reached to shake my right hand, I became flustered searching for it, and was likely to drop everything I was holding in my right hand once it was found. For me, much of life seemed oddly backward. Boys opening doors for me was a disaster. Since most doors opened the opposite of what I expected, a boy added into that confusing mix was neither helpful nor appreciated. I felt sorry for the gallant lad who then found himself dodging and parrying, desperately trying to get out of my way. Boys in junior high, who were in public school, had become particularly terrifying specters because they might ask me to a dance. Thanks to Mom, we sisters had taken dance lessons and I had discovered, quite conclusively, that I was a leader, not a follower, and that my feet were left-handed, too. Fortunately, the boys who had crushes admired me from afar. They were just as terrified of me as I was of them.

CHAPTER EIGHT

As fall advanced and shorter days descended, it became more challenging to find an opportunity to ride my horse. On school days when I arrived at our rendezvous after 3:00, by the time I finished my basic chores of grooming and feeding the paint, it was already getting dark and time for Mom to pick me up. Then, of course, there was the cheerless weather of the season, the drizzly, just-plain-miserable gray, damp days, the steady downpour days, and the blustery or downright stormy days that often put a damper on riding as well. I eagerly looked forward to the few fair-weather weekends when Shane and I had a whole day to ride together. This was especially true now that we were included in the general population of the farm and there were so many wide-open acres to roam. I had been particularly delighted to discover that, with the exception of the one pasture, the Murphy place was laid out in a free-range format. Once inside the first gate, a rider never had to dismount, as each pasture led unobstructed into the next. This all meant the Murphy place was set up for maximum riding fun.

The only gates on the property were the three that opened into the pastures from the barnyard area. The first, to the left of the barn's always-open doorway, was the entrance into the front pasture that was only used to hold sick, injured, or newly arrived horses. The second, directly opposite and to the right of the barn's doorway, was the entrance into the pastures at the rear of the property. There were always four or five horses waiting by that gate. It was the most popular place for horses to gather, as it was close to both the barn door and the grooming area. Horses, hopeful of being noticed, gathered there to watch the action. Consequently, each time the back gate was opened, these "Hopeful Horses," as I began calling them, had to be shooed out of the way. The third gate was the entrance into the pastures at the forefront of the property, located away from the barn, across the driveway, and in front of the house. I called the one or two horses that habitually frequented the front gate "Loners." The Loners were horses that, I imagined, preferred to be farther away from the action, keeping their interest more focused on the house and driveway, rather than on the barn and grooming area. Unlike the Hopeful Horses, the Loners were shy, backing away from the gate when they saw someone approaching.

On weekends, since I didn't have a set schedule, Shane was never waiting for me at any gate. It wasn't only dark days and bad weather that kept me from riding my horse. My family was another, probably the most significant, reason why it was challenging to get to the pasture anytime, but above all on weekends. That's because, on weekends, I wasn't walking from school. Therefore, I had to beg a ride to the pasture from a mom, a dad, or a handy brother, and then only after I had successfully wheedled my way out of some otherwise compulsory family function. These self-extraction maneuvers were both touchy and tricky, calling for the most savvy and subtle salesmanship. Quite frankly, the other members of my family couldn't have cared less whether I ever saw my horse or not. Saturdays were counted out of the weekend equation anyway, as presence at Daddy Ray's and at church was required. There were also many Sundays when I couldn't make it to the pasture due to an absolutely inescapable school or church activity, or family obligation. It seemed as if some thoughtless person in the family was always having a birthday, getting married, or having a baby, and, without question, these kinds of family events demanded my cheerful presence. On the inevitable days when I couldn't make it to the pasture, Pat would be called so that she could take the paint up to the barn in the evening to feed him. Since on weekends there was no way to keep to a schedule, Shane had no way of knowing when, or even if, I would pop into his day.

In late October, on a rare sunny Sunday, I was dropped off at the pasture. "Thank you, thank you, thank you," I gushed to Mom while hurriedly grabbing my things. I'd been prodding her since eight o'clock, and now it was almost ten o'clock. A whole day to spend with my horse—I couldn't believe it!

"I'll be back at two o'clock," Mom reminded. "Don't argue." Grandpa and Grandma Arend were visiting from Friday Harbor and Daddy Mike was preparing a special Sunday dinner for his parents and his sister, our Aunt Sonia, and her family. Okay, maybe it wasn't a whole day.

Hurrying, with the two o'clock deadline in mind, I went to the barn to get Shane's halter, and then, starting in the front pasture, I slowly circled the place, eagerly scanning for a spotted horse. Today he was found behind the house in the company of several mares he had successfully rounded up. When his name was called from a distance, "Shane!" his head jerked up and swung around, and he eyed me warily, with an odd start, as if he thought I might be merely a whimsy of his own inventing. When his name was called the second time, "Shane!" he snorted and shook his head, as if to say, "It really is you!" He trotted right over to me, and then, as was his way—truly right over me!

"You are such a good horse," I told him. "Such a good horse!"

Pleasant weather and Sunday morning had combined to bring more than the usual number of horse owners to the pasture. There were two horses eating grain and being groomed at the hitching posts. I tethered Shane next to a palomino gelding being readied for a ride. "Hello," I said to the girl brushing the palomino. "Do you mind?" She was a round-faced girl with short light-brown hair, dressed like me, bundled in a rather heavy-weight winter coat and wearing boots—though not cowboy boots. I didn't recognize her as being someone who attended my school, although we seemed to be about the same age. "Nice horse," I commented. "What's his name?"

"Dusty." And he was that! The girl, vigorously brushing her horse's back, was raising quite a cloud of dust. All of the horses were scruffy this time of year anyway, all with shaggy coats, muddied legs, and bedraggled manes and tails.

Introducing myself, and my school, I said, "Connie. Highland."

"Wanda. Sammamish." That was the reason I didn't recognize her. She was in high school, while I was still in junior high.

Pausing in her brushing, she asked reflectively, "You new here? Maybe it's that I usually ride on Saturdays. I can't get here much on Sundays."

"I can't get here on Saturdays," I returned.

At that moment, Pat strode past, giving me a definite scowl and shaking her head, as if she had something to say to me, but had no time in which to say it. Uh-oh, I thought, another infraction. Pat was often miffed with me about something the paint had done. Needing to get Shane's grain and brushes, I had to more or less follow her into the barn. I stalled for a minute, talking with Wanda, hoping to avoid her. No luck. Entering the barn, there she was, waiting for me, prepared to force a confrontation. I tried to side-step Pat's scolding by asking her a question—getting the conversation moving rapidly in a direction away from my horse. Thinking fast, I had noticed that the inside of the barn was undergoing some repair, and that a number of the rickety stall rails were being replaced. "What happened to the barn?" I asked, flashing a carefree smile. After all, what could possibly be wrong on such a beautiful day? I barely got the question out, as Pat's mouth was already twisted open, with her finger wagging in my face.

"Your horse happened to the barn!"

Wrong question. Swallowing hard, surveying the mess, I said, "My horse did all this?" As usual, I was so genuinely shocked and so terribly sorry that my woeful response was much like a puppy's total rollover, "Please forgive me!" belly-up submission, and it immediately stole from Pat all satisfaction of redress. Her wagging finger stopped wagging and her arms dropped despairingly to her sides.

"Yes," she said curtly. Then, taking a deep, calming breath, she continued. "Your horse did all this." We stood together viewing the damage, a swath of downed and shattered stall rails that started at the left wall of the barn and cut through to the center aisle.

"How did it happen?"

"I could draw you a picture," Pat said with annoyance edging back into her tone, "but I'd say it's pretty obvious. You can see that it started in that far stall. He pounded those rails down with his hooves."

"I don't understand."

"Well, maybe I could take a little of the blame," Pat admitted. "I might have left him in the stall longer than usual. He pounded his way through all these stalls, one by one. I guess he was scavenging for leftovers. I wanted to kill him. I really wanted to kill him! But . . . well, you can see that I didn't," she said motioning toward the paint, framed in the sunlight of the barn's big door. "He's still here."

Squinting and blinking I reentered the bright morning after having spent time rummaging through the cardboard box and paper bags filled with horse-related paraphernalia organized in a corner of the dark tack room. I was disappointed to see Shane had the hitching post to himself. Wanda and Dusty were gone. And I was surprised to see Daddy Ray waiting for me. The sunshine backlighting his fair hair gave him a halo. He was wearing his beloved work-in-the-shop clothes: worn and faded, tight-fitting, paint-stained, blue jeans; a onetime white but now yellowed T-shirt with a V-neck; and cracked and paint-dribbled, sawdust-covered shoes. "Say, can you give me a hand with this here?" he asked.

"A hand? Sure," I said. Setting down the bucket of grain and brushes, I followed him around to the back of the station wagon where the tailgate had been lowered. "Wow! What's this?" Whatever it was, it was big. It was some kind of wooden box filling up the back section of the station wagon. We eased the heavy box out slowly. It had to be turned upright before setting it on the ground because it had been lying on one side to fit in the back of the car. Once the box was turned over, knowing immediately what it was, "Wow! A tack box!" I exclaimed. Dad had built a tack box, and it was painted the most wonderful baby blue color. It was approximately five feet in height at the back and three and a half feet at the front, which gave it a sloped, hinged-at-the-top and hasped-at-the-bottom lift-up lid. A shiny new padlock was already in place.

"Grab your end," Dad said. "You can inspect it after we get it inside. I'll walk backward. Careful now." Shuffling along, unable to see our feet as we walked, "I know I got these measurements right," Dad was mumbling to himself. "But there's that sharp turn. It's a close space . . ."

"Wow!" I kept repeating as we carried the box into the barn, "A tack box!"

"Looks as if they're having to do some construction work here," Dad commented. "Isn't it always something?" He shook his head, commiserating, "Wish I had time to offer my help."

In an attempt to distract him from the mess I warned him, "Watch your step!" although there was nothing there.

The center aisle of the barn was wide, presenting no trouble. Dad went first, backing up the three narrow steps that led to the tack room. I was puzzled when the box fit sideways through the door without difficulty. It seemed so big and the door so small. The door, I now realized, only appeared smaller than a regular-sized door. Apparently, it was an optical illusion created by an average-sized door being dwarfed by an oversized barn wall. Life is filled with optical illusions, I mused, fraught with things or circumstances appearing bigger or smaller than they actually are. I felt there must be some sort of philosophical life lesson in this great insight for me, but didn't have time to ponder. We had to stand the box on end to move it fully inside the room and turn it around in the tight space.

"It's pretty hard to see in here," I commented.

"That's what Edison thought," Dad said, turning on the light. For the first time, for me anyway, the small room was illuminated. I had searched for that light switch so many times, fumbling in the dark, knowing it had to be somewhere, but never able to find it. No surprise. The switch was completely concealed behind a bundle of rope that hung from a nail on the back wall behind the ladder leading to the hayloft. How had Dad known?

The box fit into the corner spot in line with the other tack boxes. Standing back for a minute to appreciate the scene, I noted the other boxes, in the glow of their new neighbor, had lost some of their previous luster. "This is so great, Dad," I said softly.

"Here's your key," Dad said. "Let's get your things put away." It was as if he had handed me a magic key. Hesitating, I turned it over in my fingers, savoring the moment. "Don't worry," he said. "I've kept an extra, just in case."

Inside, the box was divided into two sections. On the left, taking up almost half the interior area, was the space reserved for the galvanized garbage can that held grain. The other section was open, with hooks to hang rope, halter, and bridle. There was room for Shane's grain bucket and much more. Dad passed items from the sack, while I lined up brushes, combs, and ointments on the shelf that ran the full length of the tack box under the lid. Everything had a place.

Giving him a hug, I exclaimed, "Wow! Thank you, Dad. This is great. Absolutely great!"

My exuberance embarrassed him, as it often did. Looking down for a moment, shuffling his feet, "You settling in here okay?" he asked. "Anything else you need?"

"Can't think of a thing."

"Last chance to join the family for roller-skating."

"Thanks again for the offer, Dad. Truly. But I want to stay here."

"Pizza after?"

"No, Dad."

"Sure? We'll miss you. We won't see you again until next weekend."

"I'm sure." He was breaking my heart.

"Suit yourself." He was disappointed. He was always disappointed when all his kids weren't with him. "You sure you have a ride home?"

"I'm sure."

There was a lump in my throat watching Dad drive away. I always got that same uncomfortable, constricted feeling in my throat whenever I watched my dad drive away. Deciding to indulge my guilt further, I walked after his car to where the station wagon could be seen traveling its entire lonely route around the pasture and out of site. The brush of a cold nose and a warm lick on my hand prompted me to look down into Water Dog's compassionate eyes. Automatically scratching his black head, "I'm all right," I told him. "Thank you for asking."

At last, perfect weather for riding and hours to spend with my horse. The paint needed a light brushing before our ride, and while I worked, thinking about the baby blue tack box, my self-confidence soared. Even Shane's bridle slipped on effortlessly.

The paint and I approached the front gate. I was uncomfortable using the back gate, having found I had no knack for shooing horses away—no flair for scare or whatever it took. The Hopeful Horses did not find my attempts at intimidation threatening in any way. Moreover, I found my wild waving and shouting actually served to attract them, and that I was in danger of being crushed by the resulting press of horseflesh. The fact that I regularly brought them treats surely served to frustrate my efforts. The front gate was better anyway, mostly because there was a well-placed boulder right inside that was the perfect size for mounting my horse. Further, the front pasture was almost always empty of other riders, which made it a good place to warm up and practice my mounting and riding skills. The other girls seldom used the front property, probably because it was so visible from the house, even though the house sat back behind a row of fruit trees that lined the fence. Also, it might have been less appealing to riders because much of it was sloped, as well as flanked on two sides by busy roadways. In comparison, the pastures at the rear of the property offered relatively flat, quiet, and more secluded riding.

I led the paint past the boulder so his back came alongside, bringing him into perfect position for mounting. Now the trick was speed. I had to climb up onto the boulder and jump onto Shane's back faster than he could move his rear end away, thereby moving his back ever so slightly out of mounting range. This was easy for him to do, requiring but one sidestep of a rear leg, and there would be nothing more to mount than a big, innocent-appearing, horse head. And so there it was—the head. Blocking all else, it wanted to be scratched behind the ears. This was a typical mounting scenario for us. My horse enjoyed this game so much it was almost compulsive for him. I had come to suspect that, above all, he enjoyed the part of his game where he had to keep such a stone face of disinterested innocence. Of course, he knew I was trying to mount him, and he knew that I knew he knew.

Mounting was something we needed to work on—but not today. Jumping back down from the rock, the paint was led around a second time, in a wide circle, and then along and beside the boulder. And a second time, Shane stood still, a virtual statue, locked in perfect position for mounting. Again, I scrambled up the rock. And once again, standing up, there it was—the head. It had been expected. "You again!" I said, in a mock surprised and mildly scolding tone. Then, using body language, hanging my head sadly, dropping my arms hopelessly to my sides, "I guess we won't be riding today after all," I said woefully. This was all merely tactics, pretending to be surprised at seeing him there, and then acting very disappointed. I could afford to be patient and employ psychology, for my horse was such a good-natured animal he would be incapable of keeping his game up for long, especially if he thought he was truly making me unhappy. He was not, however, in any way making me unhappy. I was having great fun whether we got to go riding or not. After all, I was in heaven—horse heaven.

Still standing on the rock, taking time to appreciate the day, I scanned the horizon and sniffed the fresh breezes. It was one of those rare days when it was possible to smell the salt air from Puget Sound, even though it was quite a distance away. Or was it Ivar's fish and chips I smelled? What a fabulous morning!

With hopes high, I led Shane around a third time.

The different speeds at which a horse moves—walk, jog, trot, lope, canter, and gallop—are called gaits. Every horse has its own distinctive way of going, and this uniqueness of movement is one of the most important things to be aware of when purchasing a horse. For example, some horses have a very slow, drag-along, drooping-head kind of walk. Their first gear is set too low. This would be mind-numbing on a long ride—or on any ride for that matter. I was lucky this was not the case with my horse. The paint had a heads-up, attentive walk. I say I was lucky, because much of what was good about my horse truly was the purest kind of dumb-luck, and had nothing whatever to do with any horse sense or savvy employed by me on the day of Shane's purchase. The paint was also blessed with an enviable jog. It was smooth and covered ground quickly. His trot, on the other hand, though faster, was jolting. Frankly, his trot was like riding on a jack-hammer. However, since most horses do have a jarring trot, my horse had nothing for which to be ashamed. Shane's canter was also pleasing. A horse may canter very slowly, loping, or it may canter quite quickly. However, in every instance, the canter is an enjoyable gait. I liked to practice transitioning the paint from the jog to the canter, omitting the jarring trot that seemed, naturally and tragically, to insert itself in between. A steady hand and a steady horse—that was my goal for us.

Shane and I jogged and cantered along the many paths that crisscrossed the front pasture. Much of the time—okay, most of the time—I had a strong grip on my horse's mane, with its long, sturdy hairs laced through the tightly clenched fingers of my right hand. I would have held on with both hands, but one hand was needed to steer the horse. We practiced stopping and backing up. Shane was a natural at backing up. It was one of the few things we did exceptionally well together up to this point.

Horseback riding isn't supposed to be all work, it's supposed to be fun, and so after practicing enough for one session, we went to find the other riders. We followed the well-trodden trail that circled around the house to the pastures at the rear of the property. With the sound of the busy roadway more distant behind us, the paint's hooves falling on the hard-packed earth could clearly be heard. Clomp, clomp, clomp. Listening, cherishing the sound, I patted the paint's warm neck, silently thanking my two fathers for making it possible to experience the joy of having such a wonderful animal in my life.

Ahead were riders in the farthest field. That was the flattest field at the Murphy place and riders used it to race their horses, sometimes competing. I wondered how fast my horse could gallop, and planned to find out sometime—but not today. Continuing to follow the well-worn path, taking a sharp right, we entered the area of the riding arena.

The riding ring was in a secluded location, set up inside the open-end of a reservoir. No part of it was visible from anywhere else on the property. The three sides of the levee formed a horseshoe and were built up in substantial dike-like fashion. The floor of the reservoir was level at the front half section, which was where the riding ring was set up. However, the second half section sloped sharply downward toward the rear of the reservoir, and consequently where water collected. It was a private world, inside the riding ring, inside the reservoir.

The minute we rounded the corner I saw two girls already using the ring, so I hesitated, keeping outside the perimeter. Although they must have seen us, we were ignored; no smile or hint of welcome was cast our way. My hesitation had everything to do with the fact that I recognized one of them as a girl whom I had seen the first day Shane and I arrived at the Murphy place—the very same redhead who had felt compelled to share her observations about my horse. She was riding the stocky buckskin mare with the shaved mane. By now, I knew her name was Gretchen, as she was one of the horse owners who regularly complained to Pat about Shane's greedy conduct with her mare. Gretchen had a right to complain. The paint had an unwavering fascination for her mare, and the buckskin did not appreciate being singled out for his attentions. Proving that fact, Shane often had bites and nicks on his neck and rump that were surely the result of his amorous encounters. The girl riding with Gretchen was unknown to me. She was younger, rather slight, and riding a small, sturdy horse, likely a Welsh pony.

I pondered whether Shane and I should go or stay. I wanted to leave, thinking that my horse could very well be an unwelcome distraction for the buckskin mare, or that her owner might decide to take this opportunity to confront me personally about my horse's behavior. I wasn't eager for another confrontation, especially after having just been the target of Pat's frustrations. At the same time, I didn't want to appear guilty or intimidated by retreating, which would have been quite obvious under the circumstances. Finally, I decided it was best to act as if nothing was amiss. For the moment anyway, Shane and I would stay right where we were to watch the girls from a respectful distance outside the boundary of the arena.

Gretchen had her mare fully rigged in fancy western gear, and she wore an outfit to match, complete with Western-style jacket, cowboy boots, and cowboy hat. She was practicing mounting, making her horse stand still by using a quirt to tap the mare's side if the horse made a move away. She was exacting with the mare, using the quirt handily. Her tactics seemed to be working well. I stayed, hoping to learn something.

Before long, Shane and I found ourselves creeping closer, until we were inside the open end of the horseshoe. Realizing we'd ventured inside the ring, I thought to back my horse a more polite distance away. The paint immediately protested, jerking his head and rattling his bridle. He didn't want to leave. Very probably, he was enjoying being near the buckskin mare. My horse's opinion was understandable, even reasonable, as we weren't doing any harm by our presence there. However, his noisy insubordination caught the attention of the two girls, now staring at us with scowls of disapproval. I took action quickly to demonstrate that I could control the situation and show my horse who was boss. I stiffened my back—good posture was important. The paint, sensing my resolve, reluctantly obeyed my heavy-handed pulling on the reins and my heels digging into his flanks.

At this open end of the reservoir both banks were flush with the surrounding terrain. Before we knew it, the paint and I had blundered onto the embankment. Naturally, we followed it, marveling at the day and the panoramic view our newfound elevation afforded. Even though the bank stayed level as we rode, the ground on both sides dropped away. It was safe to ride along the levee, although I never would have thought to do so. The embankment was approximately three yards across, solidly packed, and covered with closely cropped field grass. It was obvious the reservoir had been there for many years. Shane and I now had a much better view of the arena, and stopped to watch the interesting activity in the ring below.

The girls were preparing to jump their horses. There were two low obstacles and one higher jump constructed from boards and blocks. The low obstacles were purposely set at an easy beginner's level about a foot high. It was a height at which a horse would be encouraged to jump over, or at least be forced to pick up its step or risk a reminding tap on a sensitive shinbone. From my lofty perspective, it appeared as if any horse, even the smaller Welsh, could easily step over the low obstacles.

The redheaded girl went first, loping her horse slowly around the inner edge of the ring, keeping the mare to a well-disciplined canter. Twice around the ring they went before turning toward a low jump. The mare sailed over the obstacle, and then with hardly a break in stride, continued cantering around the ring. Twice they cantered around before again turning toward a low jump. This time, however, the buckskin changed her mind at the last second. Something, her footing perhaps not quite in sync, made her skid to a stop right before the jump. Only after much animated prodding by her rider did she reluctantly step over it. The other girl, who went next, was also wearing Western garb and riding with a saddle. The pony loped confidently around the ring, but became suspicious when turned toward a low jump, dropping his stride from a canter to a bouncing trot. Both horses inclined toward the trot after the turn. A trotting horse was more likely to high-step over the obstacle. Sometimes a horse would dribble over the jump in a painfully slow, forward-falling stumble. The dribble was unsightly, as well as loud, because it seemed as if each of the horse's four knees and four hooves individually bonged, clanked, and rattled the board. The trick to successful jumping, I soon understood, was all in timing the approach.

Now Pat and Swifty were at the outer edge of the arena. I had spotted Water Dog first, nosing around the perimeter, the faithful herald of Pat's arrival. When Pat rode Swifty into the ring, the two girls stopped what they were doing and rode their horses aside. It was impressive when the chestnut gelding sailed over the high obstacle with ease—the other girls had ignored it. Pat's gelding wasn't a particularly big horse; if anything, he was kind of scrawny. Pat jumped down from her horse to raise the high pole even higher. Then she leaped back into the saddle without using the stirrups. From a standstill, she grabbed the saddle horn with one hand and swung up as expertly as any stunt rider I'd ever seen. It was hard to refrain from clapping. Seeing Pat and Swifty in motion was inspirational. Wow! I thought. I'm going to learn how to do that.

At that point, I got to thinking that Shane and I were standing too close, mostly because the girls seemed to be taking furtive glances our way. One more sideways glance and I decided to ride a bit farther along the embankment to lessen any impression of spying. Right away, the paint didn't like the idea, again noisily protesting by stubbornly shaking his head and rattling his bridle. As before, this immediately called us to the attention of the girls, who stopped what they were doing to stare at us with stern expressions. I prodded the horse, but this time my efforts to force the issue merely served to send him into his full, spoiled-brat, "Oh, no I won't!" hoof-pawing act. I had only intended to ride a short distance away, unnoticed. Instead, I found myself arguing with my horse. Knowing only one way to deal with Shane when he was pawing, I pulled his head around to the left until he had to turn around several times, making tight circles. Once dizzy, he was pressed on his way.

Shane and I were not too pleased with each other as we continued along the embankment to the far end of the reservoir where we could view the arena from across the water. I hoped by being farther away, we wouldn't appear to stand directly over the jumpers. Thinking to minimize my high profile even further, I decided to jump down from my horse.

After jumping down, I decided that chewing on a blade of grass would serve to affect an indifferent air. The grass growing on the levee was cropped golf-green short, the same as all the other grass on the Murphy farm. However, there was long, succulent grass growing on the steep side of the bank above the waterline. It would be a bit of an over-extended stretch, but surely I could manage to pull up a nibble for Shane and for me. I imagined a fanciful scene of my sitting cross-legged, chewing on a blade of grass, detached, above the everyday world, gazing out over the vastness before me. I imagined myself to be an Apache warrior, poised on a high cliff, appreciating the canyon lands, with my horse dutifully and majestically standing behind me. Such was the idyllic scene imagined.

Well, there would be no sitting cross-legged. Jumping down, I found it had recently rained and the ground was wet. However, it would still be possible to stand, chewing on a blade of grass, looking detached and noble. I started forward, gingerly stepping down over the side, immediately hesitating, as the ground on the side of the bank was slick. At the exact moment I hesitated, Shane gave me a shove with his head right in the center of my back. Whether it was an innocent, albeit ill-timed, attempt at a head scratch, or a deliberate I've-had-enough-of-you! push, was hard to say. Either way, the result was the same, as it didn't take much to send me toppling down the steep embankment. At the sound of the splash, the three girls turned, mouths agape, to watch me slog through the waist-deep water, coming their way. Unfortunately, that was the only way out, as all the banks were so steep and slippery. Dripping wet, I had to walk past them and the whole distance back along the levee to collect my horse.

I learned a valuable lesson that day and never again stood in front of my horse near the edge of anything high.

CHAPTER NINE

It was a fluke whenever Karen came to the pasture. It only happened when something in her parents' schedules had gone awry. Something unavoidable had occurred, connections crossed, and their daughter was left with that nut and her horse.

Karen and I were hurriedly walking from school on a chilly November afternoon. I was rushing my ever-poky friend along because I wanted us to have time to ride before it got too dark and her mom came to pick us up.

Karen pointed, "There's your horse."

"I know," I said. "That's what I wanted to show you. He waits there for me every day."

"Every day? What about weekends? Does he wait down here on weekends?"

"Shush!" I told Karen. We were getting close, and I wasn't sure how Shane would react to my having brought a friend. As we got closer, I said, "Stay here." The paint was getting jittery. He had shied back from the fence, and his ears were pointing in two different directions instead of both pointing forward, which was his usual sign of confidence. Ears at odd angles meant he was trying to sort things out, but was not coming to any conclusions.

The ditch and deep grass separated us from the fence. "You hold my books while I jump over," I said, handing my things to Karen. "I'll greet my horse and then hold your books while you jump over." The ditch was so wide I had never made it cleanly across in one jump. I was glad my friend had suggested we change our clothes before coming to the pasture. Landing, as usual, somewhere halfway up the other side, I had to scramble to avoid slipping backward into the mud. The paint immediately came forward, pressing against the fence while I hugged his neck and praised him. Forgotten was any concern he might have had about my friend. "Yes, you are a wonderful horse," I told him "A wonderful horse!" It was always a magical moment for me to be greeted in such a way. "Do you see what a wonderful horse I have, Karen? Karen?" I asked again, turning back to my friend. "Do you see?"

However, my friend wasn't seeing anything except the ditch. "Yes, yes," she said half-heartedly, "a wonderful horse."

"You weren't even looking," I said, disappointed.

"I'm not crawling down in that ditch!"

"You have to come over," I urged. "I'll take your books. I'll give you a hand."

Karen stepped back, taking a defensive stance. "I'm not crawling around in that ditch!"

"You'll have to walk all the way around then," I warned. "And it's a long way."

"Walk with me."

"I can't. I have to go up this way. If I walk with you, my horse will follow us all along the fence line. He'll walk through all that muck ahead. I know him. I've tried it . . . more than once."

"Try again," Karen said.

Giving in, I walked forward along the fence, away from my horse, thinking stupidly that maybe Karen had a point. At no surprise to me, the paint came right along, staying with me as close as the fence would allow. "Satisfied?" I asked, with a bit of exasperation in my tone. It was exasperation aimed not at Karen, but myself.

"Do you want me to carry your books?" Karen offered. We each had schoolbooks and school clothes in separate bags. She didn't need anything extra to carry.

"No," I said. "Hand mine over. We'll meet you at the gate." I slid my bags under the fence. Then, I very carefully stepped through the barbed wire, directly under my horse's eagerly sniffing nose. I had to push his head aside before I could stand up.

It was natural for me to want to show off my horse. I wanted my friend to see everything that was new since the last time she had been to the pasture. I especially wanted Karen to see how the paint and I went through the gate together. Apparently, it was quite unique; I had seen folks stop what they were doing to watch us with smiles and shaking heads.

I started up the pasture with the paint, as usual, walking too close behind me, puffing his warm, sweet breath against my neck. He was so close I could kiss his velvet nose with merely a turn of my head as we walked. Even though I was determined never to show it, it was impossible for me to ignore those anvil-like hooves, visualizing them with each resounding thud as they fell not a half-inch from my heels. We were walking slowly. I was timing our progress to Karen's trek along the road around the pasture. Several times, I waved to my friend and she waved back.

By the time my horse and I arrived at the gate, although we had ridiculously dragged our steps, Karen was still just making the turn to start up the driveway. Reluctant to pass through the gate until she arrived, but too impatient to wait, I decided to walk down to meet her halfway. I wondered how Shane would react to this change in our usual routine. Knowing horses are suspicious of change, I expected the paint to wait at the gate. Staying inside the pasture, I walked down along the fence to meet Karen as she was coming up. I was actually quite surprised when my horse accompanied me.

"Wow!" Karen said. "How do you get your horse to follow you like that? The last time I was here you were chasing him all over the pasture."

"That's what I wanted to show you," I said. I couldn't tell Karen how I got my horse to follow me, because I didn't know how I got my horse to do anything.

When we came to the gate, "You'll have to stand back," I told Karen. "This gate swings wide." The gate was rickety, with a heavy post that supported tightly stretched barbed wire. It wasn't the kind of wooden gate on which one could stand. The gatepost was secured to a fence post with a double loop of baling wire at the top and at the bottom. Pushing against the top of the post to loosen the wire, I slid the wire up and off. I had to be careful to keep strong resistance against the heavy post so it wouldn't snap back to hit me in the face when it lifted out of the lower loop.

It was best to walk wide with the gate keeping the wire as taut as possible. I walked wide, my unfettered horse walking very wide with me, until the whole big horse was through. Then, when I turned to take it back, my horse turned following behind me, staying with me while I struggled to set the post into the wire loops again. It must have been particularly strange to witness. Especially since any other horse, without a lead and once through the gate, would have simply wandered over to the barn to wait for its oats. At the very least, any other horse would have wandered out into the Murphy's yard to graze on the inviting, overgrown lawn. I was sure none of the other girls would have ever thought to let their horses out of the pasture without first securing their halters and leads.

"Now, Karen, watch this," I said, as we passed my speechless friend. With Karen following, I led my horse across the gravel lot to the hitching post. "I can tell my horse to wait here while I go to get his oats. See. Watch." I petted the paint, at the same time whispering in his ear. Then, I strode off to the barn as if I were going to get his oats. The paint watched me go, waiting, untied, at the hitching post. He was such a good horse! "See," I said, returning. "Or, I can tell him that we're going to feed him in the barn today." I made much of whispering in my horse's ear again. Then, with Karen following, still speechless, my horse dutifully followed me into the barn, whereupon I pointed to a stall, and that was exactly where he went.

"Wow!" Karen exclaimed. "Wow! You're going to be a famous horse trainer for sure." I had definitely impressed my friend.

I only laughed, truly enjoying her praise. I knew, however, I wasn't any horse trainer. Shane and I simply had a routine we followed. I hadn't whispered anything into his ear except, "I love you." And the paint always went into the same stall, in the same way. I had merely pointed for effect.

It was cold and dark in the barn. I led Karen down the dimly lit aisle and up the narrow stairs, turning on the light as we entered the tack room. Swifty raised his head, snorting a greeting. The chestnut gelding, cozy in his private quarters, expected me to stop to visit with him before I did anything else—which I did. "Karen you'll have to come say something to Swifty or you'll hurt his feelings," I said. Adding, "He's the best jumper and the fastest horse on the place."

"He doesn't look it," Karen commented.

Unlocking the tack box, I said, "But he is. It's okay to pet him. He doesn't bite. We can give him a handful of oats."

"That's new," Karen said, indicating the tack box.

"My dad made it for me."

Anguished, she asked, "Which dad? Your real dad or your stepdad? Why do you do that all the time? It drives me buggy."

"Daddy Ray," I answered. As an in-between child of divorce, it could be tricky talking about my families. People got confused. I didn't like to say "real dad" or "stepdad." And I didn't like to say "real mom" or "stepmom," or "real sister" or "stepsister" or "half-sister," the point of it having become moot long ago. I had explained my feelings about this to Karen before. It wasn't my fault I had two sets of parents—and I wasn't about to apologize for it. To Cher and me, both dads were simply "Dad," and both moms were simply "Mom." Only for clarity's sake were our parents sometimes given their royal titles of Daddy Ray, Daddy Mike, Momma Darleen, and Mom-Mom.

"We can stow our books and clothes in this corner," I said, showing Karen where I kept my things. "We'll give Shane some oats before we ride." Then, turning to the expectant chestnut, I added, "And a handful for this gentleman here. See how he eats so carefully from my hand?" I was very fond of Swifty. Everyone was. It was pleasant in the close tack room. Swifty, in his adjoining stall, kept it several degrees warmer there than it was in the other, more airy part of the barn. I started pulling things out of the box, where everything was neatly arranged for easy access. There was a box of sugar cubes and I stuffed a handful into my coat pocket for the horses waiting outside by the gate.

Karen carried the brushes; I carried the bucket of oats and the bridle. The paint was glad to see us coming. He had been impatient for my return, pawing at the soft earth of his stall, and sometimes kicking the stall wall to prod me if things seemed to be taking too long. While the paint munched his small offering of oats, I brushed his back, in particular, which was always very dusty. There wasn't time to do much more than that if we were going to ride before dark. Karen helped me brush, until I stopped her, noticing the white cuffs on her coat were getting soiled. "We'll finish this after our ride," I told her.

Since Pat fed the horses later in the evening, unless she was riding, I often never saw her on school days. So with Swifty in the barn, I knew we had the place to ourselves. It was the perfect opportunity to see if Shane was a jumper.

Now my friend was riding the paint as he followed me along the trail to the arena. "I'm not jumping," Karen informed me. "I'm not jumping," she repeated.

"I heard you the first time," I said. "No one's forcing you." I wasn't at all concerned about whether she would jump, since I knew I could talk my friend into doing almost anything. I had only to pretend indifference, or better yet, object completely. "You're not ready anyway."

"What's that supposed to mean?"

Karen would jump. "It means I wouldn't want you to get hurt, that's all." I glanced back and noticed my friend was already filthy. I had forgotten brushing a horse was such a dirty job. Even in play clothes, Karen's mother had her wearing white blouses with lace collars. And her coat hadn't been purchased with horses and pastures in mind. It was lavender, Karen's favorite color, and had snow-white, fake-fur accents around the bottom, sleeve cuffs, and hood collar.

The arena had an abandoned air, like a schoolyard deserted after recess. The jump poles had been left knocked down and haphazardly scattered. "This is so cool," Karen said. "I didn't even know it was here."

"It's pretty cool, all right," I said. "Jump down and give me a hand setting this hurdle."

Karen didn't jump down. That was only an expression, anyway. Instead, after swinging her leg over, she slid down with her stomach rubbing against the side of the horse. I didn't say anything since, riding bareback, that was the way I tended to dismount as well. However, now the front of her coat had a long, grimy, furry streak that hadn't been there before. I decided not to mention it.

"Is that water always there?" Karen asked. We were setting one pole at the lowest height.

"We're in some kind of reservoir," I answered. "Maybe they had crops here years ago. Must be. I can't think what they would use it for now. I don't know if the water ever comes up this far."

"Won't your horse just step over this?" Karen asked. "It's not very high."

"That's what we plan to find out." I said. "Here, give me a leg up." Grabbing a handful of Shane's mane, I stepped into Karen's cupped hands, whereupon, she launched me upward in the direction of my horse. The paint, with precision timing at the last possible quarter of a second, stepped away. I was launched at nothing. Diving forward, sending Karen in the opposite direction, we both landed in the dust. Shane hadn't moved much; he was practically standing over me. Without effort, from my position on the ground, I could have reached out to touch his front leg. His moving away wasn't about wanting to get away, or about not wanting to be ridden.

"What happened?" Karen asked, obviously annoyed.

"Humor," I said.

"Humor? Like ha-ha? You did it on purpose?"

"Not my ha-ha. His." I rolled my eyes upward in the direction of the horse.

Karen and I were sitting looking across at each other from our positions on the ground. My friend peered skeptically up at the paint. "Horses don't laugh," she said.

"Yes, they do," I assured her. "They laugh in silence."

Several mounting attempts later, I was on. "Now we'll see if Shane's a jumper," I said, gathering the reins and feeling in control. I was envisioning myself as the heroine of the movie *National Velvet*, racing across the English countryside astride a long-legged Thoroughbred, sailing gracefully over every obstacle in sight. "You'd better stand back," I warned Karen, urging Shane forward into a jerky trot.

At first, the paint didn't catch on to the circling. He wanted to leave the arena. Every time we rode by the exit, Shane and I had a war of wills, fighting each other for control. But I was firm; we were staying. Keeping him steady at a lope was more challenging than I had imagined it would be. I had to keep kicking and jabbing him with my heels, all the time discouraging him from slowing to his beloved trot. Around the arena we went, loping, trotting, even walking, and then loping again. It was a jerky ride. Now I turned the paint toward the jump in the middle of the ring. Shane faltered at the turn, veering right. He was adjusting his timing. I almost slid off sideways as he recovered his stride. Urging him forward and leaning into the jump, I grabbed a handful of mane at the last second. We were going over. We were in the air!

No, I was in the air! Catapulted! Sent far, fast. It was a terrific jump—but I was making it by myself.

It was fortunate that I landed with a roll—an oomph, and a roll. I got up from the hard-packed ground, somewhat dazed, already checking myself for injuries, and worried about having broken an arm or leg. Hiding most bruises and abrasions from my parents was easy, but I knew I wouldn't be able to hide a broken limb. Everything checked out okay; I still had a horse.

"Are you all right?" Karen asked, rushing to me. "I guess your horse doesn't know how to jump."

"Well, now I've shown him how it's done," I said grimly, dusting myself off. "Help me back on."

Shane was waiting on the other side of the jump pole. Mounting the second time was no easier than the first. It took, predictably, three or four tries before he got bored with our troubles. I think we'll forget about the circling part," I said, gathering the reins. "That's what's confusing him. We'll take the straight on shot until he gets the hang of it." I backed my horse away from the jump. The paint arched his neck and lowered his head, slowly backing. We backed away to the outer edge of the arena, facing the jump. There it was—not far. It didn't appear to be much of an obstacle to me; I could have easily stepped over it myself.

We needed to get up as much speed as possible before the jump, which was only a short distance away. I kicked, urging my horse forward. "Come on, Shane! Let's do it! Let's go!" His ears flashed forward, then back, then forward, and then back again. He was alert, listening to my voice, yet concentrating on the job ahead. It was a promising beginning. The paint started out strong with an enthusiastic lope. Then, despite my every effort, he immediately dropped his stride to a trot, and then changed again to a stumbling sort of jog. His final steps were creeping. Now Shane stood rooted before the jump, his front legs stiff and spread wide, his head lowered, sniffing at the pole.

"That doesn't look good," Karen called from a distance.

"No. His timing's all off. Maybe if I lead him across a few times?" I said starting to dismount.

"Don't get down!" Karen said in a panic, rushing forward. "Whatever you do, don't get down. I'll lead him."

We waited for Shane to finish his sniffing inspection of the jump pole; there was something fascinating about it. He might have been enjoying the scent of many horses, maybe even the scent of horses in the distant past. For all we knew, he might have smelled the history of the arena, or maybe even the history of the whole farm. When he had finished, I said, "He's got the gist of this now. I suggest you lead him around first, though. That will give him a fresh start." Karen agreed, leading the paint away from the jump. He was glad to go. She led him away, and then back around the arena. "Get up some speed," I suggested. "That way he'll be over before he knows what's happened to him."

Now we were heading straight for the jump, with Karen running out in front and Shane following, barely jogging. I didn't dare kick at all, because I didn't want him to mow my friend down from behind. She had to watch where she was going, and so was not able to watch her back. Karen leaped over the jump. She didn't have to leap much; it was more for show. She made it look easy. But Shane slowed to a stop. No. He was going. I could feel the paint gathering himself together as if he were a crouching wildcat preparing to spring on its prey—its far off prey. Riding bareback, I could feel everything my horse was thinking through his tensing muscles. I felt his muscles tightening, their nervous twitch of hesitation, and then, just before the jump, their final bunching and powerful resolve. I held on. It felt more as if we were going straight up than over. We came down hard on the other side—far on the other side.

"Wow! Did you see that Karen? He cleared it by a mile! A mile! Wow!"

It was my first jump—together with the horse, that is. I was exhilarated. "Sure! That's been his problem all along," I said, patting Shane's neck. "Maybe he only does high jumping. Maybe we should raise the jump."

Karen appeared skeptical, very skeptical.

"Maybe not," I said. "We'll save the high jumps for another day."

"Sure," Karen said. "Besides, it's getting dark and I'm getting cold."

* * *

I hadn't noticed our house looked empty, dark, and deserted, amid the pleasant chatter of saying good-bye to Karen and her mother as they dropped me off. I never noticed the windows of the house looking ominous—sinister black holes staring—while I was standing in the friendly glow of the streetlight. I never noticed until Karen and her mother, their smiles and their car, had rounded the corner and driven out of site. Then, I turned and I noticed. Gosh! The house looked so forbidding it made my skin crawl. Something wasn't right. There were no cars in the driveway or carport. I had never seen it so. There were no cars parked at the curb edge or across the street. That was also strange. Where was everyone, I wondered? And there was something, something disturbing, about the windows. At first, I couldn't figure out what it was. Then, I realized it was the draperies, most of which had been left open; yet there was not, coming from any window of the house, the faintest hint of light. The upstairs picture window, with the draperies pulled wide, was particularly repelling. The whole house was eerily engulfed in the premature twilight of a late afternoon in November.

Maybe the house was empty—maybe not.

I wasn't afraid of the house, nor the darkness. I wasn't afraid of much. However, I was afraid of Little Mike. I knew from experience he could be hiding almost anywhere in there, waiting. He could be patiently concealed, happily hunched, in a cramped cubbyhole for hours, no matter how uncomfortable, Little Mike, waiting. A brother giddy with the thought of the possibility, the perceived hope of an opportunity to scare one of his sisters—to scare a sister to the brink of mental fragmentation—to scare a sister to emotional smithereens!

Even though I was almost certain he wasn't in there, I decided not to take any chances. I backed away from the house until my heel bumped the curb on the opposite side of the street, then I sat down. Never once did my eyes leave the house. I scanned the windows, alert for any movement, even the tiniest flicker of light or shadow. I willed my eyes to become super eyes, wide-angle eyes, taking everything in. Was there a face at that window? There? My eyes were darting, always moving. My eyes had to keep moving because I knew, from experience, that my brother could sneak out a window at the back of the house. Little Mike, sneaking, a supernatural, devil brother, sneaking. So I had to keep watch, not only on the house, but also on the area around the outside corners of the house, yard, and landscaping as well. Every bush was suspect. Did I see something move, there, at the side of the house? It was cold. I was cold. But cold was only cold. I did not budge from my out-in-the-open position of ready retreat. There was no possibility of my going inside that house.

If I did go inside, I started thinking, what if he wasn't hiding at all—that happened. But instead, what if he were lying there, out in the open—he might be lying anywhere—pretending to be dead. A corpse! Little Mike, pale and pulseless, draped hideously over the sofa, or Little Mike fallen headfirst down the stairs, splayed grotesquely across the landing. It was a game only he enjoyed playing. Shivering at the horror of it, I pulled my coat more tightly around me. There was absolutely no possibility of my going inside that house.

I was sitting outside, exposed to the elements, miserably huddled on a frozen bit of curbing, and fearful, terrified to go into my own house. Yet never once did it occur to me to lament, or wish I didn't have a brother. This was partly because I could hardly remember a time before I had a brother, a brother likely to be lurking, eager in ambush, around any corner, behind any door, inside any closet, or under any bed. So I could not think back to such serenity. But mostly, it was because we sisters loved our brother. He was as often our champion as he was our tormentor.

Beware the desperation and raving ruminations of hypothermia! I was actually starting to believe that I could go in there. After all, I told myself, it would all be over in an instant—the terror and the tickling. He would have his brotherly fix, and then I could get on with my homework. Warmth was but steps away. I imagined it—the warmth. But even with all my wanting to go, and all my self-prodding to go—not one toe ventured toward the warmth, not one toe twitched in the direction of that house. Resigned, I drew my neck further down inside my coat collar and my hands further up inside my sleeves. So this was it then, my less than memorable, final moments on earth. I thought about my death. I thought about what they would say when they discovered me—not me, but the body. "Right there," they would point and say. "That's where we found her . . . without the dollop of common sense it took to walk across the street . . . dumb ice, affixed to the curbing—had to be chiseled off!" And they would say, "Of course, we always knew she was odd. A very odd girl," they would say.

Car headlights flashed around the corner, lighting up the night. Leaping up, I rushed to confront the sole occupant of the car as it slowed to turn into our driveway. "Where were you?" I demanded, knocking loudly on the window. "Where is everybody?"

The occupant screamed, recoiling. "What on earth!" Mom gasped, rolling down her window. "You really gave me a fright! What are you doing out here?"

Ignoring her question, I demanded, "Don't you know I was worried?" I followed the car into the carport.

"I'm so sorry," a harried Mom apologized. She was getting out of the car. Utter blackness had enveloped us the moment she turned off the engine and the headlights. However, she didn't seem to notice. "Can you help me with these groceries? I'm late because I stopped to pick up milk . . . and five bags later—you know."

"Where is everyone?" I queried again, accusingly. We were groping around in the darkness getting the groceries from the back seat.

"Dad's working late . . . Here, you take this one. What's with the lights? You'll have to step back, Con, so I can turn around." I wasn't crowding her, as much as I was cowering behind her. Mom was sanctuary, for she strongly disapproved of pranksters.

"Cher?" I prodded.

"Cher had that choir thing."

"That choir thing? Oh, yeah."

"Ouch!" Mom cried. "You're on my foot!" Which might have been injurious, since my mother had petite, feminine feet, and I had average-sized feet, which were, as usual, solidly embedded in a pair of ponderous clunkers I considered to be shoes. A blast of warm air greeted us as we, as one, entered the dark house. When Mom flipped on the downstairs light, suddenly the house was a home again.

"Lindy?" I asked.

"Linda must still be at Marla's," Mom answered. I was closely following her into the kitchen. "She's in big trouble."

"And Little Mike?" I finally asked, peering around uneasily.

"Football practice."

"Ah!"

CHAPTER TEN

Winter bore down with one bleak, drizzly day heaped on another—or at least that's how it seemed. But no matter how depressing the weather, or stormy the afternoon, the day brightened as soon as I rounded that last corner from school to see Shane waiting at the bottom of the pasture. For I knew he had forsaken his precious harem of mares to meet me there. Many times I wondered what he was thinking while he was watching for me. What time did it occur to him to come down? Of course, many days I couldn't make it to the pasture. How long did he wait on those days, I wondered? Surely he would be disappointed when I didn't show up.

Since fall it had become my habit to change out of my school clothes in the girl's locker room before setting out for the pasture. Still, this time of year at the pasture, even wearing boots, my feet were perpetually damp. I had long ago given up the frustration of trying to keep them dry. If I had walked along the road on wet days, as was sensible, they would have stayed dry much longer. But no matter what the weather, I had to jump over the ditch and crawl through the fence.

Now there he was, waiting, as damp as the day. "Hi, Shane!" I called, stopping to eye the ditch, the chasm yawning between us. Holding schoolbooks, a bag of school clothes, and an umbrella, it was a forbidding jump. Yuck! If something had to get wet, or drop in the mud, it was always me, not the books. "If you had half a brain," I told my horse as I crawled through the fence, "you would have stayed under the trees with your mares. And if I had half a brain," I told him, "I would have stayed on the road."

Shane had become accustomed to the opening snap of the umbrella. It was raining, and as we walked up the pasture together, I tried to make sure the umbrella covered his head as well as mine. The way was slippery. A ray of sunlight escaped the clouds and I became hopeful, thinking we might ride, if even for an hour. The exercise would be good for us both. When sunlight spread, bathing the farmhouse on the hill, I quickened my steps.

The paint followed me into the barn. By now, I hardly paused to watch him turn to go into his stall. No need to close the gate behind him; he would wait there, like a good horse, while I went to get the grain. Padding quietly along the sawdust floor of the center aisle, I thought about the sunshine, anticipating the pleasant ride ahead.

"Look at you!" I heard someone say. "Just look at you!" It was Pat's voice coming from the tack room ahead. Her exasperated tone made me stop. I wasn't meaning to eavesdrop; my hesitation was merely a reaction to her sharp tone.

"What's wrong with you, Guth?" the girl lamented. "Why can't you stay clean? Do you want to live in the barn? Is that it? Oh, No! You'll expect to sleep in my bed tonight. Yes, you will!" Guthrie was getting a scolding. I could hear Pat so well because the tack room door was propped wide open, the way it always was, and she must have been just around the corner on the opposite side of the wall.

Suddenly, she was coming, her boot tip appearing around the corner. "How do I let you talk me into this every time?" sounded loud and near. I ducked partially into an empty stall. It was a startled reaction. Pat tromped down the three steps with a plump, muddy Guthrie tucked under her arm. Water Dog was close at her heels, peering up at her and wagging his tail, wondering what could be wrong. The tall girl stomped past, all the while muttering, "It's the bed or the barn, Guth. The bed or the barn." I was glad she'd been too distracted to notice me.

Shane ate his small offering of oats with gusto while I tried to brush his damp back until it was dry. He smelled like a wet horse—a pungent, sweet smell. Whenever possible I warmed one of my hands on his neck, under his mane, which was an especially warm and steamy spot, while brushing him with the other. He must have known we were going for a ride, as his bridle hung on a post nearby.

I led my horse out of the dark barn into the glorious sunshine. Mud puddles sparkled and old fence boards glistened. Even the gravel parking lot appeared to be strewn with diamonds.

Shane and I rode all around the farm. From the front pasture, we kept to the upper trail that wound around the backyard of the farmhouse, avoiding the more saturated ground at the base of the front pasture's downward slope. The farmhouse, which in summer and fall had been partially obscured by the row of fruit trees, was now exposed through leafless branches. The Murphy family had lost much of their privacy to winter, and so had I. Following the trail we rode to the arena, where everything was wet and the ground soggy. We would save jumping for another day. Then we rode to the very back pasture. I counted abandoned bird nests along the way, and watched for Bald Eagles. Winter was a good time for birdwatching because there were so many different species to see. Many of our resident birds had flown south, replaced with birds from Canada, Alaska, and Siberia that had also flown south to our area.

As we rode with no purpose and no particular destination in mind, I daydreamed about being an Indian—an Apache warrior. I often daydreamed about being an Apache warrior, riding my horse, enjoying the magnificence of my canyon lands. My hands were so cold I asked my horse, "Should it be 100 degrees in our canyons today? Or should it be 110 degrees, do you think?" As always, we were on the lookout for the presence of evil white men, the interlopers and land grabbers. In my fantasy I was an important scout for my people—and Shane was a swift and surefooted animal. My horse's face was painted with bright colors, and he had feathers braided into his mane. He was a warrior, too. The red land and blue sky stretched on forever, and we did not see another human being.

My vision of paradise evaporated when something big and white passed low over the treetops ahead. It was a bird about the size of a seagull. It wasn't a seagull though; its wings were too wide and not bent. The big white bird glided downward over the roof of the barn landing somewhere on the other side, tantalizingly close, yet out of sight.

A barbed-wire fence separated me from a birdwatcher's prize. I turned my horse, kicking him hard. I was in a pell-mell rush to make it back around to the other side of the pastures, hoping that the mystery bird would still be there. We raced along the trail, almost at a gallop, and still I urged my horse to go faster. We flew along, barely slowing to make the turn around the backyard of the farmhouse, and straightened out into a full gallop along the side, where the trail of the front pasture was sloped—and slippery. I wasn't watching where we were going; instead I was rubbernecking, watching for any sign of the bird in case it flew into the sky again.

That's when it happened. On the slippery trail, at almost a dead run, Shane's legs flew out from under him. He slammed down hard onto his right side—a resounding thud! It happened so fast there wasn't time for me to get my leg out of the way. I was pinned under my horse. For a second, we lay still. The fall had knocked the wind out of us both. My universe was spinning; I couldn't breath. It felt as if the entire weight of my horse was on my leg. Then, the paint began thrashing. With whole-horse, writhing heaves, and full-body flays, he was struggling to get up, grinding my already crushed leg further into the hard-packed ground. And his head—so close to mine—became a whipping weapon, a missile launch gone haywire. Trapped, I couldn't get out of its way. Then he was up, shaking his head, loose reins dangling, trotting away.

Paralyzed with pain, I watched my horse trot away, thankful he didn't appear hurt. Then I thought, stupid horse! He sure doesn't seem to be too concerned about me. Doesn't he care about me? Doesn't he wonder what happened to me? Almost as soon as I had these thoughts, Shane stopped, turned, and looked back at me. He looked back with questioning eyes. He cares! I thought. My horse cares! Then he was coming, trotting back to me. Shane was a faithful steed returning to his mistress who was lying helpless on the ground. The thought of it was so romantic. He was getting closer, and closer, and bigger, and bigger—gigantic! Stupid horse! I thought. He's fallen on me; now he's going to trample me! I tried to drag myself back with my elbows, but there was no escape.

Lying there gazing up at Shane's heaving belly I thought, at least he cares. The pain was subsiding. Groaning, I rolled out from under my horse. It was time to test that squashed leg. Once up, I hopped around on the good leg until getting the courage to set the injured one down. It was stiff, but held.

It had been all my fault—all my fault! What had been the hurry? Now, I couldn't even remember. Feeling both guilty and embarrassed, I glanced across at the farmhouse, quickly scanning the windows. It didn't appear anyone in the house had seen our fall. That was a relief. And my horse, as far as I could tell, was perfectly fine. That was even more of a relief.

Gathering Shane's reins, I limped forward, still shaky, somewhat dazed. Our ride for this day was over. All my fault! All my fault! What if this wonderful animal had been injured? And then, gulping, I quit worrying about my horse, and started worrying about Mom picking me up. I'd better lose this limp—fast! Then, I paused, inspecting myself, seeing that my whole right side was ground in grime. Well that's just great, I thought. What would she say? Maybe she wouldn't notice, as it was my right side, the side that would be turned away from her in the car. Also, the car would be dark inside. Limping forward again, I told myself even if she does notice she won't necessarily think anything amiss since this time of year I'm often muddy. Then, as we neared the gate, I saw it, the big white bird. It was on the other side of the driveway, perched on a fence post watching our approach. We stopped, keeping a respectful distance so it wouldn't fly away. The bird blinked round eyes. It was a slow, deliberate blink, done, one could imagine, as if to acknowledge us. And then, as if to dismiss us, its whole head spun around, swiveling, until we were left contemplating the back of its head. My heart was pumping. I had never seen an owl in the wild. For a few moments, we stayed perfectly still—and so did the owl. Then I ventured a stealthy step toward the gate. Immediately the owl's head spun back around. Don't go! I thought. Please! Don't go! But the bird spread its huge wings. Lifting off, facing us, he flapped with powerful sweeps, rising backwards, keeping his eyes locked on us as he rose silently into the sky.

A Snowy Owl! I had seen a Snowy Owl! My soul soared away with the owl in mindless ecstasy.

I don't remember anything for a while after that, nothing about going through the gate, or about entering the barn. The next thing I remember was turning around in the tack room—and being face to face with Shane.

Somehow, he'd followed me in. Stunned at first, I didn't realize the full horror of the situation. That is, until I tried to move. Pressed against the back wall, there wasn't room to get past or around my horse. He filled the entire space. "Isn't this cozy," I said in a cheerful, soft voice, stalling for time, trying to think. "My, my, but isn't this cozy." It was important to act as natural and unconcerned as possible. The last thing I wanted was for him to sense my total panic.

I tried to force the paint back out through the doorway, which now appeared to be more the size of a keyhole, by pushing against his head. He was reluctant to step backward down the steps, especially when he couldn't see the steps. His long neck was the problem. In the snug quarters he couldn't turn his head around to see the steps or his hooves, which was worrisome for him.

Think! I had to think!

How had this happened? Why hadn't he gone his usual way into the stall? Our fall must have knocked the sense out of him. I wasn't thinking too well myself. Studying the situation, it became clear that the whole problem of getting my horse out of the tack room lay with the turn. He had immediately turned to the right when coming in. The wall directly opposite the tack room door was a half-wall with a ladder heading up to the hayloft. So, unless he was going up the ladder to get hay, he would have had to turn sharply right when he came in. Coming in must have been easy for him, with his curious head and his twisty neck out front. First the head would have poked in and peered to the right to see me. Then the neck would have easily come around the turn, followed, naturally, by the rest of the horse. And I could see that if I were able to unscrew his head and neck, and screw them back on to that huge butt of his, he would be just as easily able to walk back out the same way. The curious head would peer back out the doorway into the barn, then the twisty neck would follow, turning sharply, and then the rest of the horse would walk right down the steps and out. That wasn't going to happen though, because the all critical head and neck were up here with me, jamming me against the back wall. Finally, the only thing to be done was to smile and relax, so as not to upset my horse, slowly drop to my knees, and then belly-crawl under the boards of Swifty's empty stall.

By the time I knocked on the Murphy's back door, I was so upset trying to figure out how we were going to get my horse out of there that, in my mind, the entire barn had been leveled. Mr. Murphy, wearing a suit and tie, listened to my desperate tale, shaking his head. I waited, near tears, while he put on his boots and coat. Mrs. Murphy, fixing dinner, nodded to me benevolently. However, Pat, sitting at the kitchen table eyeing me, only shook her head. I was just as glad she didn't seem inclined to come with us.

"How could this happen?" Mr. Murphy asked. We were hurrying toward the barn. "How could this happen?" he repeated.

Quite flustered, all I could say was, "I don't know. I don't know."

When we entered the barn, the problem was obvious. Shane's rotund rump was dwarfing the tack room doorway. Mr. Murphy was more amused than mad. "I guess you'd better watch where you're going when you have something that big following you around," he said with a wry smile. "Don't worry. This isn't so bad."

Wiping tears away, I said, "It isn't?"

"No. I'll only have to pry a few boards loose from Swifty's stall and he'll be able to walk right out the back door."

"Then we won't need to mention this to my parents?" I asked, hopefully.

"Like that spill you just took?" Mr. Murphy said, shaking his head. "We won't mention it."

CHAPTER ELEVEN

It was spring and the days were getting longer. No more did I emerge from a dark barn when my mother arrived to pick me up. Now, on school days, there was more daylight and better weather to groom my horse outside at the hitching rail.

I brushed and brushed, working hard to uncover Shane's sleek summer coat. Then, one by one, his hooves were checked. They were wonderful hooves in good condition. When at last the grooming was done, Shane was given his oats. While he ate, I held the bucket tightly so his big, eager head couldn't dislodge it from my grasp. During all this time, the Hopeful Horses were an attentive audience, not far away, on the opposite side of the fence, waiting for the sweets I always brought them. After the grooming equipment was cleaned and stowed, the patiently waiting horses were given treats, their velvety muzzles gratefully accepting my handouts with gentle regard.

I led the paint toward the gate, stopping to pet Water Dog along the way. With better weather, longer days, and more time to ride, I had decided to set up a training schedule for Shane and me. Sitting in classes that day, between daydreaming and staring out the window at the sunshine, and having my thoughts sometimes interrupted by the intrusions of lessons, I had made a list of items to be practiced each time we rode. The items on the list were arranged in the order of how Shane and I would typically expect to do things. For instance, item Number One on our list was to practice mounting. In this particular area there was so much room for improvement that surely we would quickly appreciate our progress, thereby giving our-selves a boost of confidence.

Each time I mounted the paint, we were confronted with two problems. First, because I rode bareback and didn't have stirrups, there was always the problem of finding something on which to stand. Second, Shane had to learn to remain still. Beyond those two issues, however, it wasn't merely mounting my horse that I was trying to accomplish, but rather, swinging up onto my horse with style. Pat did it so effortlessly, the stylish mount, the nimble leap from a standstill to swing on. Determined to duplicate her feat, I had studied every turn and twist of her lithe body. She made it look easy, with her long legs and not-so-tall horse. From a standing position she would grab the saddle horn and leap onto her horse as skillfully as any stunt rider in a Western movie. Even more impressive, she was able to do it while goosing Swifty into a gallop by partly using her horse's forward momentum to propel herself onto his back.

With fantastic visions of the famous cowboy, Roy Rogers, and his won-der horse, Trigger, performing in my head, I led Shane along the path a dis-tance from the gate. Trigger, a stunning palomino with a flowing white mane and tail, was easy to mount. On command, he lowered himself to a graceful curtsy. Imagining Trigger so gallantly bowing to present his ornate saddle to me—oh how I could picture the scene so clearly—made me quickly dismiss the unattainable from my mind. For although often guilty of allowing my expectations to soar unreasonably, I was quite sure I wasn't going to be able to talk the paint into doing anything that fancy.

It was tempting to simply climb up on the familiar rock and slide onto Shane's back as always—but not today. Spring had brought with it plenty of new foliage for the fruit trees that lined the fence in the Murphy's front yard. I led Shane farther along the path to a spot where we were well posi-tioned for privacy in front of the largest of the apple trees. It wasn't that I thought anyone in the house was the least bit interested in watching our exploits; it was more that I wanted to practice with complete concentra-tion, and without inhibitions, which meant no distractions from potential onlookers, however casual.

Satisfied when not a window could be seen through leafy branches, my attention shifted from the house to my horse. Shane appeared huge—shockingly huge! He seemed to have grown at least a foot taller as he was led along the path. It gave me such a start that I had to take a moment to reflect. Was there anything else that seemed out of kilter? Nothing else appeared changed. But what a fabulous afternoon! I was able to stall my first mounting attempt by appreciating the day. To think that only a short while ago, I had been desperately anchored to my school desk watching each endless second of the clock tick by.

Taking in the view and the immediate surroundings, I saw that a crow was watching us from a branch of a nearby fruit tree. "Hi, crow!" I called, pleased to see him. "What are you looking at?" He was a large, sleek bird in his prime. Immediately, the crow glanced around nervously to see whom I was talking to, assuming that someone must have sneaked up behind him. He wasn't accustomed to being addressed. "You, crow!" I said. "Yes, you!" The moment the crow realized I was speaking to him personally, he tumbled backwards off the branch in a flustered flap of black feathers, almost striking the ground before managing to get his wings untangled and spread. Then he flew to—more launched at—a distant branch. Clearly unnerved, the crow landed unsteadily on a slender, wobbly limb. Throughout all he had successfully kept a wary eye locked on me. I watched him watching me. He hunched forward on the rocking branch, cocked his head, and studied me. It was dawning on him that he might have over-reacted. However, he wasn't ready to forgive the incident until he had scolded me with bobbing head and rattling croaks. Gosh! I had only been trying to be friendly.

Turning back to my horse again, it appeared Shane had grown taller yet! How could it be? Surely it had to be my imagination—demons of doubt—but he sure looked big! Don't panic, I told myself. Horses are very large animals. That's all. That's what horses are—very large animals. Would a small horse do? No. Would it be fun to ride a tiny horse? No way! It was an attempt at mind-over-matter psychology, but the matter was definitely still towering over the mind. Well, he's not likely to shrink any time soon, I told myself—or maybe he is! It occurred to me then to lead Shane around using the sloping terrain of the front pasture to advantage. With me now shifted to the upward side of the slope, I was a bit taller, and he a bit shorter. Pleased with myself, and inspired to tongue-in-cheek gloating, I told him, "You can see why I'm in the driver's seat, with a brain like this."

This was it then. No more delay. I moved to Shane's side. At the same time, Shane's head, as always, followed me, which turned his body away. Patiently, I turned him back to his original stance. Then sneaked back into position for my next attempt. That wasn't any good though, I realized, since Shane needed to be made aware of what was happening, as that was the whole point of the exercise. The next time, stepping to his side, I gently pushed the paint's head back, keeping pressure against his neck. When he tried to turn, I said, "Stand!" in a loud, commanding voice. I thought "stand" had an authoritative ring to it. Sure enough, it got his attention; however, it merely served to confuse him so that he forgot to turn. Instead, alarmed, his head jerked up and his ears pulled back, but he stayed where he was.

I practiced moving to Shane's side many times, while at the same time, keeping pressure against his neck and saying, "Stand!" Often I gave a self-conscious glance toward the house, glad we had a bit of privacy. Finally, I pretended to mount by grabbing hold of the mane at the base of his neck, and at the same time patting his back with my other hand. It was a simple system. If we kept to a routine, I was confident that my horse would eventually make sense of what was expected of him and stand still. When our exercise went well, he was praised and given a piece of carrot reward.

Things were progressing nicely. Shane was remaining in place enough of the time that I was ready to begin the actual practice of mounting. This was it. Moving around quickly, grabbing hold of his mane, leaping high, with all my might, I bounced off my horse about halfway up his side. The paint's head swung around, questioning, but he stood his ground. I sat in the dirt only a moment. "Good horse," I said praising him. "Good horse." More determined, I tried again. The next result was the same, except that this time, I clung on longer, slipping under the paint's belly before falling. I was on the ground still clutching a handful of Shane's mane when he pawed the ground twice. It was his way of telling me the exercise was being timed, and that he wasn't going to be patient much longer. Hopping up, I deposited the clump of mane on the ground. A few more attempts had me out of breath and sweating.

Spring! Oh how I loved it! I hung my jacket on a nearby fence post. Just that act made me several pounds lighter, raising my spirits. Still overheated, I rolled up my sleeves. Shane watched my every move with expectant interest. Stroking his neck, I told him, "You are a good horse. A very good horse."

Now much lighter, and with all the confidence of an Apache warrior, I moved quickly around to Shane's side, leaping high. Moving around quickly was my way of getting a running start. Again, I landed only about halfway up my horse, and then slowly slid under the paint's belly before letting go. Then I tried a third time, with the same discouraging result.

Huffing and puffing, I sat in the dirt a little longer after each attempt. I thought if I could just get my heel up on Shane's back I could do it. There would be no need to get my whole leg over. Merely a heel hooked over his spine and then I could pull, haul, and muscle myself on, though there wouldn't be much flash in that. I tried to think what could be the cause of so much trouble. Could it be partly that left-handed thing? Maybe it would feel more natural for me to mount from the other side of my horse. This notion was quickly dismissed, however. No one mounted from the right side of a horse. It simply wasn't done. Anyway, I rationalized, surely this is more of a big horse issue than a left-handed one.

It was such a lovely day. Maybe we had practiced enough for one session. Tired and deflated, I led Shane to the mounting rock. "You are a fine, big horse," I told him. "You have nothing to be ashamed of. You did your part." At last seated on my horse, I was feeling quite woozy. My legs in particular were numb. I had truly worn myself out. My arms felt heavy. Barely able to hold on, and without even the energy to kick him forward, I sagged against the paint's neck like a wounded warrior. With the warm sun making me sleepy, it was tempting to turn around and sit backward and lie with my face resting on the rise of his rounded rump. It was something I often did when he was in his stall endlessly chewing hay. His rump made a perfect pillow.

I don't remember indulging my fantasy; however, something suddenly woke me, and one eye opened on a strange, backward world. I hardly had time to realize that my face was resting warmly atop Shane's rump, or that we were surrounded by a group of horses—Shane's harem. I woke up nearly eye-to-eye with the buckskin mare. Then, before there was time to yawn and stretch, the mare bared her teeth and flattened her ears, snapping viciously at Shane's rear hock. Without hesitation, Shane bucked and kicked at the surprise pain. He may have been napping himself. Tossed helplessly into the air, I dove face first into the rocky ground. Thrown in the direction of the downward slope, I slid downhill on my face before any of the rest of my body touched ground.

Shane's harem scattered. For a time I didn't move, couldn't move. Finally, rising slowly to sit, I inspected my hands, turning them over, and the skin of my forearms, exposed by rolled-up sleeves. There wasn't a scratch on them. Only my head was pounding and the left side of my face throbbing. Dazed, and with no idea what time it was, all I could think was it must be time to get Shane into the barn to feed him his hay before Mom arrived to pick me up.

* * *

Getting into the car, my mother's horrified expression told me something was wrong.

"You're hurt!" Mom gasped.

"Not very," I replied throwing my books in the back, settling in. It was all bravado. My whole head was throbbing.

"Yes, very!" Mom exclaimed. She wasn't going to let it go. It didn't help that the injured side of my face was fully exposed to her in the car. "I wouldn't think to touch that mess. We're going straight to the clinic."

"Really, Mom. Please, let's not make much about nothing."

An exasperated mom reached over to pull the sun visor down so I could see in the mirror. "Does that look like 'nothing' to you?"

I gulped. The left side of my face was swollen and caked with dirt. There were rocks, actual rocks, embedded in my face. I reached up to examine the damage.

"Don't touch it!" Mom cried. "You'll start it bleeding! How could this have happened?"

CHAPTER TWELVE

By the time Mom and I arrived home from the doctor's office, with my wound thoroughly cleaned and hideously exposed to healing air, I was feeling quite fragile, ego-wise that is, and ugly beyond belief.

Daddy Mike met us at the top of the stairs. "Geez, Con!" he boomed, when he saw me. "You look like hell! What happened? I thought you were a rider!"

"Aw, Dad," I said, tears welling. I was very shaken up.

"Remember old Gillette?" he then said, seeing my distress, his booming voice dropping to a conspiratorial whisper. "Remember?" he said again, jabbing me, in palsy fashion, with an elbow that knocked me sideways. He had me. I wiped my eyes, and even smiled, remembering. Gillette was our secret. Not because we wanted to have a secret, but rather because Gillette was something Dad and I had experienced together that we didn't know how to explain to anyone else. No one would have believed us if we had told them about it, anyway. "Yeah, old Gillette, Wyoming," Dad said softly. "She was the horse for you. I'll always be sorry we didn't snap up that Gillette."

"That's okay, Dad," I assured him. "I like the horse I have just fine."

"Your horse is nothing but a CLOD!" he exploded. Daddy Mike's nickname, "Boomer" was well deserved. "That horse has hooves the size of a plow horse!"

"Shane's not a plow horse, Dad!"

As usual, he wasn't hearing anything I said. Instead, he was warming to his favorite rant. "That horse can't even walk on level ground without tripping over his own big feet!" He went on, shaking his head incredulously, "I really can't believe it! I can't believe it even when I see it with my own two eyes!" Pausing, he took a deep breath, though still shaking his head in wonderment. Then, again, softly, almost reverently, "That Gillette, now . . . she was the horse for you."

* * *

Gillette happened when Dad and I were on one of our infamous country outings. Our country outings were considered to be infamous by the family because Dad and I once returned home to suburbia with honey—and beehives. Dad and I later became backyard beekeepers and purveyors of honey, to the consternation, and sometimes horror of our nearest neighbors. I remember it was on the frantic day our backyard bees became a swarming black cloud circling our neighborhood that I first mentioned writing a book. Dad and I were running, trying to keep sight of the swarm, when I was inspired to yell out, with conviction, "I'm going to write a book someday!" And I remember Dad turning back to me to yell out, with the same conviction, as we ran, "I know you will, honey! I know you will!" Anyway, it was on one of our country outings that Gillette happened.

It had been on a Sunday morning, as it had almost always been, that the two early risers finally agreed not to squander a pristine July morning waiting around for the laggards. "Those lazy bohunks can get their own breakfast," Dad said. Besides, we reminded ourselves, they were a cranky lot when they first woke up, and even under the best conditions, with the most expert prodding, they would never be ready to go anywhere until noon.

Once the agonized-over-decision was made to set out alone, our only concern became which direction to take. Living in the Pacific Northwest provided a banquet of recreational possibilities. For instance, by heading east over the Cascade Mountains and driving down into the orchards and farmlands beyond, we might return home as heroes with a load of cherries, peaches, or 'cots, as Dad called apricots. Or we might return with a fifty-pound bag of Walla Walla Sweets, prized onions to divide among our closest neighbors. By heading west, we could take a ferry ride over to the

Olympic Peninsula, situated between Seattle and the Pacific Ocean. There we might pretend to be rich city folk searching for a country estate amid the foothills of the Olympic Mountains. And to the south, the Green River Valley beckoned, with its spectacular views of Mount Rainier, our region's most prominent volcanic peak. However, on that particular day, we decided to drive north to the Skagit River Valley farmlands. We would watch for eagles and visit any number of fresh vegetable stands along our way. We'd left a note: "Heading north—don't know when we'll be back—Dad & Con."

It was our pact never to take the main highways; we only drove back roads. "Damn! I sure wish corn was in season," Dad lamented. "My mouth's watering just thinkin' about it."

We turned onto Lake Sammamish road, driving past the Indian burial ground. The Indian burial ground wasn't really a burial ground at all, since there were no graves, and no one was buried there. Rather, it was a collection of long-abandoned white survey stakes that looked like miniature crosses. The white crosses were near the side of the road, and to me, they seemed to be lined up in an orderly, cemetery-like arrangement. When younger, I had asked, "Dad, who's buried there?"

"There lie buried all that remains of the Tam-o'-Shanter Indian tribe," he had begun. Tam-o'-Shanter was the name of a residential development near ours. "Long ago," he continued, "the Tam-o'-Shanters and the Irigoosies had a war over the rights to the land here." Then Dad had paused, glancing in my direction to see if this revelation might make me cry. He knew I was very fond of anything to do with Indians. "Those little crosses are now all that's left of the once proud Tam-o'-Shanter tribe," he had concluded solemnly.

"What happened to the Irigoosies?" I had asked, my eyes filling with tears.

"This!" he had whistled sharply, goosing me in the ribs, scaring me half out of the car, while at the same time, roaring with delighted laughter.

That Gillette day, we planned to take Highway 9 north. We would drive to Snohomish, and then proceed to Arlington and Mt. Vernon, skirting the Cascade Mountains flanking our right. We were heading out of Redmond, taking a back road to Woodinville, when we came upon a sign that read ARABIAN MARE FOR SALE. It was quite early, but for some reason, Dad slowed. We could see "Farmer Jones," as Dad called him, leading a lovely, chestnut mare toward the barn, with her foal at her side. Dad and I looked at each other and back at the mare. Right away, we knew there was something special about the animal. Appreciating his daughter's rapturous face transfixed on the mare and foal, and never saying a word, Dad turned into the drive. The man leading the mare stopped at our approach.

Dad took over as we got out of the car. "We saw your "for sale" sign, partner. Thought we'd check it out. My daughter here," he motioned for me to come close, "is in the market for a horse." Smiling, he offered his hand, "The name's Mike Arend. This is my daughter, Connie."

"Glad to meet you, Mike. Parker, Frank Parker." The men shook hands. "Well, I can tell you that this here's a truly fine mare," Mr. Parker said, while patting the horse's neck affectionately. "She's half Arabian, five years old, sound, fast . . . sure on her feet. Yes, sir, Gillette here is a truly fine mare." He gave us the impression he wasn't in too much of a hurry to sell. "We call her Gillette," he added, "because she came out of Gillette, Wyoming."

The mare danced alluringly on shapely legs. Dad and I glanced at each other. Wow! we were both thinking. "Any way my daughter might take a ride?" Dad asked. "Can't tell much about a car till you drive 'er," he added.

"To tell the truth," the man said, "I'd feel real uncomfortable about it. She's pretty skittish today. I'd have to shut her foal in the barn, and Gillette here wouldn't like that one bit." The mare punctuated his words with a stomp that sent her long mane waving and her tail shimmering all the way along until it touched the ground. Mr. Parker stroked the horse's neck reassuringly. He was trying to settle her down for us, his prospective buyers.

"My daughter's been riding for years," Dad said, with a wink in my direction. I swallowed hard. What is this man getting me into now, I thought. "Con, here," he said grasping me by the shoulder, "won't be bothered by a little skittish behavior."

Gillette, eager to be on her way, pawed the ground impatiently, which called our attention to her dainty hooves. Mr. Parker rubbed his chin thoughtfully. "I don't own a saddle right now," he mused. "She'd have to ride bareback."

"That's no problem for my daughter," Dad said throwing his chest out proudly.

The man eyed me skeptically. "Okay," he finally agreed. Handing me the halter lead, he said, "You hold the mare here while I shut the little one in the barn and fetch a bridle."

The mare, anxiously watching her foal being led away, tried to follow, neighing sharply. "Easy, girl," I cooed, hoping to reassure her. "That's all right, girl." I glanced over at Dad, who was studying the distraught animal as she saw her foal disappear into the barn. He had a strange, strained, expression on his face.

"What do you think, Con?" he asked. "Maybe we'd be wiser to save the ride for another day."

"No way!" I heard myself say.

The man returned carrying the bridle. The foal, left behind, called desperately to its mother, and the mare responded with impassioned wails of her own. Mr. Parker took the lead from my hand and rubbed the horse's ears and neck while he put on the bridle. "Gillette's not been ridden in over a year," he said, "but I can tell you she's fast, and just takes a light touch on the reins. Hold her in tight," he instructed, "because she'll want to grab the bit and take you for a ride you won't soon forget. One last thing," he said, giving me a hand up. "She's a dead stop. Stay back on her and you'll do fine." He handed me the reins and gave the mare a gentle slap on the rear.

She was a dream horse, this Gillette. We rode about the yard at a slow, rocking, prancing gait. I had time to notice Dad's rueful expression when we danced past him sideways heading for the open field. He would have plucked me off the animal if I had come within his grasp. The Arabian mare felt solid—powerful. We cantered easily, smoothly, over what was surprisingly very rugged terrain. The field had been recently plowed, and it was a choppy, furrowed sea of churned up chunks. Suddenly, we wanted to race and never stop. I leaned forward, pressing close to her neck as the mare stretched out into a gallop. I felt fixed to her back. My eyes watered as the wind raced past. All too soon our ride was over. When we cantered into the yard, I leaned far back, heeding the man's warning, and slid from her back as she came to a sliding halt. For a moment, I stroked the mare's neck. I was saying a silent thank you and good-bye. Finally, I turned to the two men standing by in utter astonishment.

Mr. Parker spoke first. "I've never seen anything like it," he said. "Seems your girl really can ride!"

Dad had a puzzled, pleased, and wildly relieved expression on his face. "Well, Frank," he said, "maybe we can talk business." We three walked with Gillette toward the barn, intent on reuniting mother and child as soon as possible.

"I'll need $700 for the mare," Mr. Parker said. "That's a fair price."

Dad and I quickly shot each other a glance. We both knew we couldn't afford that kind of money for a horse—not to mention the upkeep. True, we were driving a brand new Cadillac, but that was only because Dad sold cars; it was his privilege to drive any car off the lot he liked. He was a big man who preferred a big car. However, we just as often had a Mustang or a pickup truck parked in front of our house. We weren't poor, but with a houseful of teenagers life was a daily scramble. This kind of money for a horse was an extravagance we couldn't afford. I thought of those hungry teenagers in the house. Dad and I both saw, as we locked eyes for that split second, the seven half-gallon cartons of milk going into a shopping cart already heaped high with groceries.

"We might be able to consider $600, Frank," Dad said evenly.

"I really don't think so, Mr. Arend."

"Why don't you take my number," Dad suggested. "In case you change your mind."

We drove away in reflective silence, crestfallen, yet at the same time, elated. It took a while before we were able to put our conflicting thoughts into words. Finally Dad said, "You sure rode that horse, Con," appreciably slapping me on the knee. "You sure showed that old geezer. Oh, he'll never come down in his price," Dad lamented. "I know the type. In all fairness though, I'd say that Gillette is worth her weight in gold." Soon we were both beaming. "I think I'll have a talk with your father," he then said. "Maybe we can work something out so you can have your horse. "Damn!" he exclaimed, "That Gillette was really something."

* * *

Beginning when I was eight, Daddy Mike and I drove country roads together. Mom was encouraged to come; we didn't like to go without her. However, she wasn't a morning person, and we were sometimes up much too early for her. So Dad and I were often off on our adventures alone, two pairs of starry eyes cruising the countryside with the same big dream.

"Tell me again about the farm we're going to have, Dad," I would always beg.

"Well, you know," he would begin, as always, in a hushed voice. "First thing, I'll have my tractor and you'll have your horse. We'll have several horses. I'll let you pick 'em," I watched out the window hypnotized by the passing countryside and Dad's soft voice as he continued. "We'd have to have a fair-sized barn," he considered carefully. "Several cattle. We'll raise them for food."

"What about a milk cow?"

"Oh, we'll have a swell milk cow. You'll have to milk 'er morning and night," he added glancing over at me.

"Oh, I will," I promised.

"We'll get one of them cows you like best. One of them Jerseys with the big brown eyes."

"What about chickens?"

"Rhode Island Reds," he continued. "No other chicken to have." Then reconsidering, "Well, maybe a couple bantam hens besides." And giving me a wink, "That'll keep things fair. You'll have to gather the eggs every morning before school, and lock the henhouse at night, too."

"Oh, I will," I promised. "And what about the garden?"

"Of course, we'll have the biggest, juiciest tomatoes around. We might even have a greenhouse so we can have tomatoes all year. Yes, I think we will. And a whole field of sweet corn." Pausing, he pondered the cornfield. "We'll plant two rows one week, then plant two rows the next week, and so on. That way, the corn won't all be ripe at the same time. Do you think two rows a week would be enough, Con?" he asked, giving me another wink.

"I don't know," I said seriously. "I guess that depends on the length of the rows, and whether we plan to share."

"We'd have to slip Ma an ear or two."

"That's true," I admitted.

"We'll make it three rows a week, just to make sure," he concluded.

Dad saw what appeared to be a dead animal lying in the road ahead, which he knew would upset me. "Over there!" he pointed off to our right, sounding very excited.

Turning, I said, "What is it?"

"Thought I saw a coyote in that far field."

I scanned the field carefully.

"Guess he took off," Dad said.

I studied his profile, "I love you, Dad."

"I love you too, honey."

"There's a red-winged blackbird!" I cried. I always watched for them in the cattails that grew by the side of the road.

"I love red-winged blackbirds," Dad said enthusiastically. "I've seen those blackbirds really raise hell with them crows."

"I like crows," I said slightly offended, "just as much as any other bird."

"Con! Think what you're sayin'!" He stared at me, aghast. "Those crows are nasty devils! They compete for the food chain, and they're hell on crops."

"But don't they eat lots of bugs, Dad?"

"No," he answered softly, as if he were thinking of something else. "No," he repeated absently, "I don't think they eat many bugs, Con." For a moment, we drove in silence. Dad was lost in thought, rubbing his chin, and sometimes chuckling to himself.

"Tell me, Dad," I prompted. "Tell me."

"No. I best not."

"Please. Please."

"No. I'm not. And that's final!"

"Please, Dad. Please. You can tell me."

He was chuckling to himself again. "That kid!" Dad all of a sudden burst out, shaking his head with obvious disbelief. Then his voice dropped abruptly, so low I had to listen hard to hear him. "Calvin Morrow was his name." And so began, reluctantly at first—as they often did—one of Dad's many excellent stories from his childhood at Friday Harbor on San Juan Island.

"Calvin's dad was the county auditor. So . . . you know . . . hell, he'd go off to work at 8:00 A.M. sharp and never come back home again until evening. So . . . we . . . Calvin and me . . . one day," he paused, rubbing his chin, remembering.

"So?" I prompted.

"So?" he said thoughtfully. Then boomed loudly, "So I shouldn't be telling you this!"

"So?" I prompted.

"So," he said, resuming his story, his voice becoming hushed again. "Here's what we did. Calvin's Dad had a great big fir tree . . . higher than that," he pointed. "It had no limbs down below . . . only a cluster right up there at the top. So we . . . and I still can't believe we did this . . . took some dynamite, and caps, and electrical line. You know," he said, somewhat sheepishly. "Stuff that his dad used to blow up stumps and stuff with. And we climbed that tree using climbing hooks. We wired that dynamite on there . . . and then we wiggled 'er on down. Then we wiggled 'er on over . . . hiding . . . see . . . and we waited. We waited all afternoon for them crows to come back."

My eyes suddenly flashed wide. "Dad!" I said shocked. "That's terrible!" However, I was laughing despite myself, for I was so thoroughly enjoying his story.

"We waited, Calvin and me, while they came flying in. We waited until they were all crowded in there . . . kinda settled down like," he said trying to continue, but having to stop to suppress his laughter. "Hunkered-in. Hunkered in for the l-o-n-g haul," he resumed, sobering. "KaaahBOOM!" Dad roared, raising his arms over his head. "There was crows! There was crows . . ." He broke off to stifle another outburst of embarrassed glee, wiping his eyes so that he could still see to drive. "There was crows all over hell!"

"That's disgusting, Dad," I said, laughing right along with him.

"Oh, hell!" he said defensively. "You always make me tell you! Besides, that was the valley of crows. There must have been a thousand of 'em. We killed ever' one of 'em. Ever' one that was in that tree, that is. Musta been thirty or forty."

"All the same, I like crows," I said. "I think they have lots of personality."

Dad shook his head. "Too much personality for their own good, if you ask me."

"Kinda like you. Right, Dad?"

"Maybe." He hesitated, glancing over at me. "Maybe so."

From his stories, I knew that Dad got into a lot of trouble when he was a kid. I had heard him say, when describing his inglorious adolescence, that he had been apprehended on his determined march to the pen—penitentiary, that is. Nabbed, in fixed and contented stride, by the good Brother Donnelley. Dad said he had been fortunate to spend some time, in his still formative years, with the Christian Brothers of Ireland organization. He was especially grateful to Brother Donnelley. "I'll never forget him," Dad would say. "He gave me the first real break I ever had."

CHAPTER THIRTEEN

It was summer at last, and the Horton family was busy finalizing plans. Each weekend had to be carefully scheduled to fit everything and everyone in. It was June, and a bit early in the season for waterskiing, but as usual, Dad had promised so many friends at church and at work he would teach them how to ski, that now he wasn't sure how he was going to fulfill all his promises. August would have to be a busy month of skiing, as our family was going to be gone a good part of July on our annual summer vacation. Also, we had promised our family's best friends, the Wellmans, we would go camping with them in eastern Washington at Lake Chelan. We needed to get that date firmed up as well. Anyway, it would be nice if we could go camping with them several times over the summer. A few weekends would be spent visiting Dad's numerous relatives in Oregon. Besides our Grandma Hanes, and Dad's younger siblings, Aunt Barb, Aunt Shirley, and Uncle Harold, Dad had uncles and cousins spread from Sweet Home, to Salem, to Portland.

And don't forget the ranch! And the wedding! Momma Darleen and her sister, Bonnie, had spent much of their childhood on a 64,000-acre ranch in Oregon, where their father, Silver, still worked as a ranch hand, cowboy, and sheepherder. The girls had lived in the ranch house with the owners, George and Mary Ward, and their two children, Eric and Joan. George and Mary were like second parents to them. We usually arranged our visits to the ranch during times such as cow branding, sheep shearing, or lambing. However, this summer was special because their daughter, who was like a sister to Mom and Aunt Bonnie, was getting married in August, and my little sister, Wendy, was the flower girl. The ranch was one of our family's favorite places, but it was a very long trip, south of The Dalles, near Shaniko, and an all-day drive, much of it at the end on a gravel road. Trips to the ranch required at least a four-day weekend.

Then there were all the usual summer activities at home such as hiking, swimming, picnicking, and friends from California visiting whom we would eagerly escort to all the local tourist destinations. The Horton summers weren't merely scheduled; they were choreographed.

Besides all this, Cher and I had other obligations that had to be factored into the Horton family scheduling, because the Arend family had summer plans, too. Cher and I would be spending some weekends on San Juan Island, at Friday Harbor where Daddy Mike was raised. Walt, Mike, and Lindy had lots of relatives there, grandparents, great aunts, and cousins. There we would attend huge family picnics, and visit Roche Harbor, a scenic resort on the island, where Dad had been born. Getting to the island took all day, as it was a drive followed by a long ferry ride. We needed to plan for a three- or four-day weekend to make the visit practical.

Then there were Mom's Spokane relatives, "the Swedes," the Anderson clan. Our maternal grandparents, who had both been born in Sweden, had met and married in Spokane. When the Arend family visited, which was as often as possible, we stayed at Uncle Art and Aunt Margaret's two-story white house on Maple Street. Aunt Margaret was Mom's older sister. Besides having a roomy home with plenty of spare bedrooms, and two grown children, our cousins, Sandra and Larry, Uncle Art and Aunt Margaret had a highly-trained German Shepard named Lori. Of course, Lori and I were best friends. In the evening, Grandma would tell Cher, Lindy, and me bedtime stories, which were enchanting tales of her childhood in Sweden. We three couldn't get enough because she was such a spellbinding storyteller. In the morning, Grandma would make everyone Swedish pancakes, for which we all had gluttonous appetites, especially Little Mike and me. Since our grandfather had died the previous year, Dad would talk Grandma into coming back with us to Seattle for an extended stay. Spokane was a long, all-day drive from Seattle, which meant these trips too were best planned for a three- or four-day weekend.

So exactly where in all this summer fun did a horse fit in?

Now it was the regular Sunday evening drop; Cher and I were returned to the Arend household after spending the weekend at the Hortons. "Say," Dad said to Cher and me. "Go see if your mother can come out here for a minute." The car sat idling in the driveway, and a hopeful Momma Darleen held a calendar and a pile of notes on her lap. These were delicate negotiations. The Hortons wanted all their girls with them pretty much most of the summer. This was nothing new. Mom often came out to the car when we were dropped off to trade news and haggle over schedules. We said our good-byes. The good-byes were hard. It was particularly hard leaving our little sisters.

When we entered the house with our weekend baggage, Daddy Mike was fixing dinner, and Mom was keeping him company, sitting at the kitchen bar doing her crossword puzzles. Dad liked her near, yet out of his way. Anyway, she had done her part earlier in the day by making her fabulous spaghetti sauce.

As soon as Mom had gone out I began setting the table. "So you're back," Daddy Mike said. "I'm glad." As his helper, I was missed when I wasn't around. "I have something to tell you."

Half listening, folding napkins and placing them under each fork, I answered, "What?"

"Something important."

"Important?" I went over to the stove where he was working, as much as anything hoping to sample Mom's spaghetti sauce. I started stirring the pot, waiting for him to turn away before sneaking a taste. However, he wasn't fooled for a minute.

"Don't think you're going to pick at that," he warned. "Well . . . ," he started. "And you're not going to believe this, old buddy—"

"What?"

"I bought myself two horses today."

I was more than amazed; I was flabbergasted. "I don't believe it."

"I don't believe it myself," Dad said, sounding as if he might be having second thoughts.

"Two horses? Two horses?" One horse would have been difficult enough to digest. Horses were luxury items. Starting to get excited and believe what he was telling me, I said, "Can we afford them?"

"Of course we can't afford them," Dad said with a grin, giving me one of his conspiratorial jabs in the ribs. "But it was such a great deal I had to take it. It's a mare and her foal. Kelly and Peppy are their names. The guy threw in the foal, Peppy."

Now the possibilities were truly sinking in. "We can ride together every day. And I can take care of your horses for you. I can feed them when I feed Shane."

"Well . . . ," Dad said, hedging. "Not so fast. You see, they won't be staying at the same pasture as your horse."

"No?" Long pause. "Why not? How will we ride together?"

"They'll only be a few blocks away. They'll be down by Bridle Trails. We'll be able to ride in Bridle Trails together."

I had to think about that for a few seconds. "That's a long way," I finally said.

"It's not that far," Dad defended. "We'll work it out."

* * *

One week and many arguments later, Dad and I were still both dug in, entrenched, and unbudging. "Please don't make me," Dad begged. "I can't go up there to ride with all those little girls."

"I can't ride way down there on all those busy roads," I protested. My mind was made up. We appreciated each other's positions. I was scared; Daddy Mike didn't want to be humiliated.

"You're being unreasonable," Dad said throwing up his hands in frustration. "It isn't that far."

"No. You're the one," I answered with equal frustration, stomping away.

Now there were only a few days left before Kelly and Peppy were to be delivered to their new pasture. It couldn't in all fairness be called a pasture, I told myself. It was more a small, pampered paddock with stalls attached. It wasn't a place where a horse could stretch out to run. Shane would have been miserable there. Yet even I had to admit the place had one big attraction: a convenient, direct, off-road route into the labyrinth that was Bridle Trails State Park.

Over the past week, without ever actually admitting it, or giving in, I had become resigned to the fact that Shane and I would have to ride to Bridle Trails. So on a cool, yet sunny, June day, I rode Shane down the long driveway of the Murphy place. We were making a practice run to the convenience store, which was within conspicuous sight of the farm, about the distance of one city block. Although it was our first trip off the farm, the paint plodded along as if nothing was out of the ordinary. The long grass that grew beside the driveway was a powerful distraction for him. It was the same grass that tauntingly grew a chin-hair out of his farthest reach, on the opposite side of the fence line, the flaunting grass that he and the other horses stood by the fence and longed for day after day.

We were approaching the end of the driveway. "I wish you'd watch where we're going," I said nervously. Yet again, Shane's head had to be pulled up away from the tempting banquet that was spread out so succulently before him. That's when he saw the mailbox, right at the moment when we were making our left turn onto the road. Suddenly, my horse shot straight up into the air. We came down hard, four heavy hooves hitting all at once, but somehow I was still on board, still with the reins in my hand. Then the paint began slinking backward in cowardly fashion, snorting and puffing, his neck stretched out, his head extended, and his eyes bulging, expecting who knew what from the offending mailbox. From my perspective, it was about like watching a grown man burst into hysterical tears over nothing. Ignoring my frantic attempts to stop him, as he had all but forgotten about the rider on his back, he backed away, cowering, right down into the muck in the ditch on the other side of the driveway entrance. He wasn't watching where he was going, and might just as easily have bolted into traffic. Thoroughly shaken myself, there was nothing for me to do but wait, with my horse mired in the ditch, until he regained his composure. It turned out to be a very short wait, for in a moment he forgot about the mailbox and became obsessed with the grass once again.

Determined to complete our mission, we crossed the road when there was a long break in traffic. As much as possible, I kept Shane's attention averted from the mailbox. At the same time, I tried not to focus too much on the traffic that whizzed past us as we progressed along the narrow shoulder, knowing that any apprehension on my part would telegraph loudly to my horse. It was amazing how quickly and fully Shane, now plodding along so relaxed, had recovered from his fright. Of course, my hands were still trembling from the incident. What could have sent the paint into such a panic? I shook my head. Who could know what kind of misguided reasoning went on under those pointy ears?

Thus musing, the paint and I lived to make it to our destination, the parking lot of the convenience store. Sliding down to hard asphalt, my legs felt rubbery. Anyway, why waste time trying to make sense of my horse's ridiculous phobias, I thought, when there were plenty of my own pointless fears to examine? Wasn't I the one who had squandered a week of productive thinking fretting about which side of the road we should ride? Did we want the traffic zooming straight for us, or did we want the traffic roaring past us from behind? Now the whole mind-boggling perplexity had been resolved in an instant. We would travel on the side of the road where there were no mailboxes. Case closed.

Shane was tethered loosely to the bike rack outside the store. It wasn't so much a worry that he would wander away as it was a concern that he would suddenly appear behind me inside the store. There was the usual number of feathered freeloaders all around. Crows calling for attention from the rooftop, pigeons strutting across the parking lot almost tripping the unwary customer, and brave sparrows risking their tiny bodies to be too near the swinging door, all with their eyes locked on me—the mark. They had a system that worked. Inside, I went directly to the candy counter. The horses back at the pasture had put in their orders. I chose a chewy chocolate bar and a bag of Sugar Babies for myself, and chose crunchy sweets for the horses. Last, considering the gang of winged beggars outside, a healthful loaf of wheat bread was selected. It's a good thing I have plenty of spending money from my babysitting jobs, I was thinking.

With stealth in mind, I decided to feed the birds out behind the store, but they were a ravenous, boisterous bunch, and we quickly became a spectacle anyway. The crows felt obliged to invite every other bird in the vicinity to the party. Circling high, they made themselves effective broadcasters. More crows jetted in from distant neighborhoods, more pigeons swooped down from hidden perches, and more sparrows popped out from the bushes. I tore off good-sized, crusty chunks of bread for the crows, as part of their sport was carrying off their loot with their friends in pursuit. It would be hard for them to be taken seriously in this raucous game of tag if they didn't have a substantial and sturdy prize beckoning from both sides of their beaks. The pigeons preferred medium-sized morsels. And several slices of bread were crumbled and sprinkled under the protection of the bushes for the sparrows, the smallest of the partygoers.

Once back at the pasture, all parts intact, I praised the paint for being a good horse, stroking his smooth neck. With all the brushing he had gotten throughout the spring months, Shane's coat was glistening again. No trace of winter shag remained. "Let's give you some oats before your treats," I told him. "Then we can enjoy the rest of this beautiful day together." Feeling elated over our successful adventure, and pleased with my riding skills, I gave a friendly wave to Pat who, for some reason, was watching me from the front porch. Then I turned to trip over Guthrie. It was an ungraceful sprawl as I tried to avoid injuring the small dog. "You!" I said, startled but glad to see him. His first instinct was to cower slightly, lowering his funny tufted ears. Then as soon as he saw that I wasn't upset, he rushed forward with eager tongue to lick my face, now happily lowered to his level. Petting the round, squirming body in my lap, I noted the freckled skin on his sparsely furred back had a pink glow. Guthrie was well on his way to a summer tan.

Holding the bucket for Shane as he ate his oats, I closed my eyes and lifted my face to the sunshine, a hand laid firmly against his warm neck. It was one of our ways of being as close as we could be.

At first, I had wondered how Shane and I would communicate. However, as our time together progressed, I realized we had actually, all the while, kept in close communication using body language. For my part, mostly hands were used. My hands spoke to him with lingering caresses, and a variety of pats, rubs, pushes, and swats. Also, an open hand was often pressed lovingly against his hide to reassure or comfort him. For Shane's part, he would paw, snort, playfully slap me with his tail, wag his head, bob his head, or swing his head around to make pointed suggestions, or give me significant eye contact if he thought I wasn't listening. He could be pushy, too. He used a variety of nudges and shoves to get his point across. He could also be loving, blowing sweet smelling kisses into my ears, playfully nibbling at the back of my head, or tickling my neck with his muzzle.

When Shane was finished with his healthful snack, it was time to pass out the treats. To the rattle of the brown paper bag, the Hopeful Ones came crowding in, their expectant faces in a line along the fence. They eagerly accepted whatever they were given, making funny faces and tossing their heads at some of the more sour candies. There was one particularly ratty horse that was shy and always hung back from the fence. Through persistence I made sure he got his share.

The paint and I agreed to spend the remainder of our summer day in lazy yet dogged pursuit of the best grazing grounds, which were all those tempting places that the other, confined, horses could only dream about. Today, we began in the Murphy's backyard, where Shane efficiently mowed the long grass that grew at the base of the teeter-totter and clothesline. When he was finished manicuring one spot, I would arise from a nearby station of contemplation and repose, to stretch and call his attention to the next. Circling the house, all through the afternoon hours, Shane even trimmed the grass at the base of each of the many fruit trees. In this leisurely manner we enjoyed many summer days together.

CHAPTER FOURTEEN

*I*t was a grand day when Kelly and Peppy arrived at their new pasture. Daddy Mike, Mom, Little Mike, and I pulled up in a brand new Lincoln Continental. The Lincoln was yet another company car, as Dad was now the sales manager at Pacific Lincoln Mercury in downtown Seattle. The huge trunk of the luxury car was over-stuffed with Dad's recent expensive purchases. We even had equipment on our laps, piled on the seat between us, and wrapped around our legs on the floor of the car. When I glanced over at my brother, who was sitting on the back seat with me, he had a desperate, trapped-animal expression on his face. It was probably merely a consequence of his being mashed against the car door that made him appear so anguished and put-upon. Although I had noted these past weeks that Little Mike would roll his eyes at any mention of "the girls," as Dad was fond of calling his horses.

"Okay," Dad said. "Here we go. Ma, you try to stay out of the way. Mike, you help me unload all this . . . this . . . horse shit." Predictably, Little Mike rolled his eyes. "And, Con, don't wander off, I might need you, too."

"Right, Dad," I said.

The paddock was fair-sized. It was much larger than it had seemed to me on my first inspection when I had been pouting and had refused to get out of the car. Prowling the stable alone, I realized that it too was much larger than I had thought. The stalls were roomy. Two horses stared out at me from behind the bars of their cozy, straw-lined quarters, appearing quite content. Maybe I'd misjudged the place.

Little Mike entered the stable carrying a heavy sack of grain. Dad followed, carrying two buckets filled with brushes, ointments, vitamins, bug spray, shampoo, and more. "Let me show you where our hay is kept," Dad was saying. "You never know when I might need you to feed the girls." I glanced over at Little Mike who rolled his eyes.

"They're here!" Mom called from across the paddock. "They're here!"

Dad's face lit up. Seeing him so excited, I remembered all the magic of the first day I spent with my horse.

It was natural for the horses to be excited as well. Riding in a horse trailer had to be stressful, or at least exhilarating. Add to that, stepping out into unknown territory. Kelly expertly negotiated the springy ramp, with Peppy hugging her mother closely. The foal had no intention of being left behind. Both horses were chestnuts, their tails, manes, and bodies all a solid, light reddish-brown. Right away, because of her color, and because of her closely cropped mane, Kelly reminded me of Skat Kat. And just like that infamous, crow-hopping, bucking bronco, she was powerfully built and rippling with muscle. Kelly's unfortunate resemblance to the evil Skat Kat was so shockingly uncanny it made me immediately nervous and suspicious, maybe even a little frightened, of Dad's new horse.

Dad accepted the lead from Kelly's previous owner, who, in my estimation, seemed happy to hand her over and a bit too eager to be on his way.

"Well, what do you think, Con?" Dad said, even before the truck and trailer had completely disappeared from sight. It was important to him that I like his horses.

Walking around them, I took a long assessment of the pair. Although no expert by any stretch of reality, there were obvious physical deformities I was able to check for, such as swayback, popped knees or bowed legs, and visible signs of ill health such as runny eyes, skin rashes, or rotting hooves. Overall, they were handsome, alert quarter horses with good conformation. At nearly two years old, Peppy was almost as tall as her mother, yet still retained her gangly baby appearance. Her chestnut mane grew upward before attempting to flop over, which added much to her sprightly, youthful air. Her mother was . . . well . . . even I could see that Kelly was one very serious piece of horseflesh. She reminded me of an idling jet engine.

Something I didn't want to be on when she got full throttle.

"Kelly looks to be a bit . . . energetic," I said. That was a respectful child-to-parent understatement. High-strung was more like it. The mare was tossing her head around so much that Dad had stepped back out of the way. "Did that man happen to mention whether she was trained as a pleasure horse?"

"What are you talking about?" Dad said.

"He might have used the term 'trail horse,'" I explained.

"He used the term 'highly trained,'" Dad said sounding, slightly annoyed. "Highly trained. That's the term he used."

"Did he say it like a warning?" I said. At this, Mom and Little Mike burst into barely suppressed giggles. Whereupon, Dad shot them such a disapproving and humorless arrow that they instantly sobered.

We decided to groom the horses to get them acquainted with us. Mom's job was to restrain Peppy so we could work around her mother effectively. Whenever Peppy got too fidgety or rambunctious, Mom walked the foal around the paddock until she settled down again. The mare kept a vigilant watch over these proceedings. She let us know if she thought Mom was straying too far. I admired the mare for being an attentive mother. There were other things to admire about Kelly as well. She was intelligent, obviously listening to everything we said. Also, as we three worked around her, easily lifting each leg to clean her hooves, she gave no indication that she might bite or kick. That alone raised her several levels in my esteem. "This is actually a very fine animal," I remarked to Dad.

Dad beamed. "You say that almost grudgingly," he said.

Next, with Kelly tethered acceptably close to ease any anxiety, Dad, Little Mike, and I turned our full concentration and brushes on Peppy. The foal was a bit overwhelmed by all of us admiring her and brushing her at the same time, yet friendly and curious about us in an innocent, childlike way, always sniffing at one of us, searching for some comforting smell of recognition. She had no clue what we expected of her, and kept looking to her mother for reassurance.

By the time we finished with the soothing rituals of grooming: the praising, the petting, the brushing, and the combing, we had the two horses settled down to some extent—and ourselves worn out. There would be no rest though. Dad was eager to check out his new equipment. He wanted to thoroughly examine each item from strap to stirrup in case there was any expensive little doodad that needed to be returned or exchanged.

While tending to the horses, we had noticed, and discussed, the fact that there was a good-sized cement slab near the stable. It was off to one side and not physically connected to the barn in any way. Dad speculated that it was a place where horses were to be groomed and bathed. I thought it might be a place designed for the unloading of hay onto something other than soggy ground. Either way, it presented itself to Dad as the perfect solution for keeping his new saddle and other equipment from ever touching the ground. Little Mike and I were given the task of lugging everything that was still left in the trunk over to that cement slab.

"Don't put that down!" Dad said sounding panicked. Mike had the heavy saddle hovering ready to drop. "Give me a chance to sweep this thing. Can't you see that all this dirt and gravel could scratch the leather? Just wait," he said rushing away.

We waited, although not very patiently. I had an armload of leather whatever, and it was heavy. Dad returned with a push broom, which was the first thing he could find. "I know that saddle's heavy," he apologized, while raising a cloud of dust. "I know because they charge you by the ounce!" The cement slab was such a rough pour that it took Dad some time to thoroughly sweep out the pits and crevices of a reasonable area on which we could set his equipment. Then Dad decided to fetch the saddle blanket from the trunk, something to cover the rough cement before putting the saddle down. He was so finicky about his pristine tack that he now had both Mike and me rolling our eyes in frustration. Then the saddle blanket was too nice for the task. Dad couldn't bring himself to lay it down. There was more apologizing, and more waiting, while he scurried to find a tarp or piece of plastic.

Once we finally had everything assembled, I had to ask, "What is all this stuff?"

"It's everything I was told I had to have," Dad said somewhat defensively as he led Kelly to the center of the swept-spotless slab. "This isn't some plug you can ride bareback." I understood what Dad meant. His choice of tack had nothing to do with unreasoning chance. He had been told the specifics of what he needed by the man from whom he had purchased the horse. It all had to do with how the horse had been trained. Shane had been trained without a bit, which is why I had been told to purchase a hackamore.

It became my job to steady the mare while she was being saddled. Little Mike continued as Dad's lackey, fetching this and fetching that. Mom was to keep Peppy entertained nearby. Keeping Peppy occupied wasn't an easy assignment, especially because the foal was so fascinated by mother's hair. Perhaps Mom's blond coif was being mistaken for a ready meal. For my part, I had to contend with Kelly's fitfully thrashing head. The mare's head was an unpredictable, rock hard missile, ever threatening a surprise attack. Even though I knew it could be dangerous, somehow her head always seemed to catch me off guard.

The colorful new saddle blanket in bright yellow, blue, and orange was displayed to all, shaken delicately, and applied to Kelly's back. After Dad made sure the blanket was smooth and positioned perfectly, the lackey swung the heavy saddle up onto the mare's back. Like most saddles, Dad's saddle was a beautifully hand-tooled, leather masterpiece. He didn't give Little Mike a moment's rest. "Go around to see if this strap is twisted for me, will you, pal," he said. We don't need to do a final cinching 'til we get the rest of this gear figured out. Everything okay over there? Now where the hell is Ma? Ma!" he boomed. "Where the hell are you!" Mothers in three counties stopped what they were doing.

My mother, who was wearing a bright pink, silky blouse, white slacks, and Hollywood-style dark sunglasses, with her purse dangling from her shoulder, was smoking a cigarette while leisurely walking Peppy around the paddock. "Now isn't that something," Dad said softly, stopping to wonder at his wife. "See how she hears me, but doesn't even look my way." Although he said this shaking his head, there was definitely admiration in his tone.

All this distraction almost served to take my head off. I jumped back to save myself from injury. "That was a close one!" I exclaimed. I had choked up on the halter lead, but that hadn't helped.

"Watch yourself," Dad reminded me.

The mare's eyes were wide and rolling around in her head. Oblivious to the fact that I was standing in front of her, she was only concerned with keeping an eye on her foal. Again, I jumped back, narrowly avoiding a concussion. "What's with this?" I said, startled and annoyed.

"I have a piece of gear specially designed to fix that problem," Dad said. "Get that for me, will you, pal," he added casually, tossing the words over his shoulder. "No. On second thought, bring me that bridle first." The fancy bridle had extra long, braided reins, and a bit that included a rolling toy. Kelly began rattling the roller as soon as the bit was seated in her mouth. For the moment anyway, playing with the roller was distracting the mare from throwing her head so much.

Next, Kelly was fitted with a heavy leather strap that looped around behind her rear end below and under her tail and hooked onto both sides of the back of the saddle. Then a leather piece looped around her chest and hooked onto both sides of the front of the saddle. This is a good thing, I thought. Whatever else happens, that saddle isn't coming off! Still there was more. Another strap buckled beneath the breastplate and ran down between her front legs to the cinch strap, and still another connected the top of the breastplate to a metal ring on the underside of her bridle. This all seemed comfortably familiar to Kelly, already enjoying tossing her head up as far as the strap that was hooked under her chin would allow. There was a loud snap every time she tossed her head. Toss. Snap. Toss. Snap. Toss. Snap. If Kelly had looked like a serious ride to me before, she looked downright deadly to me now!

"Well, I guess it's time to break in my new saddle," Dad said, turning to us all proud smiles and excitement. It was at that moment, that very instant, that Kelly started to go down. The mare's front legs buckled and she dropped to her knees. Hoping to change her mind, I pulled forward on the reins of the bridle. Down she went anyway, rolling over onto her right side. She was crushing the stirrup and the smooth leather fender of Dad's new saddle. Horrified, Dad and Mike tried to push and lift almost a thousand pounds of horseflesh off the rough cement. Despite their best efforts, the mare twisted and rolled onto her back, saddle and all. A full back scratching ensued. Legs kicking skyward, she was writhing with pleasure like a flea-bitten dog. All we could do was stand by and watch. "Ah . . . Now doesn't that feel good!" Dad said softly. He didn't sound angry; he was likely in a state of shock.

As soon as Kelly was finished with her moment of ecstasy and struggling to her feet, we leaped forward to inspect the damage. The fine leather of Dad's new saddle was permanently scarred. The saddle horn had a gouge in it, the tooled edge of the cantle had several nicks, and the smooth top surface of the cantle was scraped and pitted. Dad was strangely quiet, half-heartedly picking at the embedded gravel ground into the pits. Then, "What do you think, Con," he said somewhat cheerfully, which was totally out of character under the circumstances. "Do you want to take her for a test drive?"

I might have recoiled.

"How about you, Mike. Want to take her for a spin?" Dad was definitely in shock. Little Mike stared at him as if he had lost his mind. However, in studying his dad's face, he could see he was quite shaken. "Just a short spin," Dad urged. "Walk her around the paddock for me one time, will you, pal?" It was pure pity that made Mike get on that horse.

Kelly stood her ground as Mike reluctantly mounted. She stood in one place all right, but she wasn't standing still by any means. She had all four legs pumping. The mare was revving her engines. "Once around the paddock, pal. That's all I'm asking," Dad said, handing Mike the reins.

What made Dad swat the mare on the rump, albeit gently? He had probably seen it done in some Western movie, perhaps as a Pony Express rider's good luck, Godspeed. Anyway, it had been much more of a reassuring love pat than a swat. Either way, whatever the intent, it sparked an uncontrolled, premature launch.

Clinging to the saddle horn with both hands, Little Mike rode that projectile missile of a mare straight for the fence at the other end of the paddock. "She's going over!" Dad screamed. "She's going over!" She didn't. Instead, hardly slowing, she turned at the fence. The turn was such an unexpected, abrupt about-face that Mike swung wide, struggling to stay on. He was fighting his own forward momentum with one arm flung out, flailing like some wild rodeo cowboy. Kelly wasn't having any problem correcting her forward momentum though. Nostrils flaring, she was fully turned and catapulting our way. Kelly skidded to a standstill before Dad and me, both of us on the ground. We had fallen over each other in our attempt to retreat.

Getting up, Dad asked, "Geezus, Mike! What did you dooo to 'er?" He had a singular way of emphasizing certain words when he got excited. He could actually raise one word in a sentence a whole octave.

"I didn't 'dooo' anything," Mike said, mimicking his dad's cadence. "I'm just sitting here."

"You must have goosed her a little," Dad said accusingly, winking at me.

"No." Mike said. "I didn't move a muscle."

Little Mike wanted off. He kept trying to dismount; Dad kept pushing him back into the saddle. "Will you let me think a minute?" Dad said, rubbing his chin. He appeared quite perplexed. "Can't you walk her around the paddock one time for me? I want to see how she moves. I can't see a damn thing with her racing all over hell!"

Mike threw up his hands exposing his open palms. He often threw up his hands when he was with his father. It was his sign of long-suffering submission. A gesture that clearly meant, "The ridiculous things I do for this man!"

Perhaps a bit sharply, Mike laid the reins against Kelly's powerful neck. The mare instantly responded by jump-twisting around. She lifted both of her front hooves a foot off the ground, only touching them down again when she had completely turned and was nothing but a chestnut streak of tail and pounding hooves driving in the opposite direction.

"Use the brakes!" Dad screamed. "The brakes!"

It was a short, flat-out scramble to the fence at the other end of the paddock. At which point, Kelly skidded to an astonishing stop, and then, jump-twist and all, was rocketing back in our direction. Dad and I didn't have time to run. The mare came to a snappy, straight-legged, sliding stop in front of her new master. She seemed to be expecting praise.

Dad was dumbfounded. "You must have done something to make her take off like that," he accused his son.

"I hung on!"

"Did you see how well she came to a stop when you pulled back on the reins?" Dad said somewhat sarcastically.

"I'm telling you, I never pulled back on the reins!"

"That can't be!" Dad said in disbelief.

"That's it!" Mike said, jumping down. "Ride your own damn horse!" He threw the reins at his father. I rarely, if ever, heard my brother swear.

Dad stood, holding the reins of his new horse, totally perplexed. "I don't get it," he said. "I just don't get it." Kelly, eager to be ridden again, kept nudging him as if to say, "Come on! You're next!" Dad studied his horse affectionately. "No," he told her. "We'd better hold off doing any more riding 'til we get your brakes checked."

"And your head examined," Mike added.

"Don't worry," Dad said. "I'll get to the bottom of this. I'll call that guy as soon as we get home."

We were tired. Yet we had plenty of work left to do to get the horses fed and bedded down in their new quarters. After that, the tack had to be stowed and the grooming equipment properly put away. Leading the horses to the stable, Dad said, "I knew that guy was a little kinky." And Kelly, bobbing her head, seemed to be comically in agreement with what her new master said.

* * *

It was one week later and there was already a pattern developing. At around seven o'clock most evenings Daddy Mike would come trudging up the stairs sorting the mail. At the top of the stairs, he would stop to toss his car keys to Little Mike, saying, "Feed the girls for me, will you, pal?"

This evening was no different. When Dad got home, Mom was downstairs doing laundry and folding clothes. She was enjoying a moment of solitude. The basement laundry room was her sanctuary, as it was unlikely any of her kids would follow her there. Anyway, she had done her motherly duties the moment she had walked in the door from work, pacing through one teenager crisis after another. Each child had taken her time with idle chatter, frank conversation, curfew grievances, pleas for fatherly intervention, event scheduling and chauffeuring conflicts, and the endless appeal for money.

Now it was Dad's turn. Linda wanted to spend the night at a friend's house. Mom had said it was okay with her, but she still needed to get Dad's approval. Dad's concern was that his voluptuous daughter was using her girlfriend, Marla, as a ruse so she could slip out with her ne'er-do-well boyfriend. Cher wanted to borrow Mom's car to take her friends to a movie, but she had to get Dad's buyoff, as everyone agreed she was a risky, inattentive, and even dangerous driver. Both wanted money.

With Dad surrounded, fending off Linda's request and losing ground in another heated driving battle with headstrong Cher, Little Mike didn't stand a chance of arguing his case for not wanting to feed the horses. No one cared. "Come on, Con," Mike said, rolling his eyes. "Come with me."

Tired and dirty after having ridden my bike home from spending the day at the pasture with Shane, I pleaded, "Not tonight."

"Please. Please," Mike begged. "It goes faster when you help."

"No," I said again. I was truly tired, and didn't feel like spending the next hour being teased, tickled, pounced on, chased, and generally terrified by my brother. If he wasn't scaring me by jumping out at me from some dark corner of the stable, he was driving like a maniac trying to scare me in the car.

"Please," Mike begged, dropping to his knees. "Please."

"Only if you promise not to scare me."

"I promise," Mike said, leaping to his feet. It was a hollow promise.

First, and at no surprise to me, we had to take a side trip so I could see how well Little Mike could do wheelies and peel-out of a vacant gravel parking lot. By the time we arrived at the stable, I was a trembling mess. Then I had to keep Mike in view at all times. He probably wondered why I was following him around, even up into the hayloft, like a lost puppy. Keeping my brother in sight was a strategy, not a solution.

On our return home, Dad greeted us at the top of the stairs. "I finally got hold of that slippery devil!" Dad said. "And you won't believe what I found out." He was beaming with excitement. "She's trained as a barrel racer! Can you believe it? Kelly is a rodeo barrel racer!" He sounded so amazed, so proud, so . . . happy. Little Mike and I were not as impressed.

Sarcastically rolling my eyes at my brother, I said, "Oh. That's a relief. And all this time we thought there was something wrong with her."

"Well, you have to admit it explains a few things," Dad said.

"It doesn't explain anything to me," Mike said. "I already knew you were some kind of nut!"

"I mean about the horse," Dad said enthusiastically. "She's won ribbons! Ribbons!"

"We get it, Dad," I said. "We get it. But what are we supposed to do with a breakneck barrel racer?"

"I don't know." Dad rubbed his chin thoughtfully. "I don't know.

CHAPTER FIFTEEN

*I*n the next few weeks, while Daddy Mike tried to, "get Kelly's high beams and low beams sorted out," and gain enough control over his horse so we could go riding in Bridle Trails together, I was spending my summer days at the pasture with Shane.

Solitary recreation at the Murphy farm was a distant, dark, and rainy memory. Paradise must be shared. These days, the paint and I were likely to have an audience when he escorted me up the pasture. By this time, I had given up the charade of using a halter. Eyes popped wide watching us pass through the gate in our special way—how Shane, attached to me, kept his head at my shoulder to turn with me while the gate was closed. That amazed even me, though I never showed it. Then wide eyes watched him accompany me to the hitching post where he dutifully stayed without fettering while I went to fetch the brushes and grain.

To observe our rapport, few would have guessed that Shane and I had our share of disagreements and hurt feelings—but we did. Shane disliked having his tail brushed, and he hated having it combed. However, his nice white tail, long and full, was often ratty, yellow, and muddy. Consequently, there were times, like today, when I was determined to tame a particularly tangled clump of hair, that polite lines were crossed and both of us were teetering on the brink of losing our patience. Relinquishing my grasp on Shane's outraged tail, and then stepping back to pause before renewing my assault, I tumbled backward over the hapless Guthrie again. I fell awkwardly, trying to save us both from injury. Why do we always have to meet like this, I wondered? It was his stealthy way of sneaking up behind me when I was especially busy that caused the problem. Pulling him in and submitting to an onslaught of facial licks, I gave the little menace a playful roughing up. "You have no idea how wonderful you are," I said, gently tugging on the tufts of his ears. "No idea." With my good-humor thus restored, Shane's tail became acceptable—for today. We made our truce while he ate his grain. Stroking his smooth neck, I thought about how fortunate I was to have a horse I could trust. That no matter how testy things got between us, the paint didn't bite or kick.

From our position at the hitching post, I had a good view of the back pastures. There were a number of girls riding there. Although eager to join them, there was no point in hurrying with my chores because I was waiting for Karen. I spent a lot of time waiting for my friend. Today I was waiting for her at the pasture. More often I was waiting for her at her house after spending the night so we could get an early start, a strategy that was painful for both of us. It started with the fact that Karen wasn't an early riser. Then when she finally did get up, it took her forever to put in her contacts, which was always the first thing she did. It was an exasperating ordeal to witness. The contacts had to be cleaned, and in the process, since she couldn't see anything, she was likely to drop one, forcing us to crawl around on the bathroom floor. By the time she got her eyes in, as she called them, she was awake—and mad. That's because the very next thing she always did was to strap on her watch and gasp at the time in horror, realizing that I had taken advantage of her pre-contacts condition to set her bed clock ahead. At five o'clock in the morning, my friend was predictably so groggy that she fell for this trick every time. Next she had an elaborate face cleansing ritual. Then, her breakfast was always some lengthy, big, diet-recipe deal. And it never failed that her room was a mess, so we had to do her chores before she could go anywhere. Once on our way, and by that time barely speaking to each other, we had to stop by her church for Karen to practice the organ. It was easier to meet her at the pasture whenever she had a day to spend at the farm with me.

So Shane and I waited. By the time Karen's mother dropped her off, it was almost noon, the paint's coat was shining, the tack box was in perfect order, and all of my equipment had undergone an extra cleaning.

"Sorry," Karen said. "I tried to hurry. Have you been waiting long?"

"Long enough," I said, trying not to sound too annoyed.

In an attempt to change the subject, she exclaimed, "Wow! Your horse looks great!"

"He should. He had a three-hour brushing." Karen humbly followed me to the fence at the back pasture where the Hopeful Horses immediately came over to greet us. I wasn't speaking to her, only because I was busy puzzling over why Karen would wear white shorts when she knew she was to go bareback riding. I was mentally testing every cleaning method known, trying to remove the inevitable, ground-in stain on the back of her shorts. I was thinking Borax soap and a scrub brush.

"So this is it? The silent treatment? You're going to be upset with me all day?"

With the horses all in a line along the fence, I reached into my pocket to produce the treats. "I'm not upset," I said, ceremoniously handing out a candy to each horse. "Watch this. I've taught these horses to sing 'The Star Spangled Banner.'" I had Karen's attention. "Oh, say can you see," I sang, "By the dawn's early light . . ." At the same time, stepping back, I waved my arms like a chorus conductor. As if on queue, the horses seemed to be trying to sing along. They tossed their heads up and down to my singing and mouthed the words, comically exposing their teeth. My timing was precise, knowing exactly at what moment the sour Sweet Tarts would take their irresistible effect.

"So now you're training other people's horses?" Karen laughed.

And then with what must have appeared to be incredible showmanship, knowing precisely at what moment to end the performance, I began slowly lowering my arms, circling them downward with dramatic flair, until finally the singing horses once again became just horses standing at the fence.

Karen applauded. "Can I try it? Can I make the horses sing?"

Right then Pat called her horse. She called her horse with one loud, authoritative whistle. It was the kind of whistle where you put two fingers to your lips to blow—quick, sharp, and effective. So compelling was the whistle that many of the other horses stopped what they were doing to wander her way even though they knew that the come hither whistle was meant only for Swifty.

Our choir was dispersing, so, "Let's ride," I said. And Karen agreed.

I led Shane straight to our familiar rock in the front pasture. There would be no stylish mount today or any other day. Long ago I recognized that item number one on our training schedule, mounting practice, had caused me to begin our rides in a hopelessly demoralized state. The only way I was ever going to swing up onto my horse was if I sprouted wings.

"You first," I told Karen. She didn't notice that the paint stood his ground while she climbed aboard. He had learned his part of the stylish mount. "Good boy!" I praised him, handing the reins to Karen. "Good boy!"

My dark-haired friend rode down the hill urging Shane into a bouncing trot. The usually soggy terrain of the lower pasture had been baked dry by the summer sun. When Karen rode around to the side pasture and out of sight, I sat down cross-legged on the rock, leaning my elbows on my knees. The rock was warm, and the drone of traffic sounded like a distant waterfall. I listened to some happy fellow chirping in a fruit tree behind me, drifting in and out of daydreams, wishing all of life could be a sunny day.

"Hey!" Karen called. She and Shane were rounding the corner of the fence that encircled the Murphy's yard. They were approaching quickly at a jogging gait. My friend's face was flushed. "We're missing a show back there!" And then, as so often happened, Shane tripped, his knees almost hitting the ground. It was a jolting stumble, recovered, but none-the-less, it threw the startled rider forward hard. "I hate that!" Karen exclaimed, jumping down. She was puffing, out of breath. "Don't you just hate that?"

"Aw, I don't mind it so much," I said taking the reins. "Besides, if he were perfect he wouldn't be my horse."

"Meaning?"

"Meaning that if he were perfect we wouldn't have been able to afford him."

"Maybe," Karen hesitated. "But even if he didn't trip he'd be far from perfect."

"Unlike the rest of us, of course," I said. "Anyway, I happen to think there's something perfect about all his imperfections."

"You would," Karen said, shaking her head. "You would."

I rode while Karen walked ahead. We followed the trail that wound around behind the house. Shane and I were following the stain on the back of Karen's shorts. It already looked as though we'd never get it out.

"Your dad still harping on that boarding school thing?" Karen asked, glancing back.

"Sure is," I said. "He doesn't seem to hear when I tell him that I don't want to go. He says it's impossible for me to know that I don't want to go until after I've already gone. It's some kind of engineer logic. He doesn't want to say it, but he thinks I'll get a better education at the academy."

Daddy Ray had been on one of his "I've got to give my girls every opportunity" crusades for some time. It didn't help that Cher, at her request, had spent her sophomore year at a boarding school in California. She got the bright idea when the Horton family was on vacation visiting friends there. It had been a boy thing; Scott had talked her into it. Scott was one of two sons of Alan and Louise Loeffler who lived near San Diego. Dad, Alan, and Louise had attended college together. Cher was surprised when Dad had been so supportive. He was eager for her to have the experience. She loved it, and yet she hated it. Now Cher was back at public school, but she often told Lindy and me nostalgic stories about the academy and the friends she had made there. Sometimes, when she was telling her stories, she said that she wished she'd continued to go to school there.

"Would you get a better education?" Karen asked.

"Don't worry, Karen," I answered. "I'm not going anywhere without my horse." We were turning the last corner on our way to join the girls who were riding in the back pasture. An obstacle course was set up there.

The course was a combination of the three jumps that had been relocated from the riding arena, and two makeshift agility exercises. One of the agility exercises was a zigzag course made up of miscellaneous poles, barrels, and bales of straw. The other was a set of five rotting fence posts lying parallel to each other on the ground. The posts were positioned with a gap of about four feet between them.

We were in time to see Pat and Swifty give a demonstration. The three of us stopped to watch the show from the perimeter. At least I had hoped Shane would pay attention. Instead, the presence of the buckskin mare was distracting him. Shane was tossing his head and snorting at the first glimpse of her, even though she was on the opposite side of the course. Across the course were Gretchen and her, apparently, extremely sexy mare, Wanda, and her palomino gelding, Dusty, as well as Emily and her Welsh pony. They didn't acknowledge our arrival; they were enjoying the show. All the same I knew we were welcome to join them.

Gretchen, Wanda, Emily, and I sat contentedly astride our beloved steeds watching Swifty whiz his fabulous self around the obstacle course. I was welcome in this circle; I belonged. For even though it remained unspoken among us, we girls shared something very basic in common—we were all horse-crazy. That's what it's called to be haunted by horses and insane with longing. Yet there was more to our bond than that. It was more an understanding of what it had taken for each of us to be present here today that we truly, deeply shared. As children possessed, we had mercilessly inflicted our tortured selves on our parents from the moment we were able to speak and make our impossible dreams known. We begged, we schemed, we cried. Oh! did we cry! We practically gave ourselves seizures from wailing. There was no consoling us with anything less than our very own horse. It hadn't been easy to convince our suburban parents to agree to such an expensive, not to mention sometimes dangerous, folly that was contrary to all parental judgment. And I had needed to convince two sets of parents. I definitely belonged.

The obstacle course was so effortless for Swifty that Pat had added flourishes to enhance their performance. At the starting point, Pat stood beside her horse to await a signal from Wanda, who had a stopwatch. In this group, Pat was forced to compete against herself. At the go signal the arm dropped, her horse lunged forward into a gallop, and the long-legged girl grasped the saddle horn, as always, using the forward momentum of the horse to launch into the saddle. Quickly, she reined in her racing horse adjusting his timing to the low jumps. Before the high jump, a flourish, a full spin around in place, then cleanly over the jump. A relaxed and graceful winding through the zigzag followed. We all focused on Pat's boot tips, for, when it came to Pat, we were a most critical crowd. If even a toe of her boot were to graze a pole or bale, we would have considered the whole exercise a wash. However, Swifty's narrow frame made it appear all too easy. Last was a trot through the blocks, small hooves flashing. We clapped. Pat was pleased with their time.

Admiring a perfect repeat performance, I wondered at Swifty. Everyone agreed there was something extra special about the horse. Karen was right, though. It sure wasn't his looks. The chestnut gelding wasn't a particularly attractive horse. He had no unique markings, nor a shapely head or flowing mane. Nothing about him caught your eye. If you saw him standing in a field among many horses, you wouldn't even notice him. And when he was being led across the paddock, he didn't prance or call attention to himself in any way. He was small in stature, slight of build, and so narrow through the chest his front legs seemed too close together. Yet there was no question that Swifty was a superior animal. Picking out the right horse must be a lot like picking out the right car, I mused. There's a lot you can't see that's under the hood.

Gretchen moved onto the course. Even in warm weather, the redheaded girl wore a long-sleeved Western style shirt. Coming in forward of the invisible line, she backed her horse to the starting point, the mare shaking her head at the delay. There was silence around the course. With the quirt tapping the flanks of the horse, the buckskin loped to the first jump, then nicely over. Now there was that tricky timing issue between jumps. The quirt again tapping, they were cleanly over the second low jump. The higher hurdle was bypassed. Gretchen kicked, prodding the mare through the zigzag. Her buckskin was compact but stocky, so she had difficulty using the quirt between the poles. They brushed the poles several times, and rattled through the blocks. We clapped. Except for Pat, whose performance we took seriously, it was all in fun.

I was disappointed to see things breaking up. Horses and riders were turning away heading into the farthest pasture.

"Are you going to race?" Wanda called to me. It was an invitation.

I hesitated. I had a big problem steering at high speeds.

"Well, come on anyway," Gretchen called, smiling. "If you're not, you can use the stopwatch for us."

"Why don't you want to race?" Karen asked, as we followed the group.

"I do," I said, although I really didn't.

"I can work the stopwatch," Karen offered. She was trying to be helpful.

"No, I'll do it," I said. "Then I'll race the next time, before you take your turn."

The girls lined up at the back corner of the property. They were at the far end of the long, flat pasture that was used mostly for racing. Shane and I were positioned close enough so our go signal could be seen, yet far enough away so we could see the finish line and help determine the winner. (The 'winner' was always the rider who came in second after Swifty.) Keeping one eye on the starting line, I nervously fumbled with the watch, figuring out the buttons, which of course were on the right side of the watch. Left-handed, I was such a bungler I finally had to hold the watch with both hands. The racers were ready and waiting.

With the buttons sorted out, I gripped the watch firmly with my right hand. "On three," I called, "when I drop my arm. One, two . . . three!"

Swifty left the line first, the buckskin surprisingly close behind. Hooves pounded, the ground shook. Dusty was in the race, charging forward, Wanda red-faced and screaming. Emily's pony had a bad start, but she soon had him headed in the right direction. They thundered past. Urging the pony on, I was clapping, bouncing, yelling, and practically choking in my excitement. This was all too much for Shane. Rearing high into the air, he made a lunge for the flashing tails. I tried to grab the reins as I slid down his almost vertical back, but when he made his lunge forward, I was bounced back onto the rise of his rounded rump. The paint was soon fully stretched out in a powerful, pulsing, smooth-backed gallop. Even if I had managed to grab the reins, I wouldn't have been able to stop him. I was sucked into the vortex of his wake. Very shortly, I heard the all-too-familiar thud of my own body hitting hard-packed earth.

The wind was knocked out of me, and it was a few minutes before I could even manage a groan. "She's all right," Pat told the other faces in the circle looking down on me.

"Did we win?" I asked feebly. Remembering the watch, I opened my hand. "Is it okay?"

"You should have dropped the stupid thing," Pat said, helping me up. Nevertheless, she inspected the watch carefully. We all knew it had been a gift from her father.

My relief at not having broken the stopwatch was great. "Let's ride some more," I said to everyone cheerfully. Then to Karen, "It's your turn."

CHAPTER SIXTEEN

Bridle Trails State Park

*C*onsidering my poor riding record, Shane and I had no business venturing out on the roadways. All the same, I couldn't tell my parents about all the spills and thus have risked missing riding in Bridle Trails with Dad. Besides, Daddy Mike was convinced his daughter was a skilled rider, the best, the Annie Oakley of Bellevue, and he never would have listened to anything different. Further, he would have gleefully attacked the paint as being solely responsible for all our troubles. This would have been followed by the "Your horse is a plug!" tirade I was pleased to miss. So there we were.

Some drivers slowed their cars and moved over, giving us plenty of room as they passed; others did not. The paint, plodding along with ears pointing forward and head bobbing, seemed unconcerned about the traffic—almost too unconcerned. However, for me it was scary, and if I flinched when a car whizzed past, Shane's head would jerk up. Riding bareback revealed all to my horse. Deciding it was time for my most stoic Apache face, I pretended the paint and I were warrior scouts on point position of an important hunting party. On our own, we were traveling through unfamiliar territory, far from our canyon lands. We'd been chosen above all others as the two bravest members of our tribe. Shane and I were boldly riding through the Bad Lands on our way to Bridle Trails, avoiding mailboxes, mud puddles, and any other number of objects that might have sent Shane into a panic. A shopping mall became a distant, high plateau, and passing cars merely gusts of wind howling across the plains.

There was no fanfare upon our safe arrival at Kelly's pasture. Both Mom and Dad were engaged, their joint attention taken up with yet another strategy to control a touchy Peppy situation. Dad was mounted on Kelly outside the paddock, and the foal had herself in a state, convinced her mother was abandoning her. So a reluctant Mom had been recruited into service again. She was always the bystander who never got to just stand by. Mom's mission was to distract the distraught animal by leading her around the pasture. However, the foal wasn't being led anywhere. Today, instead, she was dragging Mom back and forth along the fence. Peppy was a foal in name and mental maturity only as she was almost the size of a full-grown horse, and she was much more than my diminutive mother could handle. The romance and wisdom of purchasing mother and child had long since evaporated.

Grimacing at the sight of my mother's delicate, painted toes, I made a note to remind her not to wear sandals to the pasture. Dad had bought her a stylish pair of cowboy boots, but apparently wearing her boots made too much of a statement for my mother, suggesting that she had something to do with horses.

"You could put her in the barn," I suggested by way of a greeting.

"Oh, there you are," Dad said absently. "We already tried that."

"You could tie her to the hitching post."

He replied rather grimly, "We tried that, too."

Kelly was all business, impatiently throwing her head, snapping her chinstrap, and foaming at the mouth from rolling the toy on her bit. At the slightest touch of the reins against her neck, the mare would have whirled about and been on her way. I had to admit that Shane, so relaxed, might have appeared a bit plug-like in comparison.

"Enough is enough!" Dad exclaimed. "We're going. She'll forget about us the minute we're out of sight." Mom agreed. At that, we turned our horses. We were on our way.

I followed Dad to the trailhead that was located so conveniently adjoining the parking area. We didn't dare look back as we quickly disappeared into the trees heading up a steep embankment. The surefooted quarter horse fought with Dad for more freedom to set her own pace. It was quite a climb out of the underbrush up to the level of the power lines. The actual entrance to Bridle Trails State Park was about a quarter mile ride along a dirt utility road that ran under the wires. Kelly scrambled out of the trees into the sunlight with Shane and I close behind. Dad's horse was such a handful that it was the first opportunity he had to turn in the saddle to see if we were there. "I sure hope things have smoothed out down below," he was saying.

It was at that moment that an earsplitting, unearthly bellowing came out of nowhere. Things happened fast, but out of my peripheral vision I caught sight of a charging donkey. It was rushing straight for us, its neck outstretched, its mouth wide open, blasting a trumpeting, bone-rattling bray. Both horses shot up in the air, both landing at least six feet to the right from where they had originally been standing. At that point, the only reason Dad and I were still on our horses was that we had instinctively mirrored their behavior. Now the panicked animals were off. Again, Dad and I were able to stay on only because, in our minds, we were terror-stricken and fleeing as fast as our horses—even outdistancing them! Fortunately, a fence stopped the donkey's attack, and we were able to rein in our horses and ourselves.

It was then we realized we had been joined by Peppy. "Now, what the hell!" Dad said, almost anguished. We had to take a moment to restore our wits and discuss the situation. What to do about Peppy? Nobody but nobody, not man nor horse, was eager to pass back by that donkey.

After silently reviewing all options, I finally said, very reluctantly, "We can't take her with us."

Sounding equally indisposed, Dad said, "And we have to go back anyway to check on Ma." We had to talk ourselves into going back even though there was no choice. "What's wrong with that donkey, anyway?" Dad then asked. "What do you think?"

"He must have been defending himself to have reacted so. Maybe our crashing around in the trees on our way up scared him."

"I can always count on you to get the other guy's point of view," Dad chuckled. In fact, the donkey was now watching us from across the fence in a most benign fashion. No longer ferocious, it was now merely small and cute.

Somewhat bolstered, yet still cautious, we rode back by the now completely docile donkey. Peppy followed her mother; Shane and I brought up the rear.

We met Mom coming up the trail. She was quite flustered, as she hadn't known whether the foal had caught up with us, or what. "I couldn't hold her," Mom said breathlessly. "She jumped over the fence. I've been frantic!"

"Are you okay?" Dad asked. "I never should have left you like that." For good reason, we were both feeling sheepish.

Once back at the paddock, a thankful Mom was sent home. Then Peppy was put in her stall. By now the foal had exhausted herself and was glad to go.

At last Dad and I came to one of the many entrances to the equestrian park. We had been traveling along a sunny, dusty, utility road past the back of expensive homes and stables. High-class horses, even peacocks, had graced some estates. Dad and Kelly led the way as our horses' hooves fell softly onto the shaded, beautifully groomed trails. "We made it!" Dad said, elated. And less than a minute later, when other trails began crisscrossing ours to angle off in all directions, there was apprehension in his voice. "Do you think you can find our way back, Con?"

"I hope not."

"No, really."

"Let's just have fun and try to forget about it," I said. I could be cavalier because I had a natural sense of direction, rarely getting lost.

"I'm serious," Dad said. Two steps inside the park and he was already hopelessly disoriented.

"I'm serious, too. We'll worry about finding our way out if we pass the bones of other horses and riders."

Inside Bridle Trails was much like being in another world. Without the background noise of traffic, we could enjoy the chatter of birds and the sound of our horses' muted hoof-falls under the canopy as we rode. It was especially enjoyable listening to the creaking of Dad's new saddle.

"He's still at it," I said.

"Oh?" Then, after a few minutes, he added, "Your dad only wants what's best for you. He means well."

"He doesn't say it, but of course he wants me to meet Christian boys."

Turning in the saddle, "What about your horse? Has he said anything about that?"

"He says there's a pasture two blocks from the school, and I'll be able to visit my horse whenever I want."

"You could agree to try it for one year," Dad said thoughtfully. "After all, it's only one year. Besides, maybe you'll like it."

One year sounded like forever to me. "Maybe."

For a while we rode in silence. Then, "I'm not saying you would," Dad said, turning again. "But if you do, I promise to spend the school year finding us a pasture where we can board our horses together next summer." He added, "We wouldn't be able to ride much together in the winter anyway."

At that point, we came to a particularly confusing crossroad of trails. "Which way, Con?"

"Let's keep riding toward the southwest."

"Which way?"

"Left."

"Now how the hell do you arrive at that when we're down in all these trees?" He truly wanted to know.

"Well, I figure . . . I mean, I know, that we came in near the northeast corner. So that means most of the park is laid out to the west and to the south."

"It's the damnedest," Dad said.

As we rode, I thought about all the times I had found myself in the company of someone who was going the wrong way. I usually tried to correct things without offending. I had discovered early on that most people could get very sensitive about being told they were going the wrong way. For example, it could go something like this. We would be traveling north in the car for an hour. The Cascade Mountain range, a towering landmark, would be on our right. Then we would stop for gas. When we were underway again, I would tactfully and most gently say, "Do you notice that the

Cascades are now on the opposite side of the car?" But no matter how carefully it's phrased, telling someone they're lost never goes over well.

"You know your grandma's the same way," Dad said. He was talking about Grandma Anderson. It was as if he had been listening to my thoughts. "It's uncanny how like her you are, Con."

The trail kept widening. "Let's canter our horses through here," I suggested.

Apprehensive, turning in the saddle, he said, "Canter? That sounds pleasant. But Kelly only knows one speed—flat out!"

"She does fly," I agreed. "But she does stop. And that's a very good thing." I had actually become quite fond of Dad's horses. "Let me pass," I suggested. "With Shane out front it might discourage her from bolting." It was a reasonable plan, especially since the trail wasn't quite wide enough for two horses to ride side by side. Agreeing, Dad stopped in the trail and backed Kelly off to the side. That's when his heavy horse stepped back, mashing a rear hoof right into the center of an unfortunate fern growing too close to the trail.

"Ooooh," I groaned. The groan had slipped out before it could be stopped.

Leaning out, searching around his horse to see what was the matter, Dad said, "Now what?"

"It's nothing," I answered, embarrassed to admit compassion for a fern.

"Tell me what's wrong, or we're not taking another step."

Reluctantly, very reluctantly, I admitted, "Only that fern. Kelly stepped on it."

"Geez! Con. Why do you do that to yourself?"

"I can't help it if I'm fond of ferns," I said defensively.

"Well, you should be happy then," Dad said. "Because there are about ten million of 'em in here. Not to mention the other billion trillion in the rest of the state. Now let's forget about the fern and ride."

Maneuvering the paint past Kelly, I said, "This day is like the days we've always dreamed of, right Dad?"

Knowing I was talking about our secret dream farm, he responded, "Damn close, old buddy. Damn close."

"I love you," I said.

"I love you, too," Dad returned. Then he chuckled. "What I'd give to have seen Ma's face when Peppy jumped over that fence." He added, "You'll be sure to get that in the book for us, won't you, Con?"

"Oh, I will," I promised. We frequently bantered about the content of "our" future book.

At the end of a glorious day in Bridle Trails as Shane and I traveled the busy roads back to our pasture, I didn't think much about the traffic. My mind was occupied elsewhere. I was thinking about what a wonderful time Dad and I had riding together and looking forward to the next weekend when we would be riding together again.

CHAPTER SEVENTEEN

Mexico Vacation

It was July in the Arizona desert. We were driving to Mexico for the Horton family's annual summer vacation. The six of us, Dad, Mom, Cher, Wendy, Julie, and me, along with all our vacation paraphernalia, were stuffed into the station wagon. There had been many stops along our way, including Zion and Bryce Canyon National Parks, and the Grand Canyon. However, now we were only a day away from our ultimate destination: a rented trailer on a beach near the Gulf of California coastal town of Guaymas, where Dad also had a deep sea fishing adventure planned. In Mexico we were meeting the Loeffler family. Al and Dad had been class-mates at college. Al was a doctor, his wife, Louise, a nurse. The Loefflers had two sons, Scott who was Cher's age, and Terry, my age. It was Scott who had convinced Cher to attend a boarding school with him in California during her sophomore year.

The car slowed as Dad pulled off the highway, once again, to photo-graph a possibly-never-before-seen desert flower or plant. Our vacations had to be properly documented for friends and the "fellas" back at Boeing. If Dad wasn't taking a picture of an oddly twisted tree, cactus, or flower, it was a distant rock outcropping or cloud formation.

The station wagon didn't have air-conditioning, since it wasn't a re-quirement for Seattle summers. For the little good it did, all the car windows were rolled down. The heat was barely tolerable when we were moving, blown by a hot breeze, but when we were stopped it was suffocating. For the most part those of us waiting in the oven-like car were good sports. Everyone enjoyed Dad's professional quality slide shows when we returned home. This time Mom and one-year-old Julie were the lucky ones, asleep in the front seat. We had given Mom a respite from reading *Treasure Island* out loud to the family. Her soft, lilting voice was a big hit with the whole family, and was especially valued for its soothing quality that instantly put an end to sibling squabbling. However, it was also a delicate instrument that needed frequent breaks. Now, as Dad left the car and the two up front napped, oblivious of the current photo stop, Cher and I were all too conscious and quietly playing dolls with four-year-old Wendy in the back seat.

It was never a quick trot out into the desert to take a snapshot: the masterpiece had to be set up. This would take a while; this was art. First, the Exacta had to be mounted on the tripod, and the tripod lovingly anchored. Then, after much studying of the subject and staring into the camera, Dad would decide he had the wrong lens. The different lenses were kept cleaned and carefully wrapped in the camera case. Often the right lens had the wrong filter. Which filter was best? He had a selection of colors and varying shades of those colors from which to choose. Dad couldn't decide. Then the search for the light meter began. Where was it? Groaning, those of us waiting in the car would watch the methodical search through pant pockets and every hiding place in the camera bag.

"What are the symptoms of heatstroke?" Cher asked.

"Death," I said.

"What's he doing now?" Cher moaned. I had the better view.

"He's still in the filter stage," I said. I knew this even though Dad was fifty feet away because he was hunched over the camera. There was a lot of hunching during the filter stage while he carefully screwed the filters on and off the lens without jiggling the camera, which would have meant having to reframe the composition of the picture.

"What was wrong with the last filter?" Cher asked.

"That was a sky filter, remember? Now he's taking pictures of plants."

"How many plant filters does he have?"

"Lots."

"It's amazing," Cher said, peering past me. "The heat doesn't seem to bother him. Have you noticed? I don't think he even sweats."

"And he never complains about anything," I said. "The food, the room, the road. Have you noticed that?" I turned away with a sigh, needing to pay attention to our play. My Elvis Presley doll was on a date with Wendy's Marilyn Monroe doll.

"He complains about the high cost of everything," Cher added as an afterthought.

"That doesn't count," I said. "Everybody raised during the Depression complains about that."

Dad was talking when he got back in the car. It was as if he had continued our pre-photo conversation without us. "You'll have to make up your mind soon," he was saying. "I'll have to tell them at the school if you aren't coming. Gail will be there. Gary will be there." He was talking about the Wellmans. "You'll know lots of kids there."

We were underway again; the hot breeze was back.

"It's not that," I said.

Cher was oddly quiet on the subject. It was unlike her to be quiet on any subject. Also I had noticed when I made distasteful faces at her, hoping for a measure of commiseration or support, or at least a touch of humor, she would just shrug, as if to say, "I'm out of it. You're on your own." This was very suspicious behavior for my highly opinionated sister. She had obviously made a pact with Dad to keep her mouth shut.

"Then what is the problem?" Dad asked, sounding too concerned. "Help me out here, Con. I really want to know." He was employing every Freudian tactic known. It was all so transparent.

I thought for a few minutes, not answering. What was my problem? More than anything, I worried about how being at boarding school would impact the relationship I had with my horse. Things were working for Shane and me. We had our routine. Anyway, I had asked the paint if he wanted to move to a new pasture, away from his buckskin mare. And guess what? No surprise. He didn't want to go. Dad was quick to say I would be able to visit my horse whenever I wanted. However, I knew that wasn't true. It was merely pacification.

"Well . . . I'm waiting," Dad said.

I was still silent, wanting to explain, but not sure how to express my feelings. Dad didn't know anything about my relationship with my horse. Family members only came to the pasture to drop me off or pick me up. They seldom saw me with Shane. They didn't know or care that a horse has feelings and friends—attachments.

"It's about my friend . . . ," I started to say.

"Okay," Dad said cutting me off. "Explain it to me. I don't get it. You and Karen can't go to the same high school anyway." He didn't have the slightest clue as to what I was talking about.

"It's about my horse . . ."

"Okay. So now it's about your horse."

"When would I have time to see him?" I blurted out passionately. "With all the classes, the studying, the worships, and my job?" I had talked with Cher about her experiences. And I had talked with Gail, who had already attended the academy during her freshman year.

That's when we dropped the subject. Mom was waking up. It was time to get back to the *Treasure Island* pirates.

We met our friends in the early evening after crossing the border at Lukeville. The Loefflers had driven east from San Diego in their camper, towing a small fishing boat. Caravanning through the night to beat the heat of the Sonora Desert, we arrived at Guaymas mid-morning.

Dad and Al checked in at the office. "This is a resort?" Cher whispered. "It looks more like a trailer park and campground to me."

Dad returned jingling keys. "Home sweet home," he said cheerfully, relieved the long drive was over. We waved a temporary good-bye to our friends as they headed to their assigned campsite and we went in search of our trailer.

The one-bedroom trailer had an unpleasant, sour odor that was probably a combination of heat, stale food, and the damp, salty swimsuits of previous occupants. We opened all the windows and turned on the only two fans. The refrigerator was an icebox. Dad went to buy ice and bottled drinking water while we unpacked. Mom, Cher, and I worked quickly in the overheated trailer. Wendy helped by bringing in toys from the car and keeping an eye on Julie. We were machines of efficiency. The beach was our quest.

The Loefflers were already at the beach when the Horton family arrived carrying, it seemed, everything we would need for a week's stay. They had already been swimming, and now Al and Louise were enjoying the shade provided by an expansive, thatched-roofed cabana. "We did a dump and run," Al said almost apologetically, drying his dark hair with a towel, looking refreshed. He was in good shape and very tan from living in California. Even in July, we Northwesterners were pale in comparison.

"I guess boys don't need as much stuff," Dad said, setting down his load. He had said it matter-of-factly. If Dad were jealous of other men's boys, we girls could never tell.

There were other groups of vacationers lounging under the protection of the broad palm-leaf canopy. I noted a nearby snack bar, a volleyball game abandoned in the heat of the day, and a shack on the beach renting floating toys, diving gear, and other sports equipment. The shrewd proprietors had their wares displayed in a most tantalizing manner, spread out on the sand around their shanty. The place was appearing more like a resort every minute.

We staked out a spot beside our friends, continuing an arc of low-slung wooden chairs, facing an expanse of shimmering blue. Our view overlooked a cove with a sandy beach and lapping surf sufficient for play, but nothing worrisome that could pull a child out to sea. Offshore, a small, arid island was a scenic jumble of rocks and cactus.

Something, a body, washed up on shore. It was Scott. At seventeen, he was tall and quite thin, with short, sandy blond hair. He came carrying his swimming fins, facemask lifted above his eyes, dripping wet, and beaming. "What took so long?" he said. "You have to come check out this island." Cher and Scott had catching up to do since they had not seen each other throughout their junior year. I let them walk away. "You, too," Scott beckoned. Terry was waving to us from the island.

"Go ahead," Dad said. "We'll be out in a minute."

He must have meant that he and Al would be out in a minute. It didn't look as if Mom and Louise planned to go anywhere. They had spread a blanket on the sand in front of their chairs and had covered it with toys. Wendy and Julie were already playing with their buckets and shovels right there in the shade. The ladies had reading material, binoculars, the cooler with sodas and snacks next to them, and their chairs positioned to take advantage of the slightest breeze.

It was an easy swim to the island, where we three came ashore on a pebbled beach. "Isn't this too much!" Terry said spreading his arms. I took him to mean all of Mexico, the blue sky, the gentle breeze, not merely the island. Terry was my age, fifteen. He was a cute boy, a towhead like me, with almost white blond hair. Both Scott and Terry had crew cuts and attractive, well-placed cowlicks right in front along the hairline above their foreheads. Terry had a collection of rocks and shells to show me. "I'm not going to take them," he said. "I have these same shells at home." Living near San Diego, the Loefflers spent plenty of time at the beach. "But you can have them if you want."

The sun was intense. Dazzling daggers of light reflected off wet rocks and shot up from tide pools, stabbing my eyes so I could barely see. It was fabulous!

"I hear you're going to boarding school this year," Terry said. He had said it casually as we stood peering down at his treasures, no sell intended.

"Not you, too," I moaned. "So far, that's all I've heard about on this trip."

"Are you?" Terry prompted.

"Maybe. It's sounding more likely all the time. Anyway, I'm only going the one year. If I decide to go, I mean." Five minutes on the beach and I was dry and warming, ready to go back in the water. "What about you? Will you go to the academy with your brother this year?"

"Sure," Terry said. "Why not? All my friends will be there. Do you have a facemask? There's lots of fish around this island."

"Cher has the mask. I'll have to wait my turn."

Time was forgotten as Terry and I explored tide pools. When we got too hot, we swam or lazily floated on our backs, bobbing in the gentle rollers offshore. Dad, Al, Cher, and Scott tirelessly snorkeled, diving and circling the island. Occasionally, Mom, Louise, and the little girls strolled the beach, playing in the surf.

Sometime later in the afternoon, we islanders swam back to shore when a man in a small boat came selling trinkets and shells to the tourists. I held Wendy up to choose a shell. They were much nicer specimens than anything Terry and I had found around the picked-over island. Wendy was sandy from head to toe, and her fine, long blond hair was damp and matted. She was getting heavy, as too many pretty shells to chose from confused her. It quickly became too hot standing around the boat in the sun.

"Only one, Wendy," Dad said, leaning over the boat from the other side. "How's the fishing around here?" Dad asked the man, who smiled broadly, shaking his head up and down in answer to anything that was said to him. He didn't understand a word of English.

Suddenly, not feeling well, I said, "Dad, I'm itching all over."

"You'd better get out of the sun," Dad said, taking Wendy from me. "You look a little pink, and could be dehydrated. Better get something to drink."

"Maybe you should go take a shower," Mom, holding Julie, suggested. "Get out of that wet swimsuit. Put on some lotion."

"Maybe I will." A shower and a change into dry clothes sounded like a good idea. Besides, the trailer wasn't far.

Inside, the trailer was an oven. It felt as if the door had been opened to a blast furnace, even though the fans had been left on and all the windows were wide open. The heat made my face burn hotter. Feeling desperate, I stood in front of one of the laboring antique fans and peeled off my swimsuit. Red skin contrasted with white where the straps had been. The bathroom was stifling, so one of the fans was set on a chair in the open doorway while I showered in the cramped stall.

It was when toweling off that the blisters were first noticed, as I gingerly dried my sore skin, more patting than rubbing. Gasping, I studied my reflection in the mirror. The face staring back was an angry red. What a wreck! I poked my nose. Ouch! I had been sunburned many times, but nothing like this. How could I have let this happen?

Embarrassed and disgusted with myself, I realized returning to the beach was unthinkable. I couldn't swim anyway. The thought of saltwater made me cringe. On fire, I stretched out on a bed with a fan placed on a chair directly in front of my face.

"Anybody home?" Dad called, as he came through the trailer door.

Answering weakly, I said, "In here."

"Aren't you coming back down? We were getting worried."

"I'm too burned."

"It can't be that bad."

"It's that bad."

"Let's see," Dad said, turning on the light. "Well, you knucklehead!" he exclaimed when he saw me. "What did you expect?" It was the "Well, you knucklehead" lecture. I got that a lot. Anyway, the designation "knucklehead" wasn't meant as a put-down; he was merely stating his amazement at the fact.

I interrupted his "you can't stay out in the sun like that . . ." with, "Do you see the blisters?"

"I see them. We'd better get something on this. I'm not sure what Darleen brought in the way of first aid. I'd better go up to the office before it closes to see what they might suggest. Al might have something . . ." And Dad was off.

I spent a miserable night stretched out with one of the fans directly in front of my face. The sunburn cream Dad had located did little to help. Of course, hogging one of the fans was a hardship for everyone else in the hot, crowded trailer.

The next day, Dad and Al were off on their fishing excursion. The rest of us spent the day relaxing at the beach. I stayed under the shade of the cabana, reading a book and listening to the surf. Sometimes Cher was swimming or exploring the island with Scott and Terry; however, more often she was stretched out beside me on the blanket. "You aren't swimming much today," I commented, thinking that maybe the sight of me was dampening her fun.

"You don't mind if I keep you company, do you?"

Seeing my sister, so grown up at seventeen wearing a two-piece swimsuit that accentuated her small waist and shapely legs, I asked, "Do you miss your boyfriends?" It was a casual question tossed over my book.

"No."

Closing the book, I said, "Gee. That sounded harsh." Cher was hard on her suitors. Maybe it was because she had an endless supply. It was impossible to keep track of them all.

"You're always defending them."

"Me and everyone else with a heart." Cher attracted the nicest and most sincere of the good-looking boys. Torturing them, by leading them on and then breaking up with them, was some sort of sick amusement for her. Trifling with affections—that's what it's called. Once, I actually heard her say to Lindy, regarding her boyfriends, "I treat every one badly and then discard them right away." I remembered her exact wording because I had been so impressed with how flippantly yet so aptly she had summed things up.

"They're clingy. I don't like to get too serious. That's all," Cher explained. She added, "Don't look now. But there are a couple of cute Mexican guys over there . . . by the snack bar. I think they're coming our way. They are."

"Hola," one of the young men said. Then, grimacing, he pointed directly at my nose. He was wearing a straw hat, which he removed with some flourish as he sat on the edge of our blanket. "Coke?" he asked, flashing a disarming smile of gorgeous white teeth, and motioning for his more bashful friend, who held out colas for us, to come sit down beside him.

"Espanola?" the friend asked, nodding shyly, handing us sodas. There was something about the way he asked so hopefully if we spoke his language that instantly turned Cher and me into giggling, blushing, teenage girls.

"No speak Spanish," my flustered sister said. Cher had studied French; she had to be kicking herself about that now.

"Uno, dos, tres," I managed to say as soberly as possible between giggles. I had taken Spanish in seventh grade. Now, under pressure, I couldn't remember much. With those captivating brown eyes, and long dark lashes so close to us, we were lucky to remember our own names.

"Bueno! Uno, dos, tres," The one with the hat shook his head sadly. He was mildly mocking me for my limited Spanish by saying with body language, "This is hopeless." Then, pointing to himself, he said, "Ocho."

"That means eight," I informed Cher importantly.

"Ocho," the young man repeated, pointing to himself.

"He's saying his name is Ocho," Cher said. At that point, Cher and I weren't communicating very well in English either.

Our mutual earnest yet vain efforts to understand each other became hysterically funny. We four soon found we weren't very good at charades either—another blow. And that became funny, too. They might have asked us for a date. We might have accepted. However, none of us could tell. Suddenly, it seemed important to expose, for the purpose of playful ridicule, our disappointing ignorance of each other's language. So after some good-natured prodding, Cher began the game with "tacos." That had us all rolling! We were merely being silly, venting frustrations, and making fun of ourselves. Then came my contribution, "mucho tacos." That meant the tacos tasted great, or there were lots of tacos, but I wasn't sure which. When Ocho's turn came, he took a while, thinking hard. He was being dramatic for effect. Then he said, "Coke?" I don't know why, but that had us howling, too, the implication being that he had rehearsed that one word of English just prior to approaching us.

"What's so funny?" Mom asked. She stood over us smiling, hands on hips, truly wanting to know.

"Their English is funny!" Cher said accusingly, pointing directly at Ocho, who toppled sideways on the blanket, clutching his heart, wounded to the core.

"Well, I hate to break up the party," Mom said, "but it's time to meet the boat." We were all driving to greet Dad and Al when their fishing boat came in at the pier.

Ocho and his friend understood we had to leave when Cher and I reluctantly stood and began gathering our things. Saying good-bye was awkward; we didn't know if we would see them again. Ocho said something, solemnly, in Spanish, and held out his hat to Cher. When she only appeared confused, he pressed his hat into her hand. Delighted, she accepted the hat. Then the guys were gone.

I wasn't allowed to step out from under the shade of the cabana until I had donned the oversized white cotton shirt Dad had found for me the night before. Cher insisted I wear Ocho's hat for protection to walk the few steps to the waiting car; I thought it a generous sacrifice. Even covered, being out in the heat of the sun and riding in the hot car was painful on my burned skin. Wendy was unhappy she couldn't sit on my lap in the crowded car, and Julie, eager to take her place, thought we were playing when she was passed back to Cher several times.

At the dock, which wasn't far, the boat was already there, and Dad and Al's Pacific sailfish were strung up, hanging by their tails. Both men were excited about their catch. Dad's fish weighed 115 lbs. and Al's weighed 110. It was a small but significant difference. We took lots of pictures for the guys back at Boeing. Now Dad and Al had to decide what to do with so much fish. Finally it was decided to give the Mexican fishermen one, and have the other canned or smoked. Both men leaned toward smoked. Dad's concern, causing much hesitation and vacillation, was that smoked fish might spoil before making it home to Seattle—and the guys back at Boeing. To help settle the matter, we all assured him of our cooperation to keep it well iced. Still it was evident on our drive back to the resort that Dad wasn't completely at rest with his decision about smoked or canned, as he kept counting the days until we left Mexico, and counting the days we would be on the road driving home.

Around the campfire that evening, at the Loeffler's campsite, we listened to wildly enthusiastic recounts of the day's adventure. Dad and Al's faces glowed in the firelight as they reeled in their trophies time after time for Scott and Terry, who were spellbound. As the evening wore on, stories turned to plans to take the eager boys fishing the next day. We could tell Dad was disappointed there wouldn't be enough room on Al's small boat for Cher and me to come along. However, Cher and I were secretly relieved. I say "secretly" because we didn't dare say that we didn't want to go, which, ultimately, wouldn't have gotten us out of going anyway, and which surely would have launched Dad's favorite philosophical debate, "How can you know that you don't want to go until after you've already gone?" Dad needn't have fretted, as his fishing buddy wouldn't have him disappointed for anything. "No problem!" Al said beaming. "We simply take the girls out the next day. That just means . . . more fishing for us!" Our Dad was so excited by Al's offer. Fishing in Mexico would be a life experience for his girls! Hurray! Hurray! Forgotten was my whole-body burn and Cher's notorious motion sickness.

The next day, while the men folk were off on their adventure, Ocho's straw hat accompanied the ladies on a shopping trip to Guaymas. The hat went everywhere Cher and I went; it was our prize.

* * *

There are two kinds of seasickness. There is the classic vomiting, wish-you-were-dead kind that the word "sick" could never describe. And then there is the seasickness that afflicts the rest of us. It's called "sick-of-the-seasick." The difference between the two being "suffering" as opposed to "long-suffering." The sick-of-the-seasick symptoms are hypersensitive hearing, an acute, almost primal, wolflike sense of smell, and a hellish headache.

So there we were having our life experience, communing with the elements, adrift on a rolling sea, and exposed to the fireball raging overhead. By the time Dad, Al, Cher, and I had motored out to the fishing grounds in Al's small boat, my sunburn had me banished to under the canvas canopy, and Cher was so sick even Dad was moved by compassion and ready to turn back. Then they struck! And what a bonanza! We were in the middle of a churning school of tuna. All thoughts of turning back were joyously abandoned by both men in their rush to reel in their catch. We couldn't blame them. Leaving the *idea* of fish was one thing; leaving actual fish was quite another.

So now Cher and I found ourselves together, forward, as tucked out of the way as we could be. We were under the canvas trapped next to a reeking gas can and surrounded by foul fishing gear, and bobbing and pitching on a boat so small we could have reached out to touch the legs of the two giddy men at the stern. "You look sick," Cher said again, sitting back down between hanging-over-the-side retching episodes. "Are you sure you're not sick?"

"Oh, I'm sick all right," I said, grimly. "It's just a different kind of sick." And then, "Watch out!" I exclaimed. A tuna, just landed, was flopping around in the bottom of the boat. That meant another deathblow was imminent. Cher and I turned our backs and hunched protectively over Ocho's already blood-spattered straw hat.

*　*　*

It came to pass one evening that delicious, slightly salty, slightly sweet, moist and tender smoked sailfish was delivered to the Loeffler's camp. It arrived in boxes, on ice, and was immediately divided between two coolers. There was a lot, 30 lbs. for each man.

"Wow!" Dad exclaimed. "I didn't know there would be so much!"

"It smells wonderful," Mom said. "Let's have a taste."

"Yes!" we all agreed, "let's do!"

Everyone was given a generous sample, to a chorus of oohs and aahs. We weren't sure, but we thought none of us had ever tasted sailfish before. "Let's have more," Mom said. Whereupon, a flattered Dad handed out another sample around the campfire. It wasn't lost on any of us that it was a much smaller portion than the portion we had been given before.

When we got back to our trailer that same evening, we five females wanted another sample before bed. "Not on your life!" Dad said. We understood his concern was only that there would be ample for all his friends back at Boeing. However, we achieved our bites by suggesting to Dad that he should check on his bounty. Maybe it needed to be rewrapped from too much pawing, or maybe more ice needed to be applied.

The next day, before lunch, we asked for fish. It was the perfect appetizer. Then we wanted more. "You don't want to make a meal of it," Dad said to no one listening. After lunch, it was the same. After all, it was the perfect dessert, light and sweet. Then we wanted more. "It's a taste, not a meal," Dad admonished. Before and after dinner was the same—always five to one in favor. Our appetite was enormous. Most likely the hot climate fueled our desire for the salty treat.

A few days, and surely many pounds of Dad's trophy later, when it came time to pack the car for the long trip back to Washington State, we females made sure the cooler was accessible at the rear of the station wagon. Dad was hesitant, as well as suspicious about this strategic placement. We got him to agree by suggesting that it was the only sensible location since he would need to access the cooler often to add ice as we journeyed home. Then, once underway, as we drove the long barren stretches to the border, we females feigned delight at our discovery that our wise cooler placement was also so convenient for the many times during the day that we voted—five to one in favor—for Dad to pull to the side of the road so he could go back to get us all another nibble. Dad's defensive tactics included calling our incessant pleadings "bellyaching," which was very bad. However, even that didn't restrain us.

It was on the drive home, somewhere between San Diego and San Francisco, that Dad brought up the subject of school again. "Say, Con," he began. Whenever Dad introduced his statements with the gentle word "say" his family knew that something serious and well thought out was about to follow. He instantly had our attention. "Well," Dad continued, "I've been giving a lot of thought to your concerns about school and your horse."

"So," I prompted.

"And Darleen and I have been talking about it, too."

"So," I prompted again.

"Well . . . we've been thinking it might be fun for you to do something special with your horse before you go."

"Like what?"

"Maybe a pack trip. You know. A trail ride."

Dad had been listening! "You mean like riding the Oregon Trail?" I said hopefully, with the beginnings of excitement in my tone.

"Whoa there!" Dad said quickly. "We're not talking about a multi-state, extended expedition here."

"Then what?"

"Well . . . I remember one of the engineers went on a pack trip last summer. Gosh! I should remember; he talked about it for months after . . . said it was the best thing he ever did. Let's see . . . I'm sure he said it was somewhere near Mount Rainier. Somewhere near Cascade Mountain Ski Resort, I think he said. I can ask him about it when we get home . . . If you want," he added.

"Sure!" I said enthusiastically.

"Then help me out here, Con. I'm trying to give you an opportunity. Believe me, you'll love it."

The lure of the trail ride was strong. A trail ride in exchange for one year at the academy. A trail ride in the high Cascades!

"So this is it then," Dad prompted. "Last call."

A decision about boarding school had to be made. "Okay," I said at last. "Okay. I'll go. But it's only for one year."

We celebrated my decision with fish. By that point, we pretty much celebrated everything with fish. A fine sunset, a good hamburger, another hundred miles up the road—all called for the sweet, salty treat.

It happened somewhere between San Francisco and Portland. We heard Dad's tragic moan when he opened the cooler at one of our stops. There would be no triumphant return for Dad at Boeing. It was so shocking and so unthinkable that we all piled out of the car to see for ourselves. It was true. Despite all our efforts and frequent icing between layers, all that was left of our treasure, at least fifteen pounds of heavenly manna, was irretrievably spoiled.

CHAPTER EIGHTEEN

Trail Ride

The day promised to be a warm one, but for the moment I had the car window on my side rolled up, wishing Dad would do the same. We drove along the cool forest floor slowly approaching the winding climb that would take us to Cascade Mountain Resort. We'd been driving for more than an hour, with a rented horse trailer bouncing and clanking along behind. Trees and thick underbrush formed a wall on both sides of the two-lane roadway.

"I want you to know how much I appreciate your respecting my judgment regarding boarding school," Dad was saying.

I was thinking please, please, don't let this be yet another recital of the limitless benefits of attending boarding school. "Sure," I answered curtly, suppressing an ill-humored snarl. "Maybe you could roll up your window for me then." I tried to console myself with the same worn-out words I'd been repeating to myself for a month: "After all, it's only for one year." I'd come to particularly detest that one, and rarely called upon it anymore. The current favorites: "I'll make it through somehow," distinctly dismal, yet possessing an appealing dramatic quality, and, "Maybe it won't be that bad." This last was definitely the most hopeful of the three.

"That trailer sure is a rattletrap," Dad said, rolling up his window. Then, returning to the subject at hand, he said, "I know you'll like it." Yep.

Here he goes, I'm thinking. Unprompted by any show of interest from me, he continued. "It will be the experience of a lifetime for you. Some of my fondest memories and closest friends came out of the time I spent at the academy."

Interrupting, I said, "Is that the one where you pedaled your bike twenty miles through rain and sleet every day, Dad?" I felt instant remorse for what I had said, and especially for the flippant tone in which I'd said it. He was an easy target for hurtful remarks—the people who love you always are.

"Five miles," Dad corrected, flashing a patient grin. "Yes. That's the one."

Why don't you give the poor man a break? I scolded myself. If I was going to the academy merely to please my father, couldn't I be a decent sport about it? Yet, even while resolving to project a sunnier attitude, I heard myself lament, "I'll probably have to start studying again." Then launching a second more successful effort, I informed him cheerfully, "I'll be taking driver's ed."

Dad sighed. "I hope you're a better driver than your sister."

"Who wouldn't be?"

Sunlight filtering through the treetops made shimmering patterns on the roadway. I'd seen a black bear on this particular stretch before so I was keeping a watchful eye.

"I can't understand why Big Mike continues to let her drive," Dad said. "A brand new Cougar, no less."

He had been merely commenting, not expecting any particular response; however, I offered my thoughts on the subject anyway. "Because Walt was so much worse. That's probably why. At least Cher asks to borrow the car. He appreciates that. And even with all her accidents, she's never had a ticket."

"That's no excuse," Dad said, shaking his head.

Shrugging, I said, "I don't know." Then, recalling a vision of Daddy Mike grabbing angrily for Cher's heels as she barely escaped out her basement bedroom window, I added thoughtfully, "Maybe you have to give up a part of your rational self when you raise five teenagers."

"That could be," Dad allowed.

I glanced back at the pounding trailer and wondered how Shane was surviving this ride, then turned back around. There wasn't anything that could be done about it anyway. "Trailer okay?" Dad asked, craning his neck to see. "I sure hope you have a good time. I wonder what kind of trail horse Shane will be."

"He'll be great, Dad," I assured him enthusiastically. "After all, he was a ranch horse before I met him."

"So they said." Dad sounded underwhelmed.

We were fast approaching a gas station and grocery store combination situated all alone in the trees up ahead, a last chance to use the ladies room. "Dad, Dad!" I cried. "Can't we stop?" Before the words were out we had already passed it.

"You don't want to be late, do you?" Dad asked sheepishly.

"Why couldn't we stop?" I pouted. "That's irritating, Dad." We drove in silence until I said, "Cher didn't like boarding school all that much."

"She was homesick was her problem. She should have gone to a school here in the Northwest."

"I'm just as glad she didn't like it," I said.

"Truthfully, so am I," Dad admitted. "Or she might have stayed on in California."

"California never would have been the same," we said in unison, then laughed in unison as well.

We were climbing out of the trees into bright sunlight, the scenery changing around each bend. "It's beautiful," I said softly.

"Yes, it is," Dad agreed. "Breathtaking."

On our left, the steep rock walls were adorned with slender waterfalls cascading down from melting snow packs high above. The fading wildflowers of late summer clung to narrow ledges and flowed in muted colors from every crack and crevice. I searched for the orange brilliance of Indian paintbrush among asters and bluebells. All the while ahead of us and to our right was a vast changing panorama of mountains and rocky peaks. Dark carpets of forest spread down the mountainsides. The river below was a ribbon of blue. As we twisted our way through the mountains, majestic Mount Rainier, snow-covered year round, appeared, disappeared, and reappeared again. Sometimes we could see the mountain, sometimes not, sometimes it was in front of us, and sometimes behind.

"At this elevation the leaves are already starting to turn," Dad said, pointing to a colorful splash of vine maple clinging to an outcropping of rocks. Rolling down his window halfway, he glanced in my direction to see if I would mind. The air rushing in smelled fresh. Cracking my window an inch, I wondered, where are those sunglasses? The trailer was riding more smoothly now on the uphill grade.

"You'll meet lots of Christian boys," Dad said, looking over at me with a mischievous smirk and raised eyebrows.

With little interest I said, "How exciting."

"You'll care soon enough."

"So everyone keeps saying."

"I don't understand why boys like you," Dad said, shaking his head.

Trying to explain, I said, "I'm not mean to them. I don't dislike them. They just get in my way."

"Meaning?"

"Meaning, I'm always stumbling over them." I didn't care to be discussing boys with my dad, so I quickly changed the subject. "By the way, your roses were spectacular this year." It was said with honest feeling; his roses were special every year. "Those yellow ones always seem to smell best."

"The Oregold, the bright yellow ones?"

"No. I'm talking about that big bush out front. You know," I prodded. "The one with the creamy yellow roses."

"The Peace bush," Dad nodded. "We're making pretty good time. It's not far now."

Thinking of a question I'd never asked him before, I said, "How long were you in the navy, Dad?"

"Just two years. I enlisted in 1944 when I was seventeen."

I visualized my handsome father in his dress whites. I had a treasured photograph of him taken in front of his barrack. He was down on one knee, his white sailor hat pushed back rakishly, a cocky smile on his face. He had been a tail gunner on a Martin PBM Mariner, a giant, slow-moving plane built for long distances and water landings. He'd just missed the war. "Thank you, God," I whispered at the thought of it.

Dad pulled into a turnout allowing a string of cars to pass. "Should we check on Shane?" I asked anxiously.

"We'd better wait," Dad said, watching for a chance to pull back into traffic. "We're almost there anyway." We pulled out slowly, hoping no car would speed around the tight curve. The heavy horse trailer followed reluctantly. There was a foot-thick stonewall and a sheer drop on one side, and high cliffs on the other. A sign read WATCH OUT FOR FALLING ROCKS.

"I'm sure going to miss the little girls," I said, sighing. "Let's sing "Strawberry Roan," Dad," I suggested. Humming our key, away we went.

Walkin' round town just spendin' my time,

out of a job, not earnin' a dime.

When this feller steps up, and he says, "I suppose,

you're a bronc rider by the looks of your clothes."

Well, he guesses me right.

"I'm a good one," I claim.

"Do you happen to have any bad ones to tame?"

Singing, we finally reached the summit, slowing to watch for signs of horses among the chalets and around the ski lodge, now closed for the summer. A chairlift appeared out of place strung up a barren brown slope.

"There they are!" I exclaimed, pointing off to our left. Dad turned into the gravel parking lot. A white Cadillac with a fancy horse trailer attached blocked our view of the corral. Also on the lot were two old pickup trucks and a horse-hauling truck three times their size. To our right, at a distance, was a wooden structure with a wide, covered porch where a few people were gathered, and behind that, a house trailer. Dad pulled alongside the extra fancy blue and white horse trailer with "Gates Arabians" painted in script on the side. Eager to check on Shane, I was out of the car even before it came to a complete stop, but a man approaching stopped me midway.

"You Connie?" the man asked. He was a grandfatherly sort, with thinning pure white hair.

"Yes, I'm Connie."

"We need your gear right away so the packhorses can get a head start," the man explained. He wore baggy jeans held up by suspenders. As Dad was getting out of the car, the man told him, "I'll need your daughter's gear right away."

"Everything is right here in the back," I said, turning reluctantly. Shane would have to wait.

"You two okay here?" Dad asked, opening the rear of the station wagon for us. "I'd better check in at the office." And off he went, checkbook in hand.

"Here, let me give you a hand with that saddle," the man said. We'd had to purchase a saddle for the trip; it had been on the "required" list. "There. Your sleeping bag and that pack, that's all I need." I had to hurriedly sort through things to find the sack lunch, canvas bag, and sweater that would go with me on Shane. Everything else would go with the packhorses. "The name's Stan." He was waiting while I searched the pack for sunglasses. "I'll be seeing you tonight at camp." He added, "Hope you're not one of those picky eaters."

"Not me!"

"Well, we shouldn't have any problems then," the man laughed. "Like chili?"

"If it's hot."

"Oatmeal?"

Handing him the pack, I said, "My favorite!"

He was pleased. "You'll enjoy the ride," he cast over his shoulder, hurrying away.

"Glad to see someone else has brought their own horse," a woman was saying when I finally rounded the back of the horse trailer. The woman was about my height, with short, thick gray hair. She wore a stylish Western outfit with all the trappings, and held a quirt in her hand.

I couldn't help but exclaim, "What wonderful boots!" Her cowboy boots were white leather with bright red and blue designs on the toe. The quirt she held was also white leather. "Could you help me?" I asked, struggling with the trailer latch. It was a rusted, jerry-rigged affair. "I can't seem to raise it by myself."

The woman scowled down at my moccasin-clad feet. "Where are your boots?" she demanded.

"I forgot all about them," I said, looking down at my feet while I lied. "They must be loaded on the packhorses by now." Though boots were also "required," I had no intention of wearing them.

"Dangerous riding without boots," the woman muttered to herself.

"I hear you!" I called from inside the trailer. "Watch out below!" The paint backed down the gangway, groping blindly on sea legs . . . clomp, clomp, crash, slide. "There you are," I said to him and rubbed his neck reassuringly. "Bet you didn't enjoy that ride."

"Don't see too many paints," the woman said, but made no further comment.

Pointing to a grove of trees, I told her, "I'm going to take him down there into the shade." The woman followed, turning at the corral. Reaching the shady area, thinking it was a good place to organize my gear and saddle my horse, I tethered Shane loosely to a bush. He immediately lowered his head to inspect the unfamiliar vegetation. "You wait here," I told him. "I'll be right back." He wasn't well tied, but I only planned to be gone a minute to retrieve my things, and he would never be out of sight. Turning, I saw Dad, ready to head home, waving from beside the car. I started his way. He'd have a long drive home alone with that rattling trailer. Drawing closer, I studied my dad as he stood by the car with his hands stuffed into his back pockets. Somehow, that familiar stance of his always gave him a vulnerable quality. Makes you shudder to ever disappoint him, I thought, promising myself again to truly excel at boarding school. I would make him proud. He'll sure be unhappy when he finds those boots, though, crossed my mind.

"All paid up and squared away," Dad said. "Everything under control here?"

"I guess so."

"Here's your hat." He handed me the hat, which was also on the list mailed to us of items needed for the trip.

"Oh gosh! Thanks, Dad. I must have forgotten it in the car."

"Sure," he said, shaking his head. "And where are your new boots?"

"Down by Shane," I quickly lied. I hated to lie, but it was no use worrying him every minute. Parents would drive themselves crazy if you let them.

"Need any help with this saddle?"

"I can handle it."

He shuffled his feet, looking lost. "You know if anything should happen we're only a phone call away."

"I'll never forget this, Dad. Shane either. I guess I'm about the luckiest girl alive."

Dad reached out to touch the fancy horse trailer parked beside us, and in an almost caressing fashion, traced the lettering slowly with his fingers. "I wish I could give you girls more," he said softly, apologetically, his gaze wandering somewhere beyond me. "If I'd been a doctor," he began. It was a lament I had heard before. His choice to study engineering over medicine had been an issue of economics—medical school was too expensive.

Cutting in to finish the sentence for him, "You'd have been the best doctor in the whole world, and your girls would all be horribly spoiled brats! Besides," I gave him a quick kiss as he slid behind the wheel, "Everybody knows doctors don't have much free time to spend with their families."

"That might be true," he allowed thoughtfully. "Well, I guess I'll see you back here in a couple of days. Then it's off to the academy." He hesitated. "You do understand why I want this for you, don't you?"

"Sure, Dad, I understand." And I did. "I'm looking forward to it," I lied. "I know I make a lot of jokes about it, but mostly I'm just kidding. I'm sure it will be fun . . . I mean, uplifting and all that."

"Okay, then. See you Sunday at noon. I love you."

"I love you too, Dad. Drive carefully!" There it was, that weird lump in my throat. I always got that same odd lump in my throat whenever I watched my dad drive away.

Now, hefting the saddle, which was surprisingly heavy, I staggered off in Shane's direction, dragging the leather straps behind in the dirt. I didn't get any further than the corral, when a horse there distracted me. The saddle was dropped on a patch of grass near the corral fence. "What an incredibly beautiful horse!" I exclaimed to the gray-haired woman I'd met earlier.

"Yes. He truly is," she agreed, patting her horse lovingly. "He's a full-blooded Arabian stallion."

I reached out to touch the horse tentatively; one was wise to use caution with stallions. "What's his name?"

"Oh, you could never pronounce it," she said, searching for something in her saddlebag. "We call him Sky Rocket for short." She gave me a sugar cube to offer him.

The horse sniffed my hand. "Does he bite?"

"Not this sweetheart," she said, giving her horse an affectionate stroke along his neck. "He's as gentle as a lamb." I held out the sugar cube confidently, and Sky Rocket very graciously took it from my palm. I stroked his nose, and scratched between his ears. He had huge, gentle, brown eyes. The horse was all brown, a rich chocolate brown, with a wavy mane that fell below his thick neck, and a wavy tail that almost touched the ground. "Willis thinks I'm a crazy old fool to be riding 'rambunctious' here, on this trip," the woman confided, glancing around quickly. And at that moment, her horse bobbed his head as if in hearty agreement with what Willis had said. We stood together contentedly petting and admiring her horse. "Willis is my husband," she explained. "I just want Sky Rocket to get some exercise before winter sets in, that's all. He has *so* much energy." She put a lot of emphasis on the "so." Then, "You haven't saddled your horse yet," she said accusingly, peering past my shoulder.

I turned to see Shane standing behind me with the tattered bush dragging from the end of his lead. "Shane!" I said sternly. "Aw, now that's sad," I moaned. Feeling very guilty, I tossed the plant aside. I was feeling displeased with myself because Northwesterners are taught to be respectful of fragile mountain plants.

"You'd better saddle up," the woman was saying.

"I'm not sure how to get this saddle on," I said. "I've always ridden bareback."

"You must spend a lot of time on the ground then," the woman said, not unkindly. "That's not a very safe way to ride."

"What's going on here?" a man asked. "Why aren't we ready?"

"Willis!" The woman turned. "Can you believe this? This girl doesn't know how to saddle her horse."

"I'll tend to it, Miriam," the man said waving her aside.

Willis was of medium height, with the slightest beginning of a paunch. He wore a short-sleeved white shirt, fitted corduroy pants tucked into high-top English-style riding boots, and a tweed cap.

Standing over my saddle, Willis said, "I love her dearly, but Miriam literally lives and breathes horses." We looked toward where she stood with her back to us absorbed in brushing the stallion's mane. "And I can barely tolerate the creatures," he sighed under his breath, as if he were speaking more to himself than to me. Lifting the red blanket, he spread it over Shane's back, carefully smoothing out any lumps with his hands. Then he turned back to the saddle and said, "You get on the left side of the saddle, and drape all these straps over . . . like this."

As he raised the saddle, slinging it up onto Shane's back expertly, I had to ask the obvious question. "Why did you come on this ride if you don't like horses?"

"What?" The man sounded put off, as if I had eavesdropped on his private thoughts. "Oh. You'll understand such things someday when you're married." He paused to ponder his wife so absorbed in brushing her horse. "Besides, when Miriam told me she was riding Sky Rocket," he whispered, wiggling the saddle into position, "I couldn't help myself. I had to see it with my own eyes. Hearing about it later would never have been the same." And, chuckling to himself, "With my stories, I'll be the toast of the cocktail circuit for years."

Now the man stood by instructing while I worked to get the cinch strap tight. "There's no mystery to it," Willis was saying, "simply take the time to do it right." The man had said he couldn't tolerate horses, but his manner suggested he'd put in a lot of time around them. The new leather was so stiff that all the pulling and tugging made my hands ache. Still, in spite of my Apache alter-ego misgivings, I was enjoying the smell of the leather and the creaking sounds it made. "You're getting it," the man encouraged me. "One more pull." When I finally reached to take the stirrup from the saddle horn, Willis raised a hand to stop me.

"Not finished?"

"Not quite, young lady. Now we give your horse a breather for a few minutes. Then we'll tighten that cinch one more time."

The next few minutes were spent productively checking each of Shane's hooves for stones or loose shoes. The sun was warm on the back of my neck as I worked; we were lucky to have such fine weather. Then, after digging through the canvas saddlebag, I gave Shane a piece of apple. My decision to purchase a light canvas bag from the army-navy store had paid off. The old canvas bag was soft and easy to dig through, and held more things than the traditional leather saddlebags. Miriam's stiff leather bags might look nicer but, for the money, I'd gotten the better bargain. Lastly, the bridle slipped on easily, even though while putting it on, as usual, the paint gave me several playful nudges. His soft ears were gently pulled through the straps and his fur was scratched under the leather. "What do you think of all this, big boy?" I whispered in his ear. My friend twitched his ears, bringing his head down close to my lips as I spoke. Tucking the halter and lead into the bag, I wondered where was that hat?

Willis caught hold of my arm. "Where are you off to?"

"In search of my hat."

"Let's finish up here first," he said.

Shane stood patiently. "Horses are stupid but smart," Willis explained. "When they're saddled, they fill their lungs with air. Then, after you've finished cinching them, they expel the air and you end up with a loose saddle. That means your saddle could slip sideways, or even under the horse's belly—with you in it." He said this last with great emphasis, searching my eyes to make sure he had my total attention, and that I understood. No way did I want a slipping saddle! "Your best insurance against that happening," the man continued, "is this!" He brought his knee up fast and hard under Shane's chest, giving him a sound punch. The paint whipped his head around, ears flattened, a "What was that for?" expression on his startled face. "Now, retighten your cinch and you're ready to go."

After Willis had gone I tried and struggled with all my might, but the cinch was already as tight as it was going to get. Putting the stirrup down, there was still a nagging worry about a slipping saddle. "Did you expel all your air?" I asked, eyeing my horse suspiciously. Imagining myself hanging upside-down under his belly made me vow to check and recheck the cinch, and always, but always, punch Shane, even if he didn't like it. Just to be certain.

CHAPTER NINETEEN

At last we were all in line and ready to ride. Introductions had been made, pictures taken. During the introductions, I had respectfully endured a lecture concerning my missing boots. Luther, our host and trail guide, said "in front of witnesses" that he couldn't be responsible for the safety of his guests if they weren't wearing the required equipment. Good thing I had the hat.

When we had first mounted, Willis adjusted my new saddle's stirrups to the proper length. "Hi, down there!" I called to Shane. It was a reach to pat his neck. I wasn't used to a saddle and it felt strange sitting up so high off my horse.

At my request, Shane and I were second to last in a line of eight; it seemed to me the best position from which to watch the other riders. I was only able to secure second to last because placing a guest last was unthinkable. It was a safety procedure. Luther was in the lead, riding a lanky Appaloosa. He had provided all the horses except for Miriam's and mine. Luther had a full dark beard, and was of medium height and weight. His clothes were well worn, his cowboy hat sweat-stained and dusty. Behind Luther was his twelve-year-old son, Sunny Jim, seated on a large, heavy-framed, black and white gelding. The boy had blond hair cropped close, a freckled face, and bright blue eyes. After Sunny Jim came Sara, a dark-haired eight-year-old, followed by her father, Art, a pharmacist from Olympia. Sara, who wore her hair in two braids, was seated on a buckskin mare. Her father, a slight man, wore glasses and had a camera and a pair of binoculars hanging from his saddle horn. He was riding a bay gelding, a brown horse with black stockings and a black mane and tail. Miriam was fifth in line, if you could call it that—her high-spirited horse, prancing this way and that, neck arched and tail held high, wasn't one to stay in line. I waved to the woman once when she was turned my way, but she was too preoccupied to return the greeting. Behind her, and directly in front of me, Willis was sitting smugly, very smugly, on an all-but-dozing, small, brown mare. He also had a camera and binoculars. Jessie, a seventeen-year-old, summer trail hand, was behind me bringing up the rear. He was riding a palomino gelding.

We began our trail ride on a dirt road that ran behind base camp. I had worn the hat a short time, and was now holding it on my lap unsure of what to do with it. "I think I might be able to solve your problem with that hat," Jessie called out from behind. I turned to see the flash of an amused smile.

"So can I," I said, pretending to launch the hat unceremoniously.

"You could put it on your head," Jessie suggested. The young man had almond-shaped brown eyes that turned into half moons when he smiled.

"Then I can't think," I complained, sidestepping the true and unspeakable reason—hats flattened my bangs and messed up my long hair. It was a girl thing.

"I'll tie a string to it for you when we stop for lunch," Jessie offered. "If you want." He demonstrated his offer's potential, flipping his hat off onto his back, revealing thick, wavy, auburn hair.

"That's neat!" I said. "Thanks."

Right away, Shane was walking faster than Willis's horse. He wanted to creep close, crowding. When I tried to make him keep to the slower pace, he stubbornly stretched out his neck and sped up. To make matters worse, Willis's horse was a mare. So if I let him, he would have walked along, mindlessly smitten, with his head resting on her rump. And mares, I knew, had little patience with that kind of wishful thinking. I had to hold him back. "Aw, let him go for it," Willis suggested. "He'll learn once he's been kicked in the head a few times." Oh great! I thought. I wasn't too concerned about my hardheaded horse, only his quick and violent bucking response.

Miriam, also having issues with her horse, left the line to race ahead.

The rest of us kept our pace, following the dirt road and then turning to cross the main paved highway. There we picked up a trail bordered by tall grasses and bunches of wildflowers. Very soon, however, we left that pleasant trail, which satisfied itself winding aimlessly amid the ski resort and surrounding chalets, to begin a slow, steady climb up the rocky ski slope. Luther had pointed Miriam in the general direction of our climb, and she was already high above us, her stallion prancing up the steep slope sideways. Shane, on the other hand, was laboring up the sharp incline, lagging further and further behind Willis's sturdy steed, an experienced mountain horse. Rather than fall any further behind, I decided to jump down from my horse.

"What are you doing?" Jessie reined in, disapproval in his eyes.

"I'm going to walk a ways," I said curtly, wishing no discussion.

"It's awfully steep."

"That's okay," I answered flatly.

"Don't listen to her, Jess," Sunny Jim called back. "She just doesn't want her spoiled, lazy, stable horse to have to carry her up this hill."

"He's big and strong," Jessie assured me, shaking his head.

"Leave me alone!" I cried to everyone defensively. "I'll walk whenever I choose!"

"I told you!" Sunny Jim called back.

"Pipe down!" Luther admonished his son.

"Maybe I don't want my horse to have a heart attack carrying me up this hill," I explained to all. "Is there anything wrong with that?" I had seen horses run themselves to death in more than one Western. "Besides, my friend and I came on this trip to enjoy ourselves, not to impress certain people!" I turned, glaring pointedly at Jessie.

My moccasin-clad feet took a few moments adjusting to the rocky ground, but were soon comfortably underway. Shane followed in his usual manner, more over me than behind. I consoled myself with the amazing fact that he had never once stepped on me. Fallen on me, yes, stepped on me, no. Now Shane and I were able to keep up with the other horses, as this was a grueling climb even for them. Pant, puff, and blow. Were we halfway yet? I gazed up to our far off-goal. Miriam was nowhere in sight. No, there she was, starting back down from the top. Sky Rocket was coming down sideways in that elegant gait, the same way he had gone up. Watching the stallion, mesmerized, was taking a toll on my soft-clad feet. I stumbled twice and stepped on the sharp edge of several rocks. Ouch! Still, I couldn't take my eyes off the magnificent horse dancing down the slope toward us, so sure-footed; he reminded me of the beautiful Gillette, my only other experience with an Arabian. As Miriam drew near, I saw that her face was flushed, while Wonder Horse hadn't broken a sweat.

"Try racing him back up the hill," Luther suggested.

"I guess I've no choice," Miriam agreed, mopping her forehead with a brightly colored hankie. "He's having fun," she told us. "That's the purpose." She looked over at Willis. "Don't you think he's having fun?"

"It's only the beginning of a long ride," her husband gave dubious encouragement. "He'll tire."

Miriam gulped and turned her horse. The stallion was delighted; he was definitely having fun.

Meanwhile, Shane and I, along with all the other horses, trudged on. It seemed incredible that this rocky grade would be covered with snow and skiers within a few short months. And I would be at boarding school. The unpleasant thought was quickly pushed aside. There would be no brooding on this trip. No regrets. "This time is just for us," I whispered to the paint, so close. The gear house, which marked the end of the chairlift, was only a short distance away. Surely it marked the end of this climb.

When Shane and I crested the hill, cool breezes rewarded us. Jessie's palomino came over the rise right behind. "That's quite a climb," he commented, dismounting. "Even for *our* horses." He was being nice, making amends.

"It was quite a climb, all right," I agreed, smiling. He was forgiven. My eyes followed the line of chairs downward to the distant ski lodge and beyond to the towering mountains that dwarfed the valley. "And a thirsty one."

Jessie held out his canteen. "Here, take a swig."

"Thank you," I said.

The other riders were strolling along the hilltop, leading their horses and taking in the view. Art, who had been snapping pictures in every direction, was coming our way. "Glad we came," Art said, wrapping an arm around Sara, pulling her close.

"You two look like a picture," I said, taking the man's camera.

Soon Luther clapped his hands to get our attention. "Everyone accounted for?" Riders, leading horses, had spread out along the windswept ridge. "We have a distance to go before lunch. Let's mount up."

"May I ride back with Jessie?" Sunny Jim asked his father hopefully. Sunny Jim looked exactly like the towheaded, baby-faced boy whose picture was on the Sunny Jim Peanut Butter jar label.

"No," Luther answered decidedly. "I think you two can get along without each other's company for one days ride."

It was a challenge to get back up on Shane, gracefully, that is. I was becoming aware of a flaw in the design of the saddle: the shorter the legs of the rider, the higher the stirrups were situated on the horse. Noticing Jessie watching me, I turned my horse away so he couldn't see my clumsy mount.

We formed into our already familiar line, minus Miriam and her horse. Perhaps they had gone on ahead. This is more like it, I thought, as we traveled a more level section of trail. Spectacular country surrounded us. And for the moment anyway, Shane was following Willis's mare at a respectful distance. It was time to relax. Reaching down, I patted Shane's neck, which from the saddle was quite a reach. Riding bareback, stroking my horse's neck as we rode was a frequent and unconscious act. Now it was an all-too-conscious effort. Well, I would just have to get used to it.

Thinking about the saddle had me wondering how much this trip cost. A bundle no doubt. We had to buy this saddle, the boots, this hat. At least the boots could be returned. And I knew it was going to cost big bucks for me to attend the academy. Dad had gladly paid for Cher. He might have spent his money more wisely, I thought. Cher had been on the telephone, long distance, every other week of the school year, crying, demanding to come home, her bags packed and ready by the dorm's front door. Dad had somehow always smooth-talked her into staying. "One more week," Dad had said. "One more week. And if you still want to come home then, I'll send you a ticket." The rest of us had admired his cool-headed diplomacy.

Cher had always wanted to stay at the end of the prescribed week. Once she had been grounded to the dorm for smoking in the bathroom. What had Dad thought? Now it was my turn to give boarding school a go.

Our trail wandered through stands of oddly twisted firs and across scenic, rock-strewn meadows bright with goldenrod and fireweed. Every once in awhile I would be inspired to turn back to Jessie, saying, "Wow!" and shake my head at the beauty of it all. He would grin, nodding in agreement. Occasionally, Shane slowed to sample an extra-tempting clump of grass. I gently kept his head up. With such lush vegetation passing by all around, he could hardly be blamed for trying to graze.

We entered a forest of tall fir trees. Birds chattered in the treetops. The shade felt cool on my bare arms, and the air had a moist, woodsy scent. From my position near the end of the line, I watched the horses ahead tackling the terrain impending before us. Sometimes it was a section of slippery, exposed tree roots knotting up the trail, or an obstacle to find a way around that slowed things down. Other times it was clattering hooves crossing a rocky streambed, or a quick dip into and out of a gully. Each horse, Luther's Appaloosa, then Sunny Jim's big gelding, then Sara's buckskin, Art's bay, and Willis's brown mare, expertly picked its way.

Now the trail winding through the forest unexpectedly opened up into an enchanted emerald glade. Our host stopped. "This is where we'll take a lunch break," he told us.

Miriam, already there, stood beside her horse greeting each rider, as one by one our horses filed past into the clearing. "Isn't this glorious!" she kept repeating.

For the first few seconds, I was awestruck; the whole place was so startlingly green. Overhead, leafy branches formed a high, arched ceiling. A lone ray of sunshine escaped from the canopy to light up a waterfall at the far end of the clearing, where crystalline water flowed down sculptured rocks into a small, still pool. Even the pool had a dark green cast. The verdant foliage above was so dense that a patch of snow remained by the water's edge. "Wow!" I exclaimed, again turning to Jessie. "This place is so beautiful!"

"Let's see," Jessie grinned, glancing at his watch. "It's been ten whole minutes since the last time you said that same thing."

Riders began dismounting and searching for their lunches. Climbing down, my steps felt springy. A luxuriant layer of moss carpeted the clearing. It occurred to me it was the moss that made everything appear so amazingly green. Shane and I drank from the freezing cold water. The moss carpet covered the floor of the shallow pool as well. As we were drinking, several small birds, undisturbed by our presence, argued over the lone sunspot that brilliantly lighted up the rocks at the top of the waterfall. Meanwhile, Miriam and Willis were settled on a bank to the side, under the trees, talking and munching sandwiches, their horses tethered nearby. Luther and Art were engaged in conversation. The young girl, at first patiently waiting for her father, but now bored, was leading her horse our way. "How's your horse treating you?" I asked when she came over.

"She's real nice," Sara said, turning to stroke the buckskin's neck.

"What's her name?"

"Candy." Sara had green eyes, and a sprinkling of freckles across her tan nose.

We led our horses away from the pool, scouting for a drier location to eat our lunches but where we could still sit on the pillow-soft moss. "How about here?" I asked, and without waiting for a reply, plopped down into my usual, comfortable, cross-legged position. We dug through our sack lunches, our horses standing behind us.

"Wish my mom was here to see this," Sara said, rather forlornly.

Unwrapping my peanut butter, honey, and banana sandwich, I asked, "She couldn't come?"

"She's busy with my new baby sister," the young girl explained with a frown.

"That makes you a big sister, then," I said, trying to sound upbeat. "You're lucky. But it's an important job."

Sara shrugged. "I don't like it."

"You'll like it," I assured her. "You can be her hero. She'll get into lots of trouble. You can watch out for her. Save her life even. Little sisters are pretty easy to impress."

We laughed at the antics of the birds at the top of the waterfall. "Do you have a little sister?" Sara asked, now thoughtful and somewhat cheered.

Between bites, "Two," I said. "I'm very lucky."

"Oh, look!" Sara pointed excitedly. "Are they really fighting?"

"I seriously doubt it," I said.

Jessie and Sunny Jim were wrestling on the patch of snow at the water's edge. Jessie was sprawled on his back, and Sunny Jim, who was on top of him, had him by the throat. At the same time, Jessie had managed to claw out a handful of the hard-packed snow and was gleefully rubbing it in the boy's face. "Would you two knock it off!" Luther ordered. However, our host's stern command was ignored. Jessie was sliding into the water headfirst. But when Sunny Jim struggled to stand, seeking more leverage for the final push, he lost his advantage and was flung up and over, landing on his feet in the middle of the shallow pool. The boy sloshed out of the water, slipping in the snow. The victor, who had been crowing taunts, raced away into the trees, a dripping hornet fast behind.

Crashing sounds receded into the woods until we were left listening to a hushed forest. The birds on the ledge had vanished. Exasperated, Luther broke the silence. "Where do they get all that energy?" he said, shaking his head. Then, "There's no peace," he added, almost apologetically.

Sara tugged at my arm. "Don't you think Sunny Jim is cute?" she asked dreamily.

"Very," I said solemnly. "Sunny Jim is very cute."

"Hi!" Jessie came up behind, giving us both a start. "I didn't mean to startle you," he apologized. "Thought I'd better fix that hat." Taking it from the saddle horn, he squatted beside me, pulling a long knife from the sheath at his side. "I'll have to punch two holes in it," he explained, turning the hat over to show me, leaning close, pointing with the tip of the blade.

"Well, have at it then," I said, adding, "I really appreciate this." I studied his concentrated, handsome profile under the dipped brim of his hat, so close to my face, while he worked. He was clean-shaven except for a few stray stubbles on his tan cheek.

"Here's the finished product," Jessie said, offering the hat for inspection.

Pretending to examine the job critically, I said, "Thank you!" I put the hat on and then flipped it onto my back. "Perfection!"

"Let's wrap it up!" Luther called with authority. "And let's make sure we don't leave anything behind. We'll leave this place as pristine as we found it." As we were gathering our things, he cautioned, "We'll be spending the remainder of the day riding the Pacific Crest Trail. That means some narrow, tricky places, so everyone be alert," adding, "Miriam will bring up the rear." This last surprised me; however, I knew Luther must have his reasons. Assuming Willis would ride back with his wife, that meant Shane and I would be following Art and his bay gelding.

Before we left, Shane and I took another drink from the pool. Gosh, wish we didn't have to leave this beautiful place, I thought, waiting for my horse to finish. I gazed up into the cathedral-like ceiling, where sunlight flashed in the gently waving treetops. Surely I would visit this place in my dreams during the long school year ahead.

CHAPTER TWENTY

*L*uther's Appaloosa set a steady pace, the trail winding ever upwards as it quickly left the secluded forest. Soon Mount Rainier was visible as we traveled along a ridge. At this elevation the sun was particularly brilliant, as well as magnified by the glaciers of the mountain. I was glad to have the hat.

"Bet you're glad to have that hat now," Jessie called forward, as if he'd been reading my thoughts.

The trail dipped into shade, passing around and below rocky cliffs. Sometimes the steep bank on our right was so close it would have been easy for me to reach out to tear off a blade of grass to chew on as we rode. Shane was thinking the same. Occasional wild strawberries were also a temptation for both of us.

"This is a good place to spot a mountain goat," Sunny Jim called back. "On that boulder field over there," he pointed. Everyone scanned the area carefully; no goats.

"There's deer!" Art pointed excitedly for Sara to see. The deer were far down on the valley floor to our left.

All the while as we rode, Shane had been crowding Art's horse, and the bay gelding, at first forbearing, was rapidly losing his patience. "I'm trying to hold him back," I apologized to Art. Shane wanted to snack on the scrumptious vegetation growing out from the steep bank on our right, but I wouldn't allow him to slow enough to make the grab. As a result, he was taking his frustration out on the horse ahead of him. Finally, he nipped the rump of Art's horse, which earned him a swift kick that barely missed his head. Predictably, the paint reared back to get out of the way, causing a chain reaction of startled horses behind us along the treacherous trail. If I hadn't been paying attention, I would have been thrown into the valley.

Once the excitement had passed, Luther asked, "Everyone okay?"

"I guess so," I said, looking back to see if the others were all right. Fortunately those behind—Jessie, Willis, and Miriam—were all experienced riders.

"We'll make a rest stop soon," Luther promised.

Shane's conduct only grew worse. He continued crowding, and stubbornly refused to obey my instructions on the reins. Art's gelding angrily flicked his tail in Shane's face. "I can tell Shelby's getting ready to launch another attack at your horse's nose," Art warned.

"Maybe I'd better get down and walk again for a while," I suggested.

"That isn't necessary," Jessie called forward. He was wisely keeping his palomino at a safe distance. "Besides, one good skull-cracking might cure him."

I was in a quandary: what to do? How best to handle this situation without ruining everyone else's enjoyment of the ride? I was becoming increasingly embarrassed by my horse's spoiled and bullying behavior. Nothing I did helped. When I pulled back on the reins, the universal cue for all horseflesh to slow or stop, Shane merely shook his head defiantly, stretched his powerful neck forward, and sped up directly into the rear of Art's horse. Suddenly, an irate Shelby gave another determined hop, lashing out with steel-shoed weapons. Shane reacted instantly with dramatic, snorting bucks rearward, almost sending me, and his majesty's silly self, over the sheer cliff on our left. Again, luckily, I wasn't taken by surprise, and so managed to keep my seat, although not in a particularly dignified manner.

Luther dismounted at the first wide spot in the trail. "We'll stop here before somebody gets hurt," he ordered. "Connie, you're going to have to ride up front," he added.

I was mortified. Ride up front? Up front where everyone would be watching us? Although I disliked admitting it, even to myself, the paint's past record of frequent stumbles was on my mind. It was the reason I had asked to ride at the rear of the line in the first place. Jumping down, I gave

Shane a most withering glare. Everyone began dismounting. Shamefaced to be the cause of trouble, I kept my head lowered, kicking at rocks in the dusty trail, and even kicking at nothing but air. Jessie bent down to peer under my hat. "Why so serious?" he consoled. "He'll settle down. He's not used to this sort of riding." I shook my head. I just didn't know.

"That's right," Sunny Jim volunteered. "Anyway, some horses are naturally unhappy unless they ride in the lead."

"That's true," Luther agreed helpfully. "He's most likely a lead horse." These were all encouraging things to say, but lead horse? Well, I was very skeptical about that!

"And these horses are all strange to him," Art added.

I appreciated everyone's chivalrous efforts to cheer me. "He gets into trouble with the other horses at his pasture too," I said, thoroughly disgusted. Then added, "Shane and I usually ride alone." The paint, standing behind me, rested his head on my shoulder. "Get away," I shrugged, pushing his head aside. "I don't like you anymore!" He nudged me in the back, and then returned his head lovingly to my shoulder. This time I pushed his head away more gently. "He knows when I'm talking about him," I explained. "He knows I'm upset."

Riders and horses were forced to jostle and unscramble a bit before achieving a reasonable spread along a grassy bank. I had been much too preoccupied to notice Miriam, or Willis for that matter, since lunch. It wasn't easy to twist around enough to comfortably visit with those riding behind. However, now I noticed Miriam as she led her horse my way. She looked tired. She dropped down on my left, and Sky Rocket came to stand directly in front of his mistress, his nose not a foot from hers. Similarly, my horse stood in front of me, and so on down the line. The horses and riders were resting nose to nose.

"Your horse being good?" I queried, making general conversation. Of course her horse was being good. All the horses were being good, except mine.

"He doesn't walk," she said, gazing up at her horse affectionately. "I imagined he might eventually walk." She poked at his ears with the tip of her quirt. "I wonder why I would have thought that?"

" . . . When he's never walked before," Willis added.

Miriam glanced at her watch. "Frankly, I'd expected him to be worn out by now." With effort she produced a stoic smile. Then, turning to me, she asked, "Does my head look as though it's still attached, dear?" She rolled her head from side to side. A quiet moan escaped. "Ah, yes. There it is . . . the pain."

"Let me help with that," Willis said, massaging her neck and shoulders.

"Oh, don't stop," Miriam crooned. "I guess I'm not so young anymore. I'm not a complainer though." She then repeated so all could clearly hear her down the line. "I'm not complaining. I'm having a marvelous time. I'll have it be known that I am not a complainer." At this pronouncement, the stallion tossed his handsome head high, several times, as if in accord with his mistress's speech. The silver adornments on his bridle rattled musically, his long mane shimmered in a dazzling display. It was a modest flash of his charms, but it captured our combined attention—and we oohed and aahed in concert.

Peering up and down the line, Miriam studied our faces, delighted by our admiration. Then, turning to her horse, "Don't we say 'thank you,' young man?" She mimicked a mother's tone, scolding the stallion with mock sternness in her voice. Velvet ears snapped forward to listen attentively, and intelligent brown eyes glowed. Miriam tapped the ground with her quirt. "Say 'thank you,' Sky Rocket," she said firmly. She repeated the taps with the quirt directly in front of her horse's forelegs. "Say 'thank you.'" It was a gentle command. The stallion backed slightly, both neck and tail finely arched. Then, with one foreleg left extended, the Arabian lowered himself slowly into a regal bow, his chocolate colored mane falling forward in waves along the contoured curve of his neck.

Entertained on a mountainside, we all held our breath.

"Really, Miriam!" Willis let out a huge sigh of feigned exasperation, the silence broken. "What a ham you have raised!" The stallion bounced upright at our sudden laughter and applause. The other horses weren't impressed. They casually twitched their ears and lazily switched their tails, displaying cool indifference to Sky Rocket's glitz-for-glory performance.

We rested in shade, spread out comfortably along the bank. Sara sat on my right next to her father. I felt compelled to apologize again for what had been Shane's dangerous misbehavior. "I'm sincerely sorry for my horse's bad manners," I said, turning to Art.

"Don't fret yourself," he answered kindly. "It's too nice a day for that."

Reaching out a hand to stroke Sara's mare, "Candy is behaving like a lady?" I asked the young girl, almost wistfully. The paint snorted and stomped a jealous stomp. "You!" I admonished my horse through clenched teeth, "are being a horrible horse!" While saying this, I had the most delightful image of Shane tarred and feathered. I actually smiled at the thought of it.

Luther stood, stretching, "Day's not getting any younger," he said. Then motioning in my direction, "Connie, you first."

The paint and I took the lead with Luther riding directly behind. Shane didn't know it, but he was carrying a resentful, disgruntled, and apprehensive passenger. For I was, quite frankly, convinced we were going to embarrass ourselves in front of the other horses and riders. Yes, I was expecting the worst. At any moment, I expected to be launched into some shockingly hapless demonstration of bizarre horsemanship. And I had the blame for my participation in this spectacle firmly fixed on my horse.

The image of my horse tarred and feathered had been so pleasant a distraction that I spent the next hour whimsically imagining the paint strapped into a variety of torture chamber contrivances. It was challenging fitting him onto the rack. Lying on his back, Shane's legs stuck straight up into the air, which was hardly a convenient position for stretching. Of course, the rack hadn't been designed for horse torture. Better, Shane in irons, standing on his hind legs, back pressed against a cold, dank, dungeon wall, abandoned, pitiable, head drooping, stomach protruding. I settled on the pillory as Shane's most fitting atonement. The paint on exhibit in the village square, heavy hooves locked into place on either side of a big, fat, stubborn, self-satisfied, swelled head . . .

In this way, I indulged my ill humor until fully able to appreciate the passing scenery again. Which turned out to be at the exact moment when I realized that, contrary to my fears, the paint had set a confident, light-stepping pace. With ears forward and alert, he was picking his way skillfully over and around obstructions littering the rugged mountain track. Just maybe, Shane was a lead horse after all.

The trail had been following along the top of a high ridge for some time. We were officially riding the Pacific Crest Trail. It was a section of a track that doggedly pursues the ridgeline of Pacific Coast mountain ranges from Canada to Mexico. More relaxed, I turned to see the horses and riders coming along behind. Sara and I waved at each other. Sunny Jim waved too and pointed down to our right, where a thin thread of smoke rose from a campfire at the far end of a valley.

"Let's pull up here," Luther called out. We stopped where the main trail branched and a narrower path ran off to the right, zigzagging down into the valley. Bunching close, we listened to our host's instructions. "I'm sure everyone can see our destination," he pointed. "When we reach the bottom, feel free to go exploring, if you like. We'll meet at camp . . . whenever."

Listening to Luther, there didn't seem to be any hurry to get to camp. Mount Rainier was a backdrop for the valley and a shimmering lake. "Wow!" I turned to Jessie. "What a view! Would it be okay if I stayed up here for awhile?"

"Sure," the young man answered. "I'd stay, too, if I didn't have to help with the packhorses." He added as an afterthought, "Should I leave the canteen?"

"That's okay," I answered. "I won't be long."

When attempting to dismount my right leg refused to swing up and over the saddle. Instead, a heavy, numb, wooden-like appendage dragged up and across the saddle, its dead weight forcing me off the opposite side where the left leg was also lifeless. I almost fell off my horse. Now standing, a tingling sensation returned to my tailbone. The tingling turned to pain. The paint followed his wobbling mistress off to one side.

"If you rub your legs the feeling comes back faster," a solicitous Jessie suggested.

"Maybe that's not a good thing," I grimaced. My outraged tailbone was screaming its revenge. "Thanks for the advice, though."

Riders filed past. Miriam first—the Arabian's unerring, exuberant dance steps would quickly deliver her to the valley floor. Next, Art and Sara started down, followed by Luther, then Jessie, tipping his hat, and last, Sunny Jim. Riders became smaller with every twist and turn of the switchbacks. Only Willis lingered.

Our lofty perch was a fine overlook from which the main trail could be traced crossing the valley in an almost direct line over a treeless meadow to the campsite situated at the foot of a forested hillside. The main route was crisscrossed by less defined trails that wandered over the grassland in search of some discovery. Various locations along the lakeshore and a farther snowfield were among the most popular destinations.

Willis, who had been snapping pictures in every direction, decided to dismount. Leading his mare over, he said softly, "I'm glad I didn't miss this." Our proximity to the mountain evoked a certain reverence.

We gazed to our right at Mount Rainier, the immense mountain seeming to grow out of the dwarfed lake and snowfield below. We saw a different mountain in late summer than at any other time during the year because August and September are typically the only months with no measurable snowfall. Consequently, we were treated to a much subdued and muted version of Rainier, not the usual blinding brilliance of virgin snow and luminous blue ice fields. We saw less pristine snow, and glaciers scarred by jagged cracks and dark crevasses. The mountain was deceptive in its nearness, as evidenced by the profound silence surrounding us. If we had been closer to the glaciers, we would have heard the tremendous creaking and popping noises produced by the wrenching movements of melting and shifting ice. Gazing out and away, and turning to take in the unobstructed panorama in all directions, we saw beyond, beyond, Cascade peaks fading into the blue of a cloudless day. We were above the timberline, on top of the world, Willis and I, with our faithful steeds.

Sky Rocket raced across the meadow below. In my mind for an instant in the silence, the stallion unfettered and free racing through a dreamscape. "I've never seen such a remarkable horse." I couldn't help commenting on the obvious. Willis must have heard this all the time. "He's one of a kind."

"Not really," Willis said, sitting down on the edge of a boulder to change film.

He had my attention. "Not really?"

"Not really one of a kind. He's actually an exact duplicate of his sire."

"Oh, how wonderful!" I exclaimed. "Do you own his sire as well?"

"Unfortunately . . . his sire is no longer with us," Willis said, glancing up from his task into my questioning eyes. "He was killed in a trailer accident."

"Oh, how awful," I gasped.

"Agreed," Willis said softly. "It was one of those freak happenings. A truck backfired when we were loading him. He reared up, and broke his own neck." I futilely searched for something comforting to say. Finally, Willis continued.

"You see, Connie. Sky Rocket's sire was a very special horse. A grand champion. As such, he was often, too often, on the road, on the circuit, in transit to one event or another, including journeying to international shows. And then there was frequent travel to someone else's stable to service a mare. His was a nomadic lifestyle." Willis paused again, too long.

"And?" I prompted. "You were saying?"

Haltingly, he began again. "When it happened . . . the accident . . . I thought . . . Miriam . . . would never get over it. We made our decision to quit the horse business altogether, and as quickly as possible. The 'For Sale' sign was hung. That's when Sky Rocket was born, and to one of our mares. Born an exact replica of his sire. And I mean exact. Eerie exact. Reincarnation exact. Not that I believe in any of that," he added. "I don't try to explain it. Not even to myself." Willis snapped the camera shut. 'M's pet,' I call him. No one else has ever ridden him. Or ever will, if Miriam has her way. He's kept exclusively for stud—and then only at our location. She refuses to show him because that would involve . . . a trailer. And so the wanderers wander no longer, which frankly has been a great relief to me. We're not getting any younger, she and I. That's why I was naturally surprised when she suggested this outing. You can bet she only came for Sky Rocket's benefit. She wanted him to have a grand time. That's the word she used, 'grand.'" And I do believe she's accomplishing her mission."

One by one the other riders had reached the flatland. Luther's Appaloosa, in an easy canter, was heading toward camp, with Sara's buckskin mare and Art's bay gelding trotting along the trail a distance behind him.

Jessie and Sunny Jim were going another way. They were riding together toward the lakeshore. As we watched, Willis and I chuckled to see Miriam returning headlong up the hill in our direction.

"She's determined to tire him out," Willis said, shaking his head. "Let's follow her back down," he suggested. Willis swung easily into the saddle. "Shall we, Connie?"

"How do you like your little mare now?" I asked, partly to distract him from my stiff-legged efforts to get my foot up into the high stirrup.

"I don't like to admit this," he answered, glancing around guiltily, as if someone might overhear him on the deserted ridge top, "but she's all right. And that's probably the nicest thing I've said about any horse in a very long time."

"What's her name?" I called after him as they started away.

"I haven't asked," was his reply.

CHAPTER TWENTY-ONE

*O*ur campsite was a long established refuge visited by many generations of Northwesterners before us. It was protected from weather, set back in sparse timber, and near a water source, laid out along a stream. The only permanent structure, a rough log shelter not large enough to be designated a cabin, was substantially constructed to withstand the battering of fierce mountain storms.

Shane and I must have been the last to arrive at camp. We had taken our time meandering through the meadow without seeing any other riders. Luther and Sunny Jim, wrestling a second tent to completion, waved as we approached. A tall, thin man, whom I didn't recognize, paused to acknowledge us with a friendly nod. He was working near the log structure amidst a pile of equipment that had probably been deposited there by the packhorses. Close by was, Stan, the cook. I'd enjoyed meeting him before we began our trek.

"How was the ride?" Stan asked. He was unpacking and organizing cooking implements onto a folding table.

"Fantastic!" I answered. "As if you didn't know." Jumping down gingerly, an inadvertent groan escaped. "Aack! Ouch! It feels as if I've been split up the middle."

Stan laughed good-naturedly. "Maybe you have."

"I'm not complaining," I hurriedly added, remembering Miriam's recant. A reasonable person would expect to be stiff after a day's ride.

"Need any help with your tack?" Stan offered.

"I don't think so. It looks as if you have plenty to keep you busy right here. Besides, I wouldn't want to delay dinner. In fact, I can help you as soon as my belongings are put in order, if you'll point us in the right direction."

"You ladies," he said, "will be sharing the smaller tent." Then, pointing, "Bob put your pack and sleeping bag over by that tree. Did he miss anything?"

"Nope. That's all of it."

I led Shane around Stan's makeshift kitchen and headed for a lone conifer that stood in an open area between the two tents. "Hi, there!" the tall stranger greeted us as we passed. "I'm Bob." He had an easy smile. "So you made it here alive. I'm glad."

"It was touch and go a couple of times," I admitted. "But my friend here brought us through." Shane was given an official pat of praise.

"Huh!" Sunny Jim snorted, poking his head around one of the tents. "She means to say that her horse almost got her killed! A couple of times! But she managed to hold on somehow!"

Bob and I found Sunny Jim's comments mildly amusing; Luther wasn't laughing. "Thank you so much for clearing that up," he admonished his son. "Please ignore him, Connie," he apologized. Then shaking his head, "It's just an annoying stage he's going through."

"Yeah, that's right," Bob agreed. "An annoying stage that has so far lasted his whole life!"

"Why not spread your charm around," Luther suggested, dismissing his son, "and go see if Jessie needs a hand." The boy gladly bounded away.

It didn't take long to strip Shane down. I stacked saddle, blanket, and bridle into a neat pile, and then dug through the army bag for a brush and hoof pick. All the while, the paint, though free to wander, waited for me. He was my hero, despite what Sunny Jim might think. He had carried me safely throughout a confusing day filled with new experiences, over unfamiliar terrain. The clamorous horse trailer that had sent my nerve endings sparking must have been pure agony for Shane, particularly with his sensitive hearing. I encouraged my friend to browse all around and behind the tents while I brushed his sweat-stained back and sides.

"You, dear," Miriam said, coming up beside me. "I hope you don't mind. I took the liberty of choosing the spot nearest the door." I assumed she was talking about the tent. "It would be painful for me to have to crawl over you in the night. My knees give me fits," she explained. "Anyway, I was thinking you and Sara are at a more agile age. And I put Sara between us to give her a feeling of security. That leaves you plenty of room against the back wall. But I wanted to make certain you don't suffer from some neurosis like claustrophobia. Do you?"

"Not at all," I assured her.

Inside, the tent smelled strongly of canvas and the sweet, musty odor that forever permeates all camping gear. As agreed, I unrolled my sleeping bag along the back wall. Memories could be unpredictable, reckless things, charging in at any time, summoned by the senses. I was busy about my business, yet, at the same time, visited by a host of memories. Fragmented scenes came to mind, of camping with the family, of loud, energetic, giggly girls—with a gentle Momma Darleen, sometimes overwhelmed—and of the always even-tempered, steadying presence of Dad. After the sleeping bag had been smoothed to perfection, I decided to locate some toilet articles and maybe run a comb through my hair, so I turned to the business of the pack.

Sara poked her head through the flap. "Your horse is wandering off," she anxiously informed me.

Absorbed in rummaging through the contents of the pack, I returned without interest, "He won't go far."

Sara sat down just inside the tent door. "What are you looking for?" she asked.

"A mirror. I know I packed one."

"Why do you want a mirror?"

"I want to check to see if my nose is still on straight. Or if I sprouted horns today." Sara giggled and ducked out. Several strong upside-down shakes got things moving in the right direction. Everything spilled out. Glad to see lip balm, I liberally applied the waxy substance to my sore lips.

"Connie!" someone called. "We need you out here!"

Scrambling for the opening, I said quickly, "What's the problem?"

Jessie stood waiting. "We need your halter. I'm taking your horse up with the others."

"Up? Up where?"

"To the meadow beyond those trees," he said, pointing to the other side of the creek bed. "Has your horse ever worn hobbles?" Jessie held out leather straps and chains for my inspection.

Retrieving the halter, I answered, "I don't know."

My friend had wandered a distance behind the tents to the outer edge of our campsite clearing, and had located a promising patch of green. I was not particularly eager to disturb him. "Shane! Shane!" I called half-heartedly.

The paint was grazing in a position that happened to be turned fully sideways to me, so I could clearly observe the whole horse. When his name was called, he kept his head down grazing, eyes locked on his meal. One ear, however, the ear on the side nearest me, had reluctantly turned in my direction. He was considering my request. "Now what?" he was thinking. Wasn't he the recently praised horse that had earned this bit of rest and repast? He was hoping his mistress would get sidetracked and forget about him—not likely, but possible. He was hoping his mistress would evaporate into thin air—to good to be true.

Again, I called, "Shane!" this time calling with a tone of mild commiseration, but insistent. The paint, ignoring me, continued his head-down grazing; however, the one ear that had turned in my direction now registered a barley perceptible rearward cant of annoyance.

"Shane!" I called again, this time with impatience in my tone and a shake of the halter. The paint kept grazing. But what had been the slight rearward cant of the one ear had now become more pronounced, and his annoyance was emphasized by a chopped, flick of tail. A glaring "Don't bug me!" signal if I'd ever seen one.

"He's not going easy," I remarked.

"Nope. He's not going easy," Jessie agreed.

Again, "*Shane!*" This was accented by more shaking of the halter. And the still grazing horse produced a stubborn, clipped, "I really mean it!" rear leg stomp, and an ever more dramatic flick of tail, flashing a wider, higher swath around the rump. I was certain, as an experienced horseman, Jessie was getting all of this conversation. However, to the untrained onlooker, Shane would have merely appeared to be a contentedly grazing horse flicking at an occasional fly with its tail, and one that happened to be deaf—an unfortunate circumstance for its owner.

I explained to Jessie, "He usually comes when I call. Truly. But right now, he's hoping I'll be distracted, or this tree will fall on me."

It was embarrassing as well as pointless; nevertheless, I couldn't resist one last exasperated effort. "*Shane*!!" I accompanied this with more rattling of the halter and an impatient stomp of my own foot. For this, I received the paint's full "drop dead" treatment. Concentrated, head-down grazing, with both ears forward in the "I'm not listening anymore" attitude, combined with an oh-so-subtle turn away. It wasn't a turn really, rather more a shifting of weight, executed with absolute economy of movement. Although as plain to me as a slap in the face, it would appear to anyone else watching as if the horse were merely reaching for a farther clump of grass, exposing slightly more rear to my view.

"Well, that was rude," a savvy Jessie remarked. "I guess you'll have to go get him."

"I guess so," I agreed.

Shane raised his head at my approach, resigned, thoughtfully grinding his grass.

"You sure he'll be safe up there?" I asked, handing Jessie the lead.

"He'll be fine," Jessie assured me.

I watched my friend being led away, across the stream and up the hill into the trees, until his white markings disappeared from view. Back in the tent, there were certain essentials that needed to be placed for easy access in the dark. The flashlight found a niche along the tent wall at the head of the sleeping bag. Thanks to Dad, I was an experienced camper and knew that it would get dark quickly in the mountains—dark and cold. With this last thought in mind, an extra pair of socks was tucked down inside the bag. Planning to help with dinner, scooping up soap and towel, I went to wash in the stream.

* * *

Stan sat a few feet from the campfire, with his back turned away from the fire, his chores, and my approach. He was a solitary figure, legs crossed, relaxing in a folding chair. Peering over his right shoulder, I saw he had an open sketchbook propped on one knee and was clearly reflective, pencil poised over a blank white page. "What are you going to sketch?" I asked.

He hadn't heard me coming up so gave a start. Then, turning stiffly to see me behind him, he twisted not his neck, but his entire upper body. "Any stationary object," he answered. "Might even sketch you if you hold still long enough."

"Something smells good. What is it?" I asked, taking the liberty of lifting the lid on one of two large pots heating on a gas stove.

"My special recipe," Stan said proudly. "Venison stew."

I couldn't remember having venison before so indulged in a long sniff. "Smells wonderful!"

He was rotated awkwardly in his chair keeping an eye on me as my interest shifted to the next pot. "The other's chili. Always one in every bunch won't eat the stew," he explained. "Won't hear of it. One in every bunch." That said, he turned stiffly back to his original position.

Addressing his back, I offered, "I'm reporting for duty. Anything I can do to help out?"

Stan's torso twisted stiffly around again. "You really don't mind? If you're sure you don't mind, you can stir those pots for me from time to time. I have the heat low. It's watching things don't burn on the bottom is all. That's the main thing."

There was a long-handled spoon for each pot. I began stirring the stew, bringing chunks of meat, carrots, and potatoes up from the bottom. "Where is everyone?" I asked, glancing around a deserted campsite.

Stan stood slowly. He decided to reposition his chair, which he did with much fuss so there would be no wobble on the uneven ground. That important requirement satisfied, recrossing his legs, he gathered the sketchbook into his lap, now facing my way. "Some's over there," he answered, motioning toward the lake. "Some's up there," he pointed toward the hill. "They straggle in when they get hungry." And after a thoughtful pause, "You aren't deserting me already?"

"No chance," I answered.

"Feel free to make yourself something hot to drink if you like. There's hot cocoa. Or juice if you prefer."

Stan began sketching, and I accepted his hospitality, keeping an eye on things while making us hot cocoa. I was relieved that the artist didn't seem troubled by the interruptions of our continuing banter, although courtesy demanded he look up often from his drawing. Nor did he seem bothered by my incessant questions as to where to find one thing or another, maintaining staunch good-humor throughout. Surprising, considering most of my questions were needless, if only I'd stopped to look first before asking.

Bob came striding purposely through camp heading in the direction of the small cabin. Carrying an armload of tack, but spying activity in the kitchen, he swung wide in a nosy detour. "Do I need any of that?" he inquired politely, hovering over my work and the table, scanning hopefully for anything edible.

I was mixing powdered milk in a big jar according to the cook's easy-to-follow directions. "I'm fixing hot cocoa for anyone who wants some."

"I guess that would include you, Bob," Stan added with a chuckle. "That your last load? Everything under the tarp?"

"Everything but what you see here."

"So go!" Stan waved him on. "Finish up and then come take a break."

Not needing a second invitation, Bob hurried away. I had barely gotten the milk heating in the pan by the time he made it back. The man had red hair, exposed when he tossed off his hat, a freckled complexion, and a tall, lean frame. He might have been in his late twenties. Casting about for a comfortable place to make a landing, he dropped down with care to the low spot he had chosen. Then there were a few boxes to be adjusted into a backrest before he was content to unfurl long legs and settle back. Once comfortable, he took his time lighting a cigarette, inhaling deeply, relishing the first puff.

"Those things'll kill ya," Stan warned, pausing in his drawing to administer a scowl of disapproval, which Bob cheerfully overlooked. "I thought you quit those nasty things."

"Tomorrow, old man, tomorrow." Bob grinned at me mischievously, letting me know he was fooling around, no disrespect for Stan intended. He took another long pull from the cigarette, and in a flagrant display of pleasure, dropped his head full back and leisurely blew perfect smoke rings one by one straight up into the sky.

Stan shook his head. "Bob here is a bit of a whippersnapper," he informed me. "Can't tell him much. It's his age. Or lack of. Whatever. I try not to hold it against him. This here's our fifth season together, so he's allowed to get a little lippy." He was speaking directly to me, though his remarks were entirely for Bob's benefit. The younger man, however, appeared not to be listening to a word of it. "Yep," Stan continued, "Bob here is a good worker. One of the best, I'll allow. It's been a fine thing having him help out. He makes life real easy on me." He said this last in mock doleful tones. "Pity he won't be around much longer." He gave Bob another glance, this time catching the man's eye. "Least not if he keeps up smokin' those things."

"Stop! Enough!" Bob exclaimed, grinding out the cigarette.

It was time to stir the pots again, and a tantalizing aroma escaped when a lid was raised.

"I'm half-starved," Bob moaned. "Whatcha got goin' there?" So eager and curious, he was almost ready to spring up to see for himself.

"Well, let's just see what we've got goin' here," I said, making a great show of delving into the pot. Then, intent on torment, digging and poking, I described the stew's succulent attributes in detail. "We have here a thick gravy, with oodles of big, tender, chunks of meat, and loads of vegetables—looks like juicy carrots and potatoes, and more." A cooperative victim, Bob hung on every word. Pleased with myself, I asked both men, "Now how does that sound?"

"Don't ask him!" Stan was indignant. "Food. It's all the same to him. He'd eat beaks . . . and claws!"

"I won't eat beaks and claws," Bob assured us, sounding wounded.

"Sure you would," the older man countered, giving me a wink. "If I roasted them? Roasted them over the fire? Roasted them crispy, to crunchy perfection, and seasoned them with a little salt?"

"Well, maybe," the half-starved man paused to ponder. "I don't know. Ahh! He's not roasting any beaks!"

I brought Stan his hot cocoa first, in respect for his age and cook's status, but he waved me in Bob's direction instead. "He wants his marshmallows," the younger man explained, cautiously accepting the steaming cup.

"And he'll want a second cup in two cracks of a whip!" Stan countered.

Enjoying a silent interlude, we savored our hot drinks. There was considerable heed required to not scorch our lips and tongues. Finally, "Make him show you his drawing," Bob urged between sips. "He's the best artist in the world. Go on," he prompted. "Make him show you." Stan held up the unfinished drawing for us to view. His work was indeed impressive. I moved in to inspect.

"Is that your chair at home?" I asked. Stan nodded. It was an overstuffed armchair. "Is that your cat?" I asked.

"He's a friend of mine," he answered.

"He's big."

"That's my Pudge," Stan confirmed with obvious affection. Definitely of the lazy-lounger variety, a massive animal stretched out asleep across the back of the chair.

"Pudge is a stationary object?"

"True."

"Show her the rest of the drawings," Bob urged. "Show her the picture of me."

"Nope. That's it for the present." The artist withdrew his sketchbook from our adoration and flipped it closed. "It's back to work for me. You too, Bob. We need wood cut. And I'll want kindling for morning."

There was already a double row of wood piled to the rafters of the roof's wide overhang on both sides of the log shelter. "What about all that firewood?" I asked, pointing.

Reaching for his hat, Bob handed me the empty cup. "We don't touch that."

"That wood stays right where it is," Stan explained. "Warmth for a lost hiker or hunter. A last chance for survival."

Bob added several logs to the fire, kicking them down into the bed of coals, sending a spray of sparks skyward. I sat basking in the campfire's stupefying glow, occasionally rearranging the fiery landscape by poking in the coals with a stick. Dreamily, I listened to the sounds of wood being chopped and of Stan rattling dishes nearby. I was soon dozing.

CHAPTER TWENTY-TWO

A sharp wail! A howl of pain! "YOW! OH NO! DAMN! OW! OW! OW!

Startled from my nap, I leaped up stretching to see over the fire. Something had happened to Bob.

Luther rushed to Bob's aid. "Let me see!" he demanded, grabbing the injured man's flailing limb. "Let me see! How bad is it?" And, prying the hatchet from the convulsive clutch of the opposing hand, he ordered, "Sit down right here before you fall down," and helped Bob ease to the ground, pressing him back to lean against the splitting stump. "Hold your hand up. Keep your hand up like I say."

Stan dashed forward with a handful of towels. "Let me see," he demanded. Bob kept his eyes averted while the older man took an assessment of the damage. "You're not missing any fingers," he pronounced. "That's good. Let's get pressure on it. Keep it up. I'll be able to tell more once we get this bleeding stopped." He wrapped the hand tightly in one of the towels.

Both men stood over the seated patient, Luther supporting the arm, Stan applying pressure to the wound. "How bad is it?" the injured man asked.

Stan took a peek under the towel. "You're lucky . . . very lucky. From what I see there are no crushed or broken bones. You're not going to lose any fingers. Looks like you're going to need stitches, though. Lots of stitches."

"I don't feel lucky," Bob moaned. "I feel stupid. I'm real sorry."

"Oh, all right!" Luther sounded resigned. "If I have to. If you're going to blubber." He held out his left hand for Bob's inspection. "See that?" he said. "There you are. Happy now? Hatchet wound, 1959. Fifteen stitches. A beaut, huh? I doubt you'll top that!"

"Is it bad?" Jessie asked. He and Sunny Jim were suddenly beside me. I only realized then that I had moved in close.

"Could be worse," Luther answered gravely. "He still has five fingers. Though Doc here says he'll need stitches. He'll have to ride back to base camp tonight."

"Can't it wait until morning?"

"I'm goin' tonight, Jess," the patient said. "I won't sleep anyway till this is checked out."

"I'd better get bandages," Stan said, relinquishing the wounded hand into Luther's care.

Bob grasped for the departing man, "I'm sorry, boss. I'm real sorry."

Stan turned back, "I won't let you miss out on any work, partner," he said. "You'll be patched up and back on the trail by hunting season. I promise." The older man gave his friend a paternal squeeze on the shoulder before hurrying away.

"Do you think they'll have to give me a shot?" a tragic face questioned those remaining. No one answered. Jessie gazed skyward whistling an off-key tune, and Sunny Jim did a nervous shuffle with his feet. I attempted a concerned but blank expression, and Luther, who was lowered to his haunches resting the patient's elbow on his knee, had a well-timed coughing spasm.

Stan reappeared with a bulky, metal, first aid box—ample first aid for all, including horses. The two men peeled open the towel. The bleeding had stopped enough so that we could see a nasty gash across the first two fingers of his left hand. Stan applied a compress to each finger individually, and a gauze wrap to each finger separately as well, making sure each finger was thickly padded before beginning the next step of wrapping the two bandaged fingers together.

"Do you think they'll have to give me a shot?" Bob asked his friend. Still receiving no answer, he beseeched, "Well, do you?"

"You must be feeling a whole lot better to be worrying about that," Stan answered carefully. "A shot is nothing after the damage you've done here."

"But do you?"

Stan glanced from his work into the sufferer's anxious face. "I can't think why they would," he lied convincingly.

"Well, that's a relief," the injured man said with a big sigh, color returning to his face, his breathing slowing. The danger of our patient going into shock passed.

We had stepped back to give Stan the space he needed to work from the first aid box. Capable hands wrapped the cut fingers, leaving the thumb and unhurt fingers free. This enabled a grip using the thumb, ring, and little finger. Next he fashioned a narrow splint to extend from the bandaged fingertips over the palm of the hand, and on up the inside of the arm to the elbow. The splint was secured with many layers of gauze wrap.

"We're going to want to get him out of here fast," Luther considered.

"Then we'd better come up with a horse," Jessie said. "Not Poky. That's certain." The young man removed his hat to better rub, pinch, and pound his forehead.

Our host, staring at the ground, rocked back and forth on worn boot heels. "J.P." Luther finally blurted.

"You're right! J.P.!" Jessie exclaimed.

"I'll fetch his gear!" Sunny Jim cried, rocketing into action.

"Bring me his halter first!" Jessie called after him.

The bandaging job wound to completion with a snip, a tie, and a tuck. Stan eyed his handiwork. "Not too tight? You listening, Robert? I would have preferred to put your arm in a sling, but that's impractical for riding a horse, when you might need both hands free fast. That's why the splint. You can take it off if you find yourself in a predicament where you need more wrist movement. Just pull on this string with your teeth. Don't take it off, though, unless it can't be avoided. Understand?"

Bob struggled from the ground to his feet. "Okay, boss," he said. "I won't mess with it." The patient, clearly feeling unsteady, stood only a moment before sitting down again, this time on the splitting stump.

"Too much altitude too soon," Stan cautioned. "Best take it slow." He then dipped his fingers into the breast pocket of Bob's shirt and lifted out the pack of cigarettes. "Guess there's no need for you to quit smoking today." He placed a cigarette between the man's lips, even lighting it graciously. Bob smoked with less flair than previously. His one good hand was quite shaky. "You feeling okay? Not woozy? How about I fix you something for the trail? Bring you a cup of coffee? That hit the spot?"

"Maybe." Bob considered the possibility of food. "Maybe coffee." Stan hurried off on his mission.

Luther's attention had been diverted to overseeing his son's progress assembling the gear. "Good, son. That's all of it. Good job."

When a slightly breathless Sunny Jim rejoined our small group, he asked the smoking man, "Does it hurt real bad?"

"Not too real bad," Bob reflected. "It throbs. And I get tired holding it up."

"I can help with that," Sunny Jim offered. "Rest your arm against me. Rest your elbow on my shoulder." A few seconds of silence elapsed before, he gasped, "Wow! That bandage is something!"

"Don't I know it!" Bob agreed.

"You're going to ride J.P.," Sunny Jim informed the wounded man. "Dad won't let me ride J.P." Then added, "Dad says he's a man's horse."

"Enough, son," Luther scolded. "You're only scaring him."

A few seconds later: "Do you think you might pass out on the trail?" Sunny Jim wondered. "You could pass out or fall asleep."

"Could," Bob allowed.

"If you fall off," Sunny Jim pondered, "a bear might eat you."

"Might," Bob agreed.

"Enough!" Luther repeated. "Lighten up, son."

Thoughtful silent minutes passed. Then, "You know I gave J.P. that name," the boy said.

Bob ground out his cigarette. "I didn't know."

"He's named after my favorite clown, J.P. Patches."

"He's my favorite clown too!" I exclaimed.

"Mine too," Bob admitted. Almost everyone raised in the Seattle area was a "Patches Pal."

"Mine too," Luther added, though somewhat reluctantly. J. P. Patches' local kids' TV show was very popular, even with adults.

"You're perkier," Stan said, reappearing to hand Bob a cup of coffee. "What's going on? Jolly Jim cheering you up with his graveside manner?"

"I've been keeping chuckles in check," Luther rolled his eyes, "but it hasn't been easy."

We waited, all watching for Jessie's return. Bob sipped the coffee. His hand had stopped trembling.

"Here they come!" I announced.

Jessie led Luther's Appaloosa into camp, the animal approaching with long-legged strides. "Son, fetch our buddy some grain—not much—a snack," Luther instructed, accepting the lead. Then to Jessie, "Any problems?"

"None that I could detect," Jessie answered.

Luther circled the animal with a critical eye, running practiced hands down each leg checking for unsound or tender areas, and lifting each hoof inspecting for loose shoes, wedged stones, or any hint of soreness. "Fine . . . fine . . . good," he pronounced as he went along.

The last members of our group came strolling into camp, oblivious of the mishap, Art and Sara radiant, Willis and Miriam appearing equally refreshed. "Get the kinks worked out?" Stan inquired of the group generally.

Willis left Miriam's side, "What's happening here?"

"Bob had a run-in with the hatchet," Stan said. "Fortunately, not too serious. He still has all his parts, but we've decided to send him back to base camp for some stitching up."

Willis eyed the one horse. "Alone? I'll ride down with him."

"That won't be necessary," Luther said, stepping out from behind his horse. "He's not riding alone. He'll be riding J.P. here." He punctuated his words by giving his horse a pat of confidence. "If I thought there was something more I could do for him, I'd go myself. "

Willis nodded, "He's in good hands then I take it. Hooves, I should say."

"The best!" Sunny Jim piped in.

Luther and Jessie finished the saddling. "You about ready?" Luther asked.

"About ready as I'm gonna be," Bob replied.

"Come on, then. Let's get you on your way."

Jessie held out Bob's jean jacket apologetically. "You're going to need this," he said. "Don't blame me." The left sleeve of the jacket had been amputated above the elbow to allow for the splint.

"Aw, Jess! I almost had that broke in!" came the anguished response.

"It couldn't be helped."

"Well, that's just pure meanness. Pure meanness." Stan and Jessie assisted the injured man with his coat. "Ouch! Ouch! Watch it, will you!"

"Feeling in your fingers," Stan said. "That's a good sign."

Scowling at Jessie, Bob repeated, "I said, OUCH!"

"It couldn't be helped," Jessie apologized again.

"Let's move it!" Luther urged. "Daylight's wastin'!" J.P. stomped and snorted, sensing his master's impatience.

"All right," Bob said, grumbling. "I'm coming." More grumbling. Then, "See what they've done to my sleeve?" He turned back to us. "See what they've done? It takes a year to break in one of these jackets." We all nodded, shaking our heads, agreeing. "I'll be pleased to put some miles between me and those two."

Luther, steadying Bob as he climbed into the saddle, commented, "Seems strange, someone else riding my horse." At the same time, J.P. flashed surprise, then anxiety. Realizing his master wasn't in the saddle, the Appaloosa sidestepped in confusion and threw his head back trying to figure out how his man could be in two places at once. Calming his horse, Luther made final adjustments to the equipment. The stirrups needed to be lowered for Bob's long legs. And he decided to tie the reins together so there wouldn't be any possibility of the injured man losing one in his awkward condition.

While our host fussed, good-byes were said. First, Stan stepped forward with a peace offering of crackers. "I took the liberty. Anyway, crackers are easy on the insides."

"Peanut butter and crackers?" Our patient's disgruntled face lit up. "You're forgiven!"

Then Jessie looped a canteen over the saddle horn. "You'll need to wash those down," he said. "And I'm tucking a flashlight into your saddlebag. You won't need it, though. You've still got plenty of daylight."

"Guess you're forgiven, too. Thanks, Jess."

Next a serious-minded Sunny Jim came forward to rub his lucky rabbit's foot on J.P.'s curious, sniffing nose, before ceremoniously handing it to Bob. "You hold on to this for me," he said. Nodding his appreciation, the rider solemnly accepted the rabbit's foot tucking it into the breast pocket of his jacket.

Last, Luther had advice to give. "Robert, let J.P. handle things," he said. "He knows the way. Trust him, he'll take the shortest route. Have Owen bring him up tomorrow in the afternoon. Don't worry about anything. We'll make sure Stan has plenty of help." And stepping aside, "All right then. Ready? Hang on!" he warned the rider. "Go home, boy!" he ordered his horse sternly, slapping the animal smartly on the hindquarters. "Skedaddle! Home, boy!"

"Take care! Safe journey!" we chorused. "Safe journey! We'll miss you!"

The Appaloosa was off without hesitation, quickly disappearing down the tree-lined trail heading out into the meadow beyond. We listened to the fading hoof-falls of the retreating horse until we could hear nothing at all.

"He's getting a shot for sure," Sunny Jim said, breaking the silence.

"Two," Stan confirmed. "He'll get a shot of Novocain before they sew him up. And he'll get a tetanus shot."

"I'm hungry," Sara announced to no one in particular.

"That makes two of us," the boy said.

"Food's ready," Stan said. "We can eat whenever . . . as soon as everyone's washed up."

"Fine with us," Willis spoke for his wife as well.

"Agreed," Miriam said. "I can eat anytime." Turning to our nearby host, she added, "We could use a light in our tent."

Luther, gazing down the deserted trail, pulled his attention back to the group. "A light in our tent?" he said absently. "A light in our tent?" he repeated. Then, glancing at his watch, "Let's do it," he said decisively, turning on his heel. Miriam and Willis followed.

"You want to come with me, Sara?" I asked offering my hand. "We can wash up for supper together. If it's okay with your dad?" I thought about putting some cream on my sore nose. "Did you get sunburned today?" I asked. "If you remind me, we'll put some cream on your face." We waited with Miriam and Willis outside the tent. There was still plenty of light, but inside the tent was quite gloomy as it was now in the shadow of the wooded hillside.

"I looked for you before we went walking," Sara said. "Daddy said you must be busy. Were you?"

"Probably . . . very."

"I brought you back some snow, but it melted."

"That's the way of it," I said. "I appreciate your thinking of me, though." I was distracted, noticing that Sara's braids were in need of attention. I wanted to help. But braids were a mystery to me like all knitting and knots. One of those right-handed things, I told myself. An excuse, I suppose, because I had never taken the time necessary to master them. Thinking back to past lopsided tragedies, I decided that Sara's braids were acceptable after all, at least enough for a supper eaten outdoors around a campfire.

Luther arrived with the unlighted lantern and ducked wordlessly into the tent. I gave Sara's small hand a squeeze while we waited, our eyes fixed on the dim doorway, all of us anticipating a welcoming glow. Certainly not expecting the bright flash and loud WHOOSH that followed. Flames exploded! Fire filled our night's abode! A fast moving shadow burst from the tent with the fiery lantern in tow. "Back! Get back!" Luther shouted. Instead, Willis and Miriam descended upon him, frantically attacking the flames, beating and smothering them with hats and hands. Their instant response extinguished the fire almost as quickly as it had ignited.

Afterward, carefully inspecting him, it was hard to believe our host wasn't burned, or that his hair and clothing weren't even singed. But it was true. Not surprisingly, our fireworks attracted the attention of everyone else in camp. "You're positive you aren't burned anywhere?" Art asked. "I find it hard to believe."

"Thanks to fast work by these two," Luther said, still inspecting his shirtsleeves. "I can't thank you enough," he said, turning to Willis and Miriam.

Jessie checked inside the tent with a flashlight, confirming our suspicion that, indeed, all of the fire had followed the lantern outside. He reported no damage, nothing but the strong odor of kerosene, which we would be able to air out. Racing hearts began to slow.

"Totally my fault." Luther shook his head in disgust. "I know better. I always light the lantern outside. Always. I can't understand what got into me."

"Your mind rode off with Bob and your horse . . . we can assume," Willis said.

"Sure did," Sunny Jim agreed.

"I hope this isn't one of those happens-in-threes things," Stan said.

"Don't even think it," Luther said. "We've had enough excitement already."

"What was that?" Willis broke in. "Listen!"

"What?" we asked.

"Shush! Listen!" Willis's face showed alarm. "Can't you hear . . . that?"

Only then did I hear a noise. It seemed to be coming from where the horses were up in the meadow. More sounds. It sounded as if something gigantic was crashing around in the woods up there. My heart began pounding. It could only be a bear! The crashing sounds were getting closer, approaching down the mountainside. My eyes, straining into the shadowy forest, envisioned a furiously crazed monster, a grotesque, hulking creature baring slathering fangs, rampaging through the underbrush. Then I saw something high up, glimpses of light in the shadows. Immediately, I recognized Shane by his telltale white markings. He was staggering and reeling, careening down the steep slope. Gravity was sending him downward. Part free-fall, part floundering, with his front legs shackled together, he was hopping and lunging, coming fast. The paint plunged out of the trees onto the open flat.

Jessie was quick to react, gallantly sprinting across the rocky streambed, slipping and splashing, sacrificing his boots. He was down on one knee removing the leather straps before Shane even had time to recover his dignity.

"Wowser!" Sunny Jim exclaimed. "What did I just see?"

"That was a belly-churner," Stan said shaking his head.

"Nauseating," Miriam agreed. "Amazing he didn't break his fool neck.

You okay?" she asked turning to me. I had swallowed a welling hysteria in one mighty gulp, so may have appeared to be in distress. "You see he's fine. Best not make over him," she advised. "That will only encourage unwanted behavior."

The desire to run to my horse, in a melodramatic display of motherly emotion, was strong. "Something c-c-could have spooked him up there," I said, half choking out a possible explanation.

"Yeah! Sure!" Sunny Jim snorted. "A spooky marmot!" Then he turned to the others. "That's right, her horse was attacked by a marmot!" And to me, "Nah! Your horse is a crybaby. Look at him. He wants his mommy. He's a sissy!" The boy wagged his head in knowing disgust and moved to join his companion across the creek.

"I hope your boy isn't planning a career overseas," Willis said, turning to our host, "things touchy the way they are over there."

"You mean to say you think he'd set off World War III?"

"I mean to say, I'm afraid your son could be that 'last straw' people talk about." Then, turning to me, he said kindly, "Miriam's right, Connie. Your horse isn't doing himself any favors. Best to ignore this."

"Sound advice," Luther agreed. "He's going right back up where he came from. It's good pasturage, and he'll need all his strength for tomorrow's ride."

"Is there a chance he'll try to come down again?" I asked.

"Not likely! I'd say he gave himself a serious scare. He's not stupid enough to try that stunt again."

"You sure?"

"We'll make sure," Luther promised. "We'll hobble both his front and his back legs. He won't be going anywhere."

Miriam put a consoling arm around me. "There's nothing to be done here. Let's go get ready for supper."

CHAPTER TWENTY-THREE

Nearing the campfire, I heard talking. "J.P. can get you home in a snowstorm," Sunny Jim was saying.

"Sounds like legend material," Art said.

"Though true," Luther said.

"He saved my dad's life."

"It's true," Luther confirmed.

I joined the end of the two-person line waiting for food. Stan was dishing up a plate of venison stew for Willis, and Miriam was next in line, standing very close to her husband, hovering actually, eyeing the proceedings. "Enough," Willis said. "Smells good."

When it was Miriam's turn to be served, she bent sniffing suspiciously at the contents of the pot. "What exactly is this again?" she asked.

"Venison stew," Stan said simply, neither defending nor offering further explanation. "Or chili if you prefer." Then, winking at me, he lifted the lid on the other pot. As he held the lid up for her to see, I noticed his hands were gnarled and trembling.

"Chili," Miriam decided quickly, sounding relieved. "And one biscuit, please."

As soon as Miriam had gotten far enough away for me to have a whispered confidence with our cook, I leaned close. "One in every bunch," I marveled. "Just like you said."

"Sometimes I tell 'em it's rattlesnake stew," Stan said, keeping his voice down. "I can't stop myself." He ladled me a helping. "I've laughed myself to sleep nights remembering some of those recoiling faces. One guy pulled his head down inside his shirt collar, and we didn't see him again for two days!"

"Aw! That can't be true," I said, but appreciating the story all the same.

"You look like a good eater. One biscuit or two?"

"I can eat ten Swedish pancakes."

"Better take two."

I chose a spot to sit next to Sara. We sat holding the plates on our laps. "Do you think Candy is okay up there?" she asked me, her green eyes filled with concern for her horse. "With the marmots around?" A mouthful of stew prevented me from answering before we were interrupted by a merry laugh.

"Candy made friends with the marmots long ago," an amused Jessie assured her. "They don't bother her."

"Do the marmots come into camp?" Sara wondered. "Can they get into the tents?"

"They usually mind their own business," Art scolded, "and they don't ask so many questions. Now watch your plate before it ends up in the fire."

Luther glanced down at his watch, the firelight glinting off the silver metal when he turned his wrist.

"Think he's there yet?" Willis asked.

"Not yet," Luther answered. "Not yet."

We all ate, enjoying our food. The stew was delicious. "Anybody need a refill," Stan called, "before I sit down?"

"He means, speak now," Sunny Jim informed us between bites, "or expect to serve yourself." Sara giggled softly beside me.

Stan sat down next to Miriam. "You don't seem to have much appetite," he said. "Is there a problem?"

"Not with your cooking, believe me. Frankly, I'm too tired to care about food."

"You'll feel better after a night's rest," Willis said. "I have to say you've been a hardy soul, M." There was a murmur of agreement among us. "By the way, Luther," Willis continued. "What horse will you be riding in the morning?"

"I've been giving that some thought," Luther said absently, glancing again at his watch. It was a noticeable gesture because he habitually stretched out his arm to free the watch from his sleeve.

"What time is it?" I was prompted to ask.

"Exactly two minutes and a lifetime since the last time I looked," Luther said, sounding disgusted with himself.

"You could ride Sparky," Sunny Jim offered. "And Jessie and I could double up."

"That's a generous offer, son. A very generous offer. But I'm afraid that wouldn't make for a very peaceful day, now would it?"

"Think he's there yet?" Willis asked again.

"Not yet," Luther answered. "Not yet."

"You two are compulsive," Miriam said. "Willis, he just said he's not there yet."

"Wait! Hush!" Willis held up a hand. "Don't you people hear that?"

We fell silent, all listening. I held a bit of unchewed biscuit in my mouth, my ears concentrating. I didn't hear anything, and searched the other anxious faces aglow in the firelight. There was nothing out there. Relief! Thankful, I began chewing and breathing again. Then, I heard something—the dreaded sound—a distant yet unmistakable racket. There was definitely some commotion coming from where the horses were up in the meadow. This time I prayed it was a bear!

I stood. Everyone stood. With trembling hands, I set my plate down. Everyone set his plate down. I started for the stream, moving into the cool air away from the campfire. Everyone started after me. Bright spots danced before my eyes obscuring my vision. It was twilight, and the brilliance of the firelight had dazzled much of my ability to see. I groped my way, tripping over the uneven ground, stumbling to the edge of the streambed.

There, teetering on the bank of the stream, focusing my eyes in the half-light, I swept the hillside for any sign of my horse. At first I saw only flickers of white, high up, but soon saw a horse shape. Shane was coming down cautiously, not straight down as before. This time, he was traversing the steep slope, picking his way. Still, he was struggling to stay upright. With both his front legs and back legs hobbled, he was forced to move in stiff-legged hops. Snagged! The bulky animal slipped sideways into a tree. A shaking blow! He pushed off hard, escaping the tree, though as a result pitched himself forward into a straight-legged leap, a flying, sliding, head-long plunge. Shane was an out-of-control, one-horse-din of resounding cracks and thunderous snaps falling down through the underbrush. It was a certain tailspin to a crash landing. And then the paint dropped out of the woods onto the flat. It was more a dribble than a drop, a kind of "here's your horse" plop.

I clasped my breast. Somehow he had landed in an upright condition, seemingly dazed and wobbly, but standing. At that point I would have re-sponded, dashing the distance to my friend, but there was never time. He staggered once, hopping sideways, adjusting to the level surface, and then he came on fast. Heading in our direction with determined leaps, crossing the slippery streambed in a spray of reckless bounds, my wild-eyed horse came skidding to his knees directly in front of me.

Tears of relief flowed. I kept wiping them away, hoping no one would see. Shane's breath was hot on my neck. "No good up there, huh?" I man-aged to choke out the obvious. In answer, he heaved a huge sigh, which in horse talk surely meant, "Thank God! Thought you'd be upset, but you're glad to see me!" I was glad to see him safely grounded, but not pleased to see him arrive back in camp. I plucked bits of wilderness from his forelock and mane.

"It's okay," Luther said. "He's okay."

My eyes were swimming.

"I for one vote her horse ought to stay in camp tonight," Sunny Jim pro-claimed.

"And I second it," Jessie said.

"All in favor say 'aye,'" Luther said, resigned to the situation.

"Aye," everyone said. It was unanimous. I whisked away a gusher.

"Your horse can have J.P.'s grain in the morning," Luther said kindly.

"And I can wake you early, when I get up, if you want," Stan offered. "We can take your horse over by the lake to graze before breakfast. If you want."

I nodded numbly.

After the hobbles were removed, Luther and Jessie thoroughly checked Shane for injuries. Thankfully, there were none, at least none we could see.

I led the paint over to a pine tree between the two tents. He was tethered with a lead long enough for him to relax in head hanging luxury, but not, I hoped, long enough for him to get into trouble. Having no wish to encourage further antics, I hardly spoke two words to the horse. I had to be tight-lipped because words of praise were eager to gush out. Uncalled-for words such as, "Oh, you wonderful horse! You didn't break a leg! Good horse! Great horse!" So instead I blurted, "Do you know what they do to a horse that breaks its leg? Well?" I had to tell him. "They shoot you in the head, that's what! They shoot you in the head! And that's doing you a favor!" Somehow I felt better having shared my worst fears.

* * *

"Everything okay?" Jessie asked, stepping out of the shadows. "We were wondering about you."

"I think so."

"You didn't finish your supper."

"No."

"Standing around in the dark helping anything?"

"No."

"So you can come back with me then?"

All talk silenced at our approach, the faces around the campfire friendly and expectant. "He'll live," I pronounced, trying to put them all at ease. Then added, "Of course, maybe that's not such a good thing."

"Sure, that's a good thing," Stan assured me. "Here, you sit right down, and I'll get you some hot food."

"Not much," I said, sitting down again next to Sara.

"Your horse isn't anything different," Willis said. "All horses are unpredictable. Witless wonders, all! One can never tell what they'll take into their heads next. Why I . . . "

"Really, Willis!" Miriam interrupted. "Don't start."

Willis sat beside his wife. "I'm not going to start. But we can all agree that horses don't have a lick of common sense . . . and for that matter neither do the people who ride them!" He added, "And the more purebred they are, the less common sense they seem to have!"

"That's nothing to say about Sky Rocket," Miriam disputed.

"I wasn't talking about your horse, M."

"Really, Willis!" Miriam giggled. "Please stop." They smiled at one another, as a private joke passed between them.

Sunny Jim poked at the fire with a stick. "This is the last ride of the season," he said woefully.

"Yes," Stan said, handing me a plate of food. "You have to go to school. And brooding won't change it."

"We've had a safe season," Luther said. "And speaking of safe seasons," he glanced at his watch, "I'll bet J.P. has Bob back at base camp by now."

"Agreed," Jessie said. "I was thinking the same thing."

"He'd take the fast route that we came up," Stan said.

"Owen will run him down to the hospital straight away," Luther said. "He'll be patched up by the time we turn in."

"I'm just glad that we'll be up here when he gets that shot," Sunny Jim exclaimed.

"And he'll have some time to forget about it before we get back," Jessie added.

Miriam stood, stretching. "I'm bushed," she said and yawned. "I hate to be a party pooper, but I'm going to call it a day. I can't wait to get these boots off." And then more to herself, "My horse has never ridden trails before, so he's sure to be stiff and sore on the ride tomorrow."

"But not you?" Willis asked, now also standing.

"He won't appreciate a cranky rider," Miriam continued, finishing her thought, and ignoring her husband's comment completely.

"I'll get you tucked in," Willis was saying as they disappeared into the night, "And then I'll check on His Highness . . ."

"I'll go have a last check on our friends upstairs," Jessie said. "And I'll make sure Candy is safely bedded down for the night," he said to Sara.

"May I go too?" Sunny Jim asked his father.

"Sure," Luther said. And to Jessie, "Take dreary drawers with you." Then, "But don't dally," he said to his son, "Stan can use some help with clean up."

"I'll help with that," I said. "But didn't I hear Willis say that he was going to check on the horses?"

"He's checking on their horses," Jessie explained. "Their stallion and that old mare. He has them picketed together out back of camp." A picketed horse is tied, usually to a stake driven into the ground.

"He seems to think that mare has a calming affect on the stallion," Luther said. "Maybe he's right."

Art stood, taking his daughter's hand, "Let's put you to bed, little miss," he said.

I started gathering plates; supper was over.

"Is picketing safer than hobbling?" I asked Stan. We were very close to finishing the dishes. I was drying the last pan.

"No," Stan said decidedly.

"Oh?"

"Either way, things can go wrong. We prefer to hobble our horses. It gives them the opportunity to forage."

"Oh?"

"You're fading, kid," Stan said, taking the pan from my idle hands. "Thank you for all your help. Now off to bed with you." I didn't argue.

I crawled along the inside edge of the tent to my assigned spot at the rear. Miriam was lightly snoring; Sara was still. I decided to sleep in my clothes, an old camping habit, except for my moccasins, which were stowed where they would be easy to locate in the dark. Then, I put on a sweater over my shirt and slipped on the extra socks as well. For a short time, muted talking and rustling sounds could be heard around camp, and then, absolute silence.

There is no other silence like the silence one experiences when camping in the mountains. When at last the final camper had gone to bed and that profound silence descended, I did not dare to cough or blow my nose. For I could imagine one cautious nose blow, sending herds of elk stampeding and old owls dropping from the trees. Silence.

Suddenly, PAW, PAW . . . POUND, POUND.

Miriam sat straight up. "What!? What!?" She lay back down almost as quickly. She must have thought she was dreaming.

PAW, PAW, PAW . . . POUND, POUND. The sounds echoed, reverberating in the quiet night.

I realized it was Shane. I had left him tied to the tree between the tents.

Someone in the men's tent called out, "What's that!?"

I answered, not loudly, "I think it's my horse."

Silence again. One minute. Two.

PAW, PAW, PAW . . . POUND, POUND, POUND.

"Now, what the hell!" I recognized Luther's voice, sounding disgruntled.

"It's my horse," I told them again. "He doesn't like being left tied up."

Silence again, but only for a moment.

PAW, PAW, PAW . . . POUND, POUND, POUND.

"He won't quit until he's untied," I called.

"Untie him then!" Luther ordered.

Someone else in the men's tent voiced concern. "Won't he run off?"

I heard Luther answer, "If he runs off it will be a blessing!"

Crawling past Sara, I heard a giggle, and punched her sleeping bag playfully. Miriam didn't move; nothing was bothering her. I was as stealthy as I could clumsily be in the dark, understanding that everyone would appreciate some sleep before the night was over. It didn't feel right leaving my friend untied; however, I was fairly certain he wouldn't run off—unless a bear startled him—but then one could never know. By that point, I was wholly with Luther, thinking, if he runs off it would be a blessing! Leading him a distance from the tents and pointing him in the general direction of the lake, I whispered, "Please be quiet," and gave him a gentle swat on the rump.

Back inside the tent, I quickly fell asleep dreaming of a strikingly marked paint roaming the hillsides alone and forlorn. He had a sign hanging from around his neck: FINDERS KEEPERS it read.

It was sometime early, long before dawn, when Miriam jerked upright. "Something dripped on my face! Something dripped on my face!" She sounded as if she were quelling a mild hysteria. Grabbing the flashlight, I lit up the tent to see that Shane's head was stuck inside the flap drooping directly over Miriam, who gave a startled jump at the sight. Shane never moved or opened his eyes.

"We're switching places," Miriam ordered. "Connie, you're switching places with me right now." There was no argument. I set the flashlight down positioning it to dull its light. "I thought I heard someone snoring over me,"

Miriam said, muttering to herself. "I could have sworn I heard someone snoring over me." We were moving our sleeping bags around. "But I was wrong. Wrong!" She continued her muttering, glancing over at me accusingly. "It wasn't someone. It was something! Some . . thing . . . snoring over me." Our places were traded as smoothly as possible under the confined circumstances. Sara never woke up. I fell back to sleep immediately. Shane dripped and snored over me too, but I was just too tired to care.

CHAPTER TWENTY-FOUR

After a leisurely morning in camp, we climbed the switchbacks out of the valley. Shane and I were in the lead position again, with Luther behind us riding Sparky, Sunny Jim's black and white gelding. Next came Sara, followed by her father, then Willis, Miriam, and Jessie. Stan was next to last in line leading the packhorses. Sunny Jim was riding Poky bringing up the rear. Several times while climbing I looked back to watch the other riders following behind on the switchbacks. We were a fortunate group of trail riders, enjoying another cloudless and relatively windless day in the high mountains, yet appreciating enough of a breeze to stay any haze that might have obscured our pristine mountain views. Once the ridge was reached we were able to see beyond Mount Rainier to the snow-capped peaks of the region's other volcanic mountains: Mount St. Helens and Mount Adams to the south, and Mount Baker to the north, with a stunning expanse of peaks stretching between.

Our trail followed the ridgeline for several miles. As on the previous day, I soon found there was plenty of time to sightsee, ponder, and reminisce while trail riding. Shane was doing such a superb job of concentrating on the rocky trail that there was little directing of him required. Besides, whenever I did try to direct my friend, he instantly reprimanded me with a much deserved, "Chill, Hopalong! There's only one trail!" response, which usually took the form of an annoyed, snapping tail. Encouraged to keep my hands to myself, I just sat back and enjoyed the ride.

Gradually the trail dipped downward, winding its way through a forest of alpine fir trees. Patches of snow remained in a few perpetually shady areas, and there were muddy stretches of trail where the snow had recently melted. Occasionally, on the muddy stretches, Shane and I had disagreements—which I invariably lost—as to how best to navigate around the muck. Shane let me know when he got fed up with my meddling. His ears would shoot back at that odd cant, and he would bend his neck around enough in my direction to make sure I was getting his message. At those times he seemed to be saying, "Would you like to climb down for a while, or what?" By patting him on the neck, I assured him I had no desire to climb down, and that he was handling things just fine. Again, as a result, there was nothing for me to do but enjoy the ride. No complaints from me. I let the reins relax in my hands and the straps rest softly against my horse's neck.

"Hey," Luther called. "Wait up!" We had been climbing again, the trees thinning out. I reined in my horse, turning in the saddle. Because of a bend in the trail, I could only see the first several riders in the line. "We're waiting for the packhorses to catch up," Luther explained.

"We're waiting for Poky," Art called forward. "He's been lagging further and further behind." The voices of Miriam, Willis, and Jessie could be heard down the trail.

"Okay," Luther finally said, "let's go."

In the next few minutes, we were above the tree line traveling the ridge again. When the trail straightened out sufficiently so I could hope to see our whole group, I looked back, prompting everyone behind to do the same. Sunny Jim waved. Then, clowning around for us, he pretended to be riding a racehorse. He leaned far forward against Poky's neck, wildly whipping the reins, and pretended to flail Poky with a switch he had torn from a passing tree. This was quite amusing to watch, especially with Poky merely ambling along paying no attention to the antics of his rider or the laughing appreciation from onlookers.

"Let's take a break here," Luther called out.

It was a perfect place for a rest stop, a wide-open area with a spectacular view and a convenient seating area in a jumble of boulders off to one side. Jumping down, I led Shane aside, nodding to Sara and Art as they passed. Jessie tipped his hat in greeting, riding his palomino over to a nearby rise.

"There's elk down there," he turned to inform us.

"Elk?" Willis said, dismounting then leading his horse that way. Art and Sara hurried past.

"What about you?" Miriam asked, dismounting. "Don't you care about elk?" I didn't answer because as she dismounted I was distracted, noticing that her stallion arched his neck even more tightly, bringing his muzzle up and pulling it in as she was getting down. For some reason, that act particularly struck me, for it appeared to be a gesture of gentlemanly regard for his lady.

"How's Sky Rocket enjoying the day?" I asked.

"Our slow pace hasn't dampened his spirits, if that's what you're asking," Miriam answered, groaning and rubbing her lower back with both hands. "I'm not sure how he does it, but somehow he's able to do a full gallop yet still stay in one place." Then, "Of course, Willis is loving it. Don't think I don't know."

For some unknown reason, I blurted out, "Does Willis really dislike horses so much?"

"Oh?" Miriam seemed taken aback. "Did he tell you that?"

"Yes," I said.

"Well, dear," Miriam said quickly, glancing in the direction of her husband. "I don't know what Willis told you, but do you see how special this horse is to me?" She underscored her words by caressing her pet. "Well, that's how special another horse, just like this one, once was to him."

"I don't understand," I said.

"Willis doesn't dislike horses, dear. It's that . . . well . . . sometimes people lock up their hearts for safekeeping."

"Oh," I said, nodding.

"See those rocks over there? I know there's a seat with a backrest waiting for me somewhere in those rocks, and I'm going to find it."

I did want to see the elk, but I had no intention of leading my horse near the edge of anything high. Deciding that it would be a good time to give Shane a carrot, I dug one out of the canvas bag.

"Can I have one of those?" Sunny Jim asked, leading his horse my way. "Poky loves carrots."

"Your horse doesn't seem to be in much of a hurry," I commented, giving him a nice one.

"Poky isn't one of our horses," Sunny Jim said. "He's Bob's horse."

"Oh," I said. "And Bob doesn't mind that he's slow?"

"Nah. He doesn't mind. He says he's not in much of a hurry either." Then, "Don't you want to see the elk?"

"Sure she does," an eavesdropping Jessie called. "Come on."

"Huh!" I said aloud, but to myself. "I'm not falling for that old trick!" Knowing that, to see the elk, I would have to get very close to the edge of the precipice. And I did not intend to be the victim of Shane's sick horse humor. "I don't want to look over," I answered.

"Come on!" Jessie prompted again.

"Well," I said, giving in, "only if you come hold my horse back while I look."

"One of those, huh?" Jessie laughed. He was a very horse savvy guy.

Once we were underway again, Shane and I were third in line behind Luther and Jessie. Our host had decided to take the lead, explaining to our group that the next part of the ride might be tricky—nothing dangerous but a bit rough going. He had asked Jessie to ride forward with him, the young man explaining that since part of our journey would be on a seldom-used route, he might need to help Luther clear debris from the trail.

At first, we continued along the ridge, but soon, at a fork in the trail, we left that high tract, and began descending into a thickly forested region. Continuing downward, true to Luther's warning, the terrain became more rugged. That was fine with me, since the paint had to pay attention to his own business, instead of pestering Jessie's palomino. "We won't be on this trail long," Jessie turned to inform me. "We don't usually come this way, but it'll be worth the detour." Then, in a whisper, "Going this way has a special surprise for . . ." he pointed right behind me, "Sara." He whispered her name so she would be certain not to hear.

Another mile up the trail, Shane suddenly balked. I quickly cried out, "Wait!" to Luther and Jessie before they disappeared around the next bend.

"What is it?" I asked my friend, leaning forward in the saddle to see what was holding him back.

"What is it?" Sara called as her horse, Candy, pressed from behind.

"Uh-oh!" I exclaimed to everyone waiting. "My horse is nervous about this water on the trail."

"That's okay," Luther called. "Let him take his time."

The way had been muddy and a small pond had collected on this low section of trail. It was merely a puddle. Luther and Jessie's horses had trudged through giving it little heed. For my horse, however, standing water presented a problem. Shane had it worked out that mud puddles were some kind of trap door entrance to hell. Nearly panicked, my horse was hemmed in by horses pressing from behind and by high banks and underbrush crowding in on both sides. I braced myself for what I knew was coming. The paint crouched at the edge of the puddle, dramatically gathered himself into a great bunch, and then powerfully thrust into space. When he landed, hard, far past what would have been reasonable to clear the other side, I was thrown forward against the saddle horn. "Oof! Ugh!"

"Are you all right?" a concerned Jessie asked.

I felt for broken ribs. All right? Was I all right? What does that truly mean, I asked myself. There was time to ponder since I couldn't answer anyway, as the saddle horn had punched the wind out of me. Surely, there are degrees of all right, I thought. If I hadn't been killed, but merely wounded, was I all right? Finally, I nodded. It was all I could do.

Soon we rode out of the trees and into an open meadow. Acres of tall grass stretched before us. Our host reined in his horse, moving off the trail, wordlessly signaling for us to do the same. There we waited for the others to emerge from the forest. Once most of our group had come together, Luther pointed to a nearby area where the grass had been flattened, trampled down and used as a bed by deer or elk. Keeping his voice low, he told us this was an area where, if quiet, we might see deer up close. So we were being very quiet when Stan and the packhorses joined us.

"What's up?" Stan asked.

"Waiting for you," Luther said. "There's deer in the area, so we're keeping the noise down."

"I haven't seen the kid for a while," Stan said softly, scanning back down the trail. "Guess this is as good a place as any to let him catch up."

We waited, watching the last bend in the trail. Shane spent the minutes trying to graze. When I wouldn't let him, he shook his head and stomped his rear leg in frustration. Reacting to my horse's impatience, Jessie told us, "One more minute and I'll backtrack." That's when we saw the carrot coming around the bend. Sunny Jim had rigged a carrot to a long stick and was dangling it in front of Poky as they rode. We all laughed at the sight.

"That's funny!" Luther said, slapping his leg. As they came closer, he said with a smile, "Now that's what I call damn funny. But does it help?"

"Not one bit," Sunny Jim replied with a good-natured grin.

"Well, we probably scared any creatures that might have been in the area," Stan commented.

"Let's go," Luther said. "Try to keep up, son," he added. "We worry when we can't see you."

We rode through that meadow and another, silently watching for deer. It was such an exceptional day, cliffs above jutting into a clear blue sky. As we rode, I listened joyously to the sounds of creaking saddles, and our horse's hoof-falls on the trail. Even without talking, we weren't a very stealthy group.

We traveled over meadows, passed through forests, and crossed streams with rushing currents. Twice we paused to water our horses at still pools. At those times, the paint acted as any other horse, confidently crossing the rocky streambeds, and eagerly drinking from still pools at the water's edge. But when there was standing water on the trail, even the smallest of puddles, he shied, sometimes to the extreme of leaving the trail to blaze a new route. In his zeal, he'd scrape my leg against a passing tree if I couldn't get my foot out of the stirrup fast enough. I didn't complain though, since the alternative would have been the inter-planetary leap, which neither my friend nor I enjoyed.

Luther reined in his horse, moving off the trail, and signaling for us to gather round. "We're about to stop for a lunch break up ahead through these trees," our host told us. "If we keep our voices down, it's more likely we'll see some of the inhabitants of this meadow. Also, this is a fragile place, not suitable for these big guys. So feel free to stroll, if you like, but let's confine our horses to the one area I'll indicate. Any questions?" No one spoke. "Then let's go."

Barely emerging from the trees, we heard a kind of whistling call, an alarm that was a warning of our arrival. That shrill call attracted our attention so that we were able to catch the scurry of small creatures diving for their holes. We stopped our horses, watching the furry faces peering out at us from many of the burrows dotting the landscape.

"Oh!" Sara cried excitedly, clapping her hands. At that, the startled little faces popped out of sight further into the safety of their holes. "Oh no!" Sara realized her mistake, covering her mouth.

"It's okay," Jessie whispered. "They'll be back. They want to see you just as much as you want to see them."

Then, when a cautious face or two could again be seen, a flustered Art began fumbling for his camera—and they were gone. Sara cast her father a look of stern disapproval.

"Art, you'll have plenty of time to take pictures, " Luther promised the disappointed man. "But first, let's get our horses settled."

We followed Luther a few more yards before he turned into a campsite. The clearing was only steps from the trail, yet completely hidden by trees. After dismounting, we led our horses out of the way of other riders coming in. "You can tie your horse here beside Gertrude if you want," Jessie offered, as Shane and I were passing.

"Gertrude?" I laughed before I could catch myself. I hadn't meant to be rude.

"That's okay," Jessie grinned, shaking his head, putting me at ease. He seemed to have enjoyed my candid mirth. "It gets a chuckle every time. Besides, I agree."

"Where did he get a name like that?"

"Same place J.P. Patches got his name, I suppose," Jessie mused. "Although I've never asked.

"Ah!" I said, then understanding. Gertrude was another beloved Seattle clown, who helped out at the city dump on J. P. Patches' popular kids' TV show. Gertrude was a man dressed up as a lady. He was supposed to be J. P.'s girlfriend—let's say he had a crush on J.P.—but along with the polka-dot dress and the generous smear of red lipstick, the burly Gertrude had a husky voice, thick, hairy forearms, and plenty of dark facial stubble.

The campsite was quickly filling with horses, so after assisting me, Jessie was kept busy helping everyone else find a place to tie up. Amid the bustle, Stan handed out sack lunches.

Sunny Jim was last to arrive. "Did you see the marmots?" he asked Sara as he dismounted.

"No," Sara answered nervously. "I hope they're not around here."

"Sure she saw the marmots," Luther said, smiling broadly.

"I did?"

Art looked up from changing the film in his camera. "She did?"

"Sure," Luther laughed. "Don't you remember all those bashful ground dwellers we saw when we came in?"

Father and daughter glanced at each other sheepishly. "Well, I guess the joke's on us then," Art chuckled, snapping the camera shut. Then to his daughter, "Let's go get some pictures for Mom, honey," he said, taking her by the hand.

"And for my new baby sister too," Sara added.

"Don't forget your lunches," Stan called. "Sara will want to share her potato chips with her new friends."

I found a large, flat boulder at the edge of the meadow and sat down to eat. Art and Sara had walked a short distance into the meadow. The others spread out in small groups scouting for perfect lunching and viewing spots. As I had, they elected to stay along the edge of the meadow. I guessed everyone had the same idea—to eat our lunches at a respectful distance, with the hope that Sara could enjoy the shy marmots.

"Do you mind?" Jessie asked, sitting down to join me before I had time to answer. "We usually see people in groups of two or three," he commented.

"Oh?" I said, not understanding what he was talking about. Anyway, I was distracted by his good looks, thinking the more I looked at him, the better looking he got!

"On the ride," he explained. "People usually come in groups."

"Oh," I said lamely, after spending a moment searching for an intelligent response. Jessie merely smiled. It was a pleasantly amused kind of smile.

We watched Sara place potato chips at the entrances to the burrows and on the rocks surrounding her. She sat down to wait, her father ready with the camera.

"This will definitely be the highlight of her trip," Jessie whispered.

Marmots are a large, ground dwelling variety of squirrel. Naturally curious, it didn't take long for them to emerge. Hikers visiting this campsite had been feeding these characters for years. The young girl sat very still as one by one her treats were snatched. Creeping closer, keeping wary eyes on Sara, they eventually sat up very near her, exposing their rotund bellies while turning the potato chips in their tiny paws as they ate. Occasional giggles sent them all scrambling, but they were quick to return.

"I'm surprised you didn't want to feed the marmots," Jessie commented.

"I've had my turn," I answered. "Now I'm enjoying watching Sara take hers."

Across the meadow, the activities of the marmots resumed. Roly-poly pups tumbled in play, while vigilant family members sunned themselves nearby. Jessie stretched out behind me on the rock. "You're quiet," he said. "Is there something wrong?"

I wasn't about to tell him his mere presence had me flustered, so I answered, "Maybe I'm thinking about being dumped off at boarding school tomorrow."

"Dumped?" Jessie queried, concern in his voice.

Ugh! I immediately regretted that such a misstatement, for it was so untrue, had somehow inadvertently popped out. "Actually, 'lovingly left' is more like it," I quickly admitted. "You see, my parents met at boarding school, so it's practically a family tradition. Anyway, that 'dumped' thing? Forget it. It's just me. I have a tendency to over-dramatize," I lamely explained. "I'm never hot; I'm burning up. I'm never tired; I'm exhausted. I can't help it. It's the way I think. It's some weird quirk with my personality." Tongue-tied before, now I was babbling.

Jessie laughed. "You're funny," he said.

That had me wondering. Does he mean good funny? Or does he mean bad funny? Wow, this whole boy-girl thing is terribly confusing. There was never a chance to sort it all out though. Our host called to us, "Time to go, gang!"

CHAPTER TWENTY-FIVE

We arrived at our day's destination in the late afternoon, a campsite situated on a gentle slope near a lake. A dark-haired man, wearing a red plaid shirt and suspenders, stepped out from a good-sized cabin. "You're late," he accused. "I was about to get worried."

"We came a roundabout way," Luther said, dismounting. "How's Bob?"

Rolling his eyes the man answered, "He'll live. Nothing broken. But what a fuss he made!"

"How's J.P.?" Luther asked, glancing around for his horse.

"That reminds me. Bob says thanks for the loaner, and that he hopes he never has to ride your horse again!"

"Little zippy for him, huh?" Luther chuckled.

The man introduced himself to me as I climbed down. "Owen," he said. "We must have missed each other before. I'm Luther's brother." And addressing us all, "Did you have a nice ride?"

"Sure did!" Sara responded enthusiastically.

"Wonderful!" Art agreed.

"What a beautiful spot!" Willis exclaimed. "Any fish in that lake?"

"You bet," Owen answered. And then he turned to our host, saying, "But we'll have to hurry if we're going to catch enough for dinner."

"Then let's get these packhorses unloaded," Luther said.

At that the work began. Luther, Owen, and Sunny Jim helped Stan with the packhorses. Jessie helped us guests get sorted out. Following Jessie, we led our horses to a wooded area behind the cabin where there was a corral and several hitching posts. "There's fishing, hiking, or riding," he told us. "If you think you'll want to ride more today we'll just loosen these cinches for the time being. With everyone staring at him as if he'd lost his mind, he added, "There's a real nice trail around this lake, so you might want to give it a moment's thought."

"I'm pooped," Miriam said. "Done in."

"Oh, come on, M," Willis surprised us all by saying. "Let's go for a stroll around the lake. You can have a stretch. We'll lead our horses, then if we want to ride at some point, we still can."

Miriam said, aghast, "You think you might want to get back up on that mare . . . again . . . today?"

Turning to affectionately stroke his horse's nose, Willis said, "I've had a relaxing ride. I'm not that tired."

"We'll go," Art said. "We'd like to come. If you don't mind the company."

"I'll take pictures of you and your daughter, " Willis offered, leading his horse away.

"And I'll take pictures of you too," Art said.

Once the four had gone, Jessie asked, "What about you? Will you be wanting to ride some more today?"

"If I do," I said, "I'll ride bareback. Right now, I'm going to get this saddle off and find a sunny place to brush my horse." Jessie assisted with my gear. "We've been lucky to have such nice weather," I commented. "Bet you guys have been in some hellacious storms up here in these mountains."

"Sure have," Jessie answered. "And they come up fast."

It was common knowledge in the surrounding Seattle area that this whole region near Mount Rainier had its own weather systems, and was prone, even in summer, to unpredictable storms. So unpredictable were these storms that even though forewarned, savvy climbers and hikers were frequently caught off guard. We were so aware of this weather phenomenon because, from the city, even on the most clear and sunny days, the towering mountain could be invisible, veiled in clouds or haze. It was a fact highly frustrating for locals when first time visitors came to stay, as we were eager to show off our spectacular mountain. "There it is!" We would point to its exact location. "It's huge, right there, but you can't see it." It was as frustrating for us as it was for the hopeful tourists. At the same time, it was that amazingly fickle, enshrouded quality that never allowed it to be taken for granted. It was merely part of the mystique of "The Mountain," which is what locals call Mount Rainier. Then, when the mountain did reappear, it was so breathtaking that no matter how many times you had seen it before, you were awestruck. If our beloved Seattle was but the diamond on the finger of our beautiful Pacific Northwest, Mount Rainier was surely her crown.

"Don't you want your halter?" Jessie asked, watching me paw through the canvas bag for a brush.

"No point," I answered.

The paint followed me around the cabin to a sunny spot near where Luther and Sunny Jim were erecting a tent. "You women are sleeping in this tent tonight," Luther said. "We men will sleep in the cabin." I peeked in a window of the cabin to see three walls lined with bunk beds.

"It's going to rain tonight," Sunny Jim informed me. "But you'll stay plenty dry."

Pondering a clear blue sky, I commented, "There aren't any clouds."

"If Stan's old bones say rain, it'll rain," the boy assured me.

While I brushed Shane, Jessie was brushing his palomino nearby. Several times, while working, I became aware that the young man was watching me. I could feel it. The feeling that he was watching made me take a quick side-glance his way even though I didn't really want to. Then, when sneaking a peek at him, I would catch him in the very act of staring at me. I was surprised when he didn't look away. Instead, smiling broadly, he gazed straight into my eyes. His behavior was very disconcerting. It made me uncomfortable, even downright squirmy. Jessie was very handsome—any girl with a beating heart would be sure to notice. I continued brushing Shane, trying to remain calm—acting nonchalant. Somehow, I couldn't keep myself from sneaking a peek at him again when I got that . . . squeamish feeling. Finally, I made myself meet his eyes with a steady gaze. I needed to see if he was truly watching me, or if it was merely my overly self-conscious imagination. He was. Gosh! Blushing, I hurriedly turned away.

Suddenly, I was assailed by rampaging emotions. Embarrassment. Dismay. Maybe there was something like pleasure, but it made me sick to my stomach. I was accustomed to boys harboring crushes. However, this situation felt very different. Continuing to brush Shane, I became more and more annoyed with myself, hoping I wasn't becoming boy-crazy like my obnoxious older sisters. With these thoughts in mind, I was determined not to look over at Jessie again, even if burning hot knives were stabbing at the back of my neck. I didn't even notice him leave when he finished his grooming session.

By the time Shane's coat was glistening, the campsite was deserted. Luther and Owen had gone fishing, and Stan had taken a camp chair down by the lakeshore to watch them. Jessie and Sunny Jim were roughhousing. They had been banished by the men and were off chasing each other through a wooded area farther around the lake. Thinking about organizing my things in the tent, a shadow caught my attention as a bird passed overhead. Clouds were definitely moving in. Deciding that we too should take advantage of the remaining sunlight, Shane followed me on a walk to a lush patch of grass not far from the forested area where Jessie and Sunny Jim had last been seen.

I was sitting comfortably on a log at the water's edge, enjoying solitude, while Shane grazed behind nearby, when Sunny Jim approached. He was giggling, out of breath, and his cheeks were flushed scarlet. "Jessie likes you," he blurted. "He told me he thinks you're pretty." Then the boy fled, his mischievous mission accomplished.

Jessie immediately came up red-faced and apologetic, embarrassed by Sunny Jim's betrayal. "That little brat!" he exclaimed, sitting down beside me. "If I catch him, I'll hold him down, and you can kick him . . . preferably in the head!" he added. Meanwhile, the boy was lurking and taunting, but careful to stay clear of Jessie's grasp.

At first, I didn't know what to say as we sat watching the boy, so pleased with himself and so obviously eager for us to chase him. "I don't have any little brothers," I finally said, "so I'm not sure how they work. Maybe if we ignore him, he'll go away."

Jessie was skeptical. "I don't think little brothers work that way, but I'm game to try. Let's go for a walk." At that, turning our backs on the boy, we began walking in the opposite direction, hoping he would get the hint. We strolled slowly along the lakeshore past the fishermen and a napping Stan.

"Your horse seems to like you . . . a lot," Jessie said.

"It's mutual," I answered.

"I mean he's following us."

I glanced back to see that Shane was following us closely. "Oh, he would. I guess he doesn't have anything better to do. Do you mind? I could tie him up."

"Mind?" Jessie chuckled. "No, I don't mind. I've never been chaperoned by a horse before."

I giggled. And blushed, I'm sure. I had to be a mess—camping always does that to a person. And I couldn't remember having combed my hair all day. My face was sunburned and my lips were dry and chapped. Even my voice sounded oddly high-pitched to me. I was worrying about how I looked, and of course, it was making me shy and tongue-tied. And this wasn't a time for acting shy and tongue-tied. So that's when I decided to take a large dose of my Swedish grandmother's cure for shyness. She had told me, "Shyness is easy to conquer. The trick is to not think about yourself when you're with somebody else. If you aren't thinking about yourself, you can't be shy, and you might actually learn something interesting about the other person." It was good advice.

"Were you raised around horses?" I asked. "You seem to know everything there is to know about them."

"I guess you could say that," Jessie said. "I've worked for Luther the past few summers. I've been saving for college. I start in a few days, at Washington State, at Pullman. I'm going to be a veterinarian."

A college man, I thought. A college man! "I can tell you'll be a good one."

"I hope so," Jessie said. "That's very kind of you to say."

My mind pretty much went blank when I gazed up into his soft brown eyes. Those long dark lashes pretty much sucked every intelligent thought right out of my head. If my sisters could see me now!

"And what about you?" Jessie was saying. "You seem to have a special way with horses."

At first, I thought he might be joking, not sure what "a special way with horses" meant. I answered carefully, "I've never had a riding lesson. Guess it shows."

"No. I mean that you have a special relationship with your horse."

Glancing behind to my faithfully trailing friend, I said, "Do I?"

At that moment, a "whoop!" was heard. Luther had a fish on the line, the tip of his pole bobbing downward. Immediately snapping the pole back, he began reeling and, in his excitement, upset his balance. He almost tumbled from the log perch into the lake. Then Owen's pole bobbed. Tossing a nice sized trout onto the bank, Luther called excitedly. "Dinner is served!" He then began preparing his line for another cast.

The action woke Stan, now stretching. Luther had another fish on the line. "It must be time for me to start cleaning fish," Jessie said reluctantly.

"And for me to help with dinner," I added, seeing Stan heading for his cooking chores.

Before assisting Stan, there were chores of my own to do. I needed to wash up and get my things organized in the tent before dark. Also, there was the issue of where to tie up my horse. As it had become a cloudy evening and rain seemed assured, I went ahead and tied Shane under the protection of the trees behind the cabin. Once in the tent, I donned a sweatshirt, combed my hair, and found the soap.

By the time I arrived at the kitchen area, the campfire had become a popular place. Willis, Miriam, Art, and Sara were all there. "You, dear," Miriam greeted me. "You should have come on our walk. We had a marvelous time."

Sunny Jim dropped off fish. "They're still fishing," he told us. "They're determined to fish until it gets too dark."

"Well, that won't be much longer," Stan said.

I got busy fixing hot drinks. Stan appreciated my help. As we worked, guests came and went from the campfire, washing for dinner and putting on warmer clothes. Jessie stopped by a few times for short visits but, for the most part, he was away getting gear stowed and the horses grained and settled for the night.

We ate trout and biscuits, all of us thanking Luther and Owen for the special treat. "We've had a wonderful time," Willis said. "We plan to come on the ride again next summer. Sunny Jim showed a delighted Sara how to roast a biscuit on a stick. Watching them giggling, their faces so close together, eyes shining in the firelight, Jessie was inspired to scoot over my way to whisper, "I think the marmots have been upstaged." We stayed cozy around the campfire late into the evening, roasting marshmallows and talking about our day.

Gathering plates, Stan said, "Thanks for your help, Connie. Seems like no one ever eats as much as I expect."

As on the previous evening, I noticed his hands were gnarled and shaking. "Do they hurt much?" I asked. "Your hands?"

"More when the weather changes. They've been complaining all day. It's old age." He held out his crippled hands for me to see. "I don't mind so much. These hands have worked hard for a lot of years. Besides, this shaking gives my paintings an abstract flare I enjoy. Art dealers think so, too. I've sold a few."

When we started washing dishes, I asked, "Have you always been a cook?"

"Was I always a cook?" Stan repeated, with some surprise at the question. "No. I was nothing resembling the sort. I was a mechanic. Could fix anything. Still can. Don't want to, though. I had my own repair shop. Actually enjoyed it the first twenty years or so. Then the fumes started to get to me, and customers, too. Nobody's happy when his transmission goes out. I stopped when my hands lost their strength. Arthritis. This is my fifth season cooking. Couldn't spare the time till I retired. But it was always a dream of mine, coming out here like this. Life begins again at sixty-five, you know. No. I guess you wouldn't know at your age." Stan paused, then continued. "I'm almost seventy now. I spend most of the year painting my cat, Pudge. Cats make great models. I like to paint him staring out the window at a bleak winter landscape, or stretched out across the back of his favorite chair. Pudgy is old now, like me. I'd never picked up a brush until I retired. Never had the time . . . nor the notion. That's why they say life begins again at sixty-five." Then, after a pause, "What about you?" he asked. "What's your story? Tell me about your family."

"Huh! I don't like to talk about them much," I said. "They're a confusing lot. I'm going to write a book about them someday, though. That way, if someone asks me about my family, I'll simply hand the book over and say, "Here they are, if you're truly interested—as sorted out as they ever can be!"

"Well, okay then," Stan laughed. "At least you can tell me if you have any brothers or sisters."

"Plenty."

"Then you'll probably want to have children of your own someday?"

"Huh! I'm not having kids. I can tell you that much for certain. I can't keep a pet turtle alive!"

"Your horse seems healthy enough."

"He's just been lucky so far," I said grimly. Stan laughed. Maybe what I said had been a bit overstated. However, I wasn't laughing, as I remembered back to my gentle parakeet that had been killed by my cat, and to discovering my turtle friend lying dead in his small, tropical bowl. Emotional traumas mirroring the goldfish Harold incident, with Daddy Mike ranting, "This child is to have no more pets!"

Jessie came up carrying a lantern. "You two about finished here?" he asked. "Anything I can do to help?"

"You? Since when do you care about kitchen chores?" Stan answered, surprised. "Ah, I get it! Yes. Miss Connie is free to go."

"I knew she'd want to check on her horse one more time before bed," the young man explained somewhat defensively. "That's all."

Walking into the cool darkness away from the campfire's dying glow, Jessie swung the lantern, humming. "Watch this dip," he cautioned. "It's rough going here. Maybe you'd better take my hand." I glanced up at him sideways to see he was grinning. I think I was grinning myself.

"I don't see any dips," I said, stooping suspiciously to study the ground, though still offering my hand.

"It's a war zone," Jessie assured. "You'd best hang on tight." And as easy as that, we were holding hands. The young man kept a firm, yet comfortable, grip as he led me through camp and around the back of the cabin. At that point, his support was needed, for now my head was reeling, and I couldn't feel my feet at all. All I could feel was his grip on my hand.

Jessie set the lantern on the ground near Shane. "I gave him extra grain. Should we try leaving him tied up tonight?" he asked. "Or? What are your thoughts?"

Thoughts? I didn't have any thoughts. Desperately, searching a vacuum, I finally answered, "He won't go anywhere. Let's leave him untied. I wouldn't want him to wake everyone if he starts pawing." . . . It's a bad habit," I added. "Of course, Miriam won't like it if he sleeps with his head in the tent."

"Well, I have an idea about that," Jessie chuckled. "We'll get you settled in the tent, and then I'll wait awhile to come back to untie him. I'll do it last thing before I go to bed. That way, he won't see you go into the tent. Anyway, he's more likely to hang around under these trees tonight when it rains."

Teeth chattering, I said, "Agreed."

"Cold?" he asked, putting both arms around me, pulling me close. "I can feel you shivering."

"I don't know what I am," I stammered.

Jessie gently pushed me back against the tree, studying my face questioningly.

"I'm almost sixteen," I blurted, for some strange reason.

"And I'm almost eighteen," Jessie countered, with an amused grin. He seemed to find something amusing in every stupid thing I said. Thinking he was going to kiss me, I got so flustered that I basically just freaked out and bashfully lowered my head, even though I wanted him to. "That's okay." The young man put me at ease. And when I dared to peer up at him again, he searched my eyes, took my hand, raised it to his lips, and kissed it. It was a lingering kiss that brushed the back of my hand and caressed my fingertips. "You'll be at your new school tomorrow," he said softly. "Promise you'll think about me."

"I promise," I said, solemnly.

The sound of rain woke me for a time in the early morning hours. Snuggling further down into my sleeping bag, listening to the pleasant patter of the rain, I thought about Jessie. I could still feel the brush of his kiss on my fingertips.

CHAPTER TWENTY-SIX

The next morning, while packing my things, I experienced a strong feeling of regret that our adventure would soon be over. It was a strange, sad longing for this place, a place we hadn't even left yet. Soon, we'd all be riding back to reality, back to other lives. It seemed that everyone was thinking the same, about their worlds, worlds away. At breakfast there was little conversation. Willis and Miriam were quiet. Sara and her father were pensive, as if they too were trying, in some way, to say good-bye to this place. Sunny Jim was sleepy-eyed and grumpy. He lived with his mother in Seattle during the school year and was letting his dad know he wasn't happy about it. As I handed Jessie a cocoa, even he seemed distracted, smiling at me somewhat sadly. He was probably thinking about starting college in a few days. Luther and Owen appeared thoughtful as well, perhaps heavy-hearted at seeing another summer season come to an end, or perhaps remembering past seasons, ghost guests haunting the cold breakfast firepit. Only Stan was chipper, humming as he poured coffee. He was eager to get home to his cat.

As we rode out of camp, I turned back, whispering good-bye to the trees, the lake, and the mountains, taking a picture in my mind, an impression to carry during the coming school year. The window to our campsite was closing, the trees of the thickening forest enfolding us, cutting off our view. Through the branches, the lake became a final speck of blue. Our host led the way. Today I was riding toward the rear of the line, which pleased me. It was the best position from which to watch the other horses and riders. Luther had granted my request because Shane had done so well minding his manners the day before. Luther was in the lead, followed by Willis and Miriam, then Sunny Jim. Sara, Art, and I were next, followed by Jessie, and then Stan with the packhorses. Owen brought up the rear riding Poky.

The damp morning had me dreaming about a hot bath. My feet in particular were wet and cold. The soft soles of my faithful moccasins were worn thin and had become saturated walking on the wet ground around the campsite. And there were thoughts of school. Sometime today I would be at my new school. Sometime today Shane would be at his new pasture. I hoped it would be a good one. Quickly, I pushed all thoughts of the coming school year away, or at least tried to. No point in mimicking Sunny Jim's sorrowful laments. Besides, I wanted to enjoy this last morning of riding. Still, thoughts of boarding school kept coming. Saying our good-byes, Mom and Daddy Mike had promised they would visit me. Dad said they would come to take me out for Chinese food or a good rare steak. And I knew they would. It was thoughtful of him to be concerned that it might get boring eating the vegetarian fare served at the school cafeteria. Most heartening, Dad had promised to find a place where we could board our horses together next summer. Cher and Lindy would come to visit, too. They'd want to check out the boys at my school.

Backtracking out on the same trail, things were familiar, a boulder, a stump, a boggy area, a nest that Jessie had pointed out the day before. I entertained myself by watching the riders and horses ahead. For instance, I noticed that Luther turned often in the saddle to keep an eye on his charges. And I enjoyed watching Sky Rocket, behind Willis's mare, the prancing stallion, tail held high, frequently rubbing his handsome head against her rump. The mare always answered his attentions with a gentle switch of her tail. Miriam had complete control of her horse, though it was a control that allowed the Arabian to show his spirit. Many times she used the quirt to reach forward to tickle her horse's ears, or run it lovingly along his neck. However, I never saw her use it for any other purpose when riding. Behind her, Sunny Jim wasn't wearing a hat, and his short blond hair lit up brightly whenever a ray of sunlight escaped from the branches overhead. Behind him, Sara and Art were relaxed in their saddles. I too was feeling more at home in the saddle, now that Shane had finally settled into the pace set by the other horses. Suddenly, I caught my breath. Something, a thought, made me turn back with a feeling almost of panic. Jessie smiled and then, with questioning eyes, turned as well to see what was wrong behind him.

"It's okay," I explained. "I don't know what came over me. I just got this crazy feeling that I've left something back there—something important."

"What could it be? I checked the campsite carefully before we left."

"Oh. Then it's probably nothing," I assured him. But the feeling was still there. It was such a panicky feeling, so intense, that I turned again, even though reluctant to further concern Jessie. I searched beyond him, past the packhorses, down the trail. What had been left at that campsite? What could it be? Again, forward in the saddle, I told myself to forget about whatever it was. That's when it donned on me that it must have something to do with all the thinking about boarding school, leaving home, learning to drive, and thinking about Jessie and the evening before. Then suddenly, I knew what had been left behind. Yes!

I twisted again in the saddle. "Turns out it was something important," I informed Jessie. "But don't worry, I won't be needing it anymore." For the last time, gazing back down the trail somewhat longingly, I said a silent fare-well to my childhood.

The trail emerged from the shadowy forest to begin climbing out of the lake basin. We climbed switchbacks, taking in the grand view, while over-head the sun shone amid fair weather clouds. Again, I found myself think-ing about school, already missing the little girls. Dad and Momma Darleen would bring them to visit. The whole family could come down for church service; it wasn't so far. Momma Darleen's cooking would be missed: her tasty casseroles, fancy Jell-O molds, and scrumptious desserts. Oh well, there were always vacations. And time to see Karen then, too.

We came to a place of steep descent. Here the trail was quite treacher-ous, with loose rocks making it easy for any horse to lose its footing. I had never felt confident riding Shane on a downhill grade, always afraid he would trip. Adding to this anxiety, up ahead, Luther's experienced moun-tain horse lost his footing, sliding for a few feet before sitting down on his haunches to arrest the slide. That sight made me lean far back in the saddle, even hanging on to the back of the saddle. If Shane did happen to trip, which frankly I believed likely, I would sail straight out over his head for sure, shot out into space like a human cannonball. Or worse, if the saddle slipped, it would slide down over Shane's neck and head and become entangled around his front legs. Then Shane and I would become an out-of-control, tumbling juggernaut, wiping out all the other horses below us on the trail. Despite these fears, the paint was paying close attention to the terrain, taking his time, picking his way, ears forward, head down, eyes locked on his work. He didn't trip, and, fortunately, the saddle didn't slip. When we safely reached the bottom of the hill, relieved, I patted and praised my friend, not caring who overheard. He was a great mountain horse. The best!

Once the packhorses had safely negotiated the hill, Luther had everyone gather around. "This is where Stan, Owen, and the pack animals say their good-byes," he told us. "From here they'll be taking a somewhat longer but easier route." We said our good-byes, each guest thanking Stan for his cooking.

Now a smaller group, we continued our descent by increments. Always, there was a refreshingly flat bit of track, followed closely by another sharp, downward grade. The lower we got down the mountain, the muddier the flat stretches of trail became. The rainfall of the night before had run freely down the slopes to collect on the more recessed line of trail. When we came to the last, big, downward grade, Sunny Jim called out. "This is a bad one," he warned. "We call it Monster Hill."

I gulped as I watched the horses and riders in front appear to drop from sight over the side. When it was our turn, as Shane and I came to the edge—vertigo! Pulling up short, I assessed the situation. The trail down was wide enough for me to walk beside Shane. Jumping down, I signaled for Jessie to pass. "We'll come down last," I told him. Then Shane and I grimly undertook Monster Hill. Making our way cautiously, I kept to the side of my horse in case he had a misstep. On the long way down, I slipped several times. However, my friend did not. Instead, he came down steadily, carefully planting each mighty hoof. My hero horse was staying right beside me.

We were almost to home base. Through trees the ski slope and lodge across the roadway could be seen. Here the well-worn trail was particularly muddy. I was daydreaming, anticipating a hot bath, when suddenly there was a holdup ahead. Willis's mare balked, refusing to step into a particularly mucky stretch of trail. Confused by the mare's behavior, Sky Rocket danced a nervous two-step pressing behind her. Willis urged the mare forward. After all, Luther's Appaloosa had trudged through the muck without incident. The mare took one step, then balked a second time. "Well, I'll be!" Willis proclaimed, surprised by the usually tractable old mare's stubborn response. Farther up the trail Luther and J.P. turned to wait. Willis urged the mare a third time. This time she decided to go, though reluctantly. She had only gone three steps into the thick ooze when her rear legs slid, sinking down deeply into the mire. The frightened animal immediately tried to lunge forward, and then began desperately fighting to free herself. Something had her caught. Willis leaped from the horse, himself sinking far beyond his high boot tops. An experienced horseman, he took control of the situation instantly, grabbing hold of the struggling animal's head to impede her attempts to go forward.

Jumping down from his horse, Jessie rushed forward to help. He plunged into the ooze, reaching down along the mare's trapped right, rear leg, trying to free it, but with no success. When he finally pulled out his long hunting knife, Willis's face paled. Of course, Jessie wasn't cutting the mare's leg, he was cutting and sawing on whatever had her trapped. We were thankful that for the moment, the mare was still. She seemed to know these men were trying to help her. Waiting, I couldn't help wondering why such a terrible thing had to happen to this little mare that we had all come to admire. With much effort, Jessie was finally able to saw off the offending snag. He held it up for all to see. It was a jagged piece of tough root end. Willis then tried to lead the mare forward out of the mire, but she was having none of it. She wanted to go back to where she had been safe only moments before. Finally, he let her have her way. When we saw the horse returning, everyone quickly dismounted, moving our horses down the trail to make room for the injured animal.

The three emerged from the muck a mess. Though the mare was covered in mud, we could see that her right rear leg, starting above and behind the hoof, had a long, vertical cut. Jessie tore off his T-shirt, quickly wrapping it tightly around the bleeding wound. Then Willis very gently twisted the mare's head until she slowly eased down on her side. They wanted to keep her quiet while deciding what to do next.

Willis was quite distraught. "It was my fault," he kept saying. "My fault. She didn't want to go, and I forced her."

"It's nobody's fault," Jessie assured. "Things just happen."

Luther left his horse up the trail, and hurriedly forged a new path through the underbrush and around the mud. "Is it bad?" he asked Jessie.

"Not life threatening," Jessie said. "It appears to be only a cut. It's a vertical cut. I didn't see any damaged tendons."

Luther was relieved. "I'll take over here, Jess," he said. "You ride. Bring the horse truck. Put as many blankets in the back as you can find. Get Bob to help. Don't forget the bandages, and bring the tranquilizers."

"Miriam," Willis called. "Give Jessie my jacket."

Jessie gave me significant eye contact and quickly tipped his hat as he pushed past. "Take care at school," he said. Then, turning back, he added, "I'll be thinking of you."

When Jessie had gone, Sunny Jim helped the rest of us tether our horses wherever there was a spot handy along the trail. Then everyone drew close, gathering around the injured animal. Each of us hoping there was something he or she could do to help. We needed assurance the mare would be all right. Willis was hunched down beside the mare's head, a knee planted securely on her neck, while soothing her with gentle rubs. It was important that the horse remain quiet. Luther kept pressure on the wound.

"Do you need a break?" Miriam asked her husband. "That's a pretty uncomfortable position for you."

"Not yet. Maybe soon." Willis shook his head. "This mare has more sense than I do. She didn't want to go. But I forced her."

"This isn't your fault," Luther assured him.

"Is she going to be okay?" a sad-faced Sara asked.

Luther answered the little girl kindly. "Sure. She'll be okay."

"What's your horse's name?" Sara asked Willis. It was a thoughtful attempt by the child to distract the distraught man.

"Don't know," Willis said.

"Maggie," Sunny Jim answered. "Her name is Maggie."

"Maggie!" Miriam declared, with obvious delight in her voice. "What a coincidence! That's our daughter's name."

"Well! That about tops it!" Willis exclaimed, watching with amusement his wife's beaming countenance. "Maybe . . . Maggie," he said thoughtfully, "had better winter with us. We have the best vet around."

"And we have plenty of empty stalls," Miriam added quickly. "Maggie will need the extra care we can give her. And, lord knows, "rambunctious" over there won't complain," she added, indicating her horse.

The unfortunate accident couldn't have happened at a more fortunate location. We were only twenty-five yards from the dirt road that ran behind base camp. The mare wouldn't have to hobble far to make it to the horse truck. Luther sat down on the ground and tried to make himself more comfortable. "Son," he said. "Why don't you get busy widening that path around this mess? We're going to have to help this mare out of here." He added, "Then the rest of you might as well ride on into camp. There's no point in everyone standing around here. It's going to be a while."

"I can help with that," Art offered.

"Me too," I said.

We worked well together clearing the underbrush and widening the path that Luther, only moments before, had so hurriedly forged around the slop, and that Jessie had just used. The boy hacked and sawed with his knife, while Art and I cleared brush away. Several times my moccasins sunk below the ooze. Those missing boots would have been useful more than once on this ride.

When it was time for us to go, Miriam decided to stay with Willis, Luther, and the mare. She wanted to be able to help out as necessary. Art shook our host's hand saying, "You've given us the most wonderful memories. Wonderful! We can't thank you enough."

I too shook Luther's hand. "Thank you," I said. "Thank you so much for watching over us." After everything we had been through together, it was an emotional moment saying good-bye to these people.

Sunny Jim led Sparky over the rough path first, Shane and I next, then

Sara and Candy. Art and Shelby brought up the rear. We led our horses past where Luther had tied J.P. Then it was a short ride through the trees, and we were once again traveling on the wide dirt road that would take us straight into base camp. I thought of the group still waiting in the forest, confident that the little mare had found a new home, and a loving one.

Rounding the last bend, I saw Dad. He was standing alone in the middle of the dirt track, squinting up the road watching for me. We were late and he was probably worried. Even at a distance, I recognized him by the way he always stood with his hands sunk into his back pockets. Gosh, I thought, he looks so vulnerable standing like that. He waved when he saw me. And just as we got closer and I waved back, Shane tripped. He stumbled forward, right down to his knees. Dad grimaced at the sight shaking his head. I was so disappointed for my friend. The paint had gone the entire long ride without one misstep. Now Dad would never believe it when I told him what a terrific trail horse he had been. Well, I thought, maybe he'll believe it someday when he reads about it in the book.

The End

AN ADDITIONAL NOTE OF THANKS

It was a privilege and a pleasure to work with my editor, Barbara Fandrich, of Fandrich Publishing Arts in Aberdeen, Washington. She is truly talented at her craft. Her thoughtful insights and gentle advice helped to make this book the best it could be.

I would also like to thank the folks at Gorham Printing in Rochester, Washington, for their expertise. With so many exciting choices, the production and printing process can be confusing for clients. Kurt and Norma Gorham made it easy; Kathleen Shaputis made it fun. Choices for artwork and layout can get downright heady. Kathy Campbell, graphic designer, is the best.

ABOUT THE AUTHOR

CONNIE RAE STRAIN is a passionate writer who grew up in the Pacific Northwest. Her first book, *Perfect Imperfections*, was a labor of love squeezed in around a professional career as a partner in an international executive search firm. She is currently a full-time writer working on her next book *Gibson Hall*, a novel. Connie and her husband, Joe, enjoy life with three cats, and frequently travel between San Diego, London, and Seattle. The photo above shows the author with her mother's dog, Hans.